THE TRUTH ABOUT
MY FATHERS

ALSO BY GABY NAHER

The Underwharf
Bathing in Light

Gaby Naher

the truth about my fathers

a memoir

VINTAGE

A Vintage Book
Published by
Random House Australia Pty Ltd
20 Alfred Street, Milsons Point, NSW 2061
http://www.randomhouse.com.au

Sydney   New York   Toronto
London   Auckland   Johannesburg

First published in Australia by Vintage, 2002
This Vintage edition published 2004

Copyright © Gaby Naher 2002

National Library of Australia
Cataloguing-in-Publication Entry

    Naher, Gaby, 1967- .
    The truth about my fathers: a memoir.

    ISBN 1 74051 228 6.

    1. Naher, Gaby, 1967- . 2. Authors – Australia – Biography.
    3. Fathers – Australia – Biography. 4. Father and child.
    I. Title.

    A823.3

Cover and internal design by Greendot Design
Typeset by Midland Typesetters, Maryborough, Victoria
Printed and bound by Griffin Press, Netley, South Australia

10 9 8 7 6 5 4 3 2 1

For Jackie,
who shared so much of this journey with me
and
for Isla, Freya and Niamh,
the grandfather they never knew

This project has been assisted by the Commonwealth Government through the Australia Council, its arts funding body.

Shortlisted for
the Nita B. Kibble Literary Award 2003 and
the Westfield/Waverley Library Award 2003.

Acknowledgments

THANKS TO PAUL Watchman, whose support and sound judgment have kept me steady. Thanks to Jackie Naher, who has entrusted me with so much of our family story.

My agent Tony Peake's enthusiasm for this memoir has helped me keep the faith. I greatly appreciate his work on my behalf.

I've had a bevy of talented readers who have contributed so much to this book but Mandy Sayer and Glenda Adams deserve a special mention. Amanda Ressom has been instrumental in helping me find this story.

Thanks to Jane Palfreyman for her passionate commitment to this memoir and her publishing acumen. I am grateful to Jane Gleeson-White for her keen editorial eye and unwavering support.

I have a debt of gratitude to the Monettes—to Mark, Richard and Kate—for sharing their family stories with me. Without them, Gus might never have truly lived for me. Each of them gave me permission to quote from their letters and emails. Thanks to the Estate of Gus Monette for permitting me to use his letters in this book.

In Switzerland my thanks go to Elisabeth Kopp, who helped me research family history, who translated for me and who was an exemplary host. Thanks also to Monica and Benny Lanz, and to Trudi Aeschlimann-Müller. Thanks to Mary Bryan of the Irish Georgian Society for sharing her Fitzwilliam Square research with me.

My thanks go also to Paul Bourke, Katherine Bright-Holmes, Ros Burrows, Anna Cody, Dorji Dolma, Kathy Golski, Kate Grenville, Anne Held, Jill Hickson, Phyllis Miller and Michael Shmith.

The following books and documents have guided me: *Burgdorfer Jahrbuch, 1995*; *Inside Ireland* by Eilis Dillon; *Grace Gifford Plunkett and Irish Freedom* by Marie O'Neill; *Dublin* by V.S. Pritchett; *Eamon de Valera* by The Earl of Longford and Thomas P. O'Neill; *The Voyage Out* by S.B. de Courcy-Ireland; letters written on the *RMS Otway* by Henry Corrigan; *Kings Cross Album* by Elizabeth Butel and Tom Thompson; the diary of Robert Jellie from his migratory journey of 1927 as transcribed by Patricia Summerling; *Memories of Kings Cross 1936–1946*, published by Kings Cross Community Aid and Information Service; *Thomas West of Barcom Glen* by Edward West Marriott; *The Birth of Sydney*, edited and introduced by Tim Flannery; *Kings Cross Sydney* by Rennie Ellis and Wesley Stacey; and *My Town, Sydney in the 1930s* by Lydia Gill.

Late Fragment

by Raymond Carver

And did you get what
you wanted from this life, even so?
I did.
And what did you want?
To call myself beloved, to feel myself
beloved on the earth.

Author's Note

The people portrayed in this book are real and the events described took place, but fictional names and descriptive detail have sometimes been used as literary devices, or to protect the privacy of certain individuals.

Prologue

MY FATHER'S NAME is Georg Johann Gustave Alfonse Friedrich.
My other father's name is Gustave John. One is my father by name
and act alone and the other one fathered me and so became my
father. I am my fathers' daughter.

George, my adoptive father whom I call Daddo, was always
trying to lure me from my desk at which he feared I would go
mad. Having returned to Sydney after time spent working
abroad, I was living temporarily in the cabana in front of his
house at Lodge Road while I sought work that would pay my
rent elsewhere. At night the dark water of the bay outside
reflected the light of my desk lamp and slapped against the crum-
bling pink sandstone of the convict-built wall. Perhaps Daddo
had walked by and heard me reading aloud to myself—which I
do when I'm editing my own work—or perhaps it was the late
night telephone calls I received from across the world that had
him worried.

One morning he came to my door and said, 'Let's go out. Let's
go to the art gallery.'

I surprised us both by looking up from the tower of manuscripts I should have been reading for a publisher and saying yes.
Perhaps Daddo was right, perhaps I was going loopy down there.

Daddo was wearing light trousers and an embroidered Indonesian shirt which Jackie—my adoptive sister—and I described as hideous but which he admired for its workmanship. We walked slowly up the slight incline towards the gallery and I held Daddo's arm just above the elbow. The top of his head reached my shoulder. He was seventy-four and his frailty—which I'd only started to notice since my return to Sydney—made me nervous. My vigorous, indomitable father had grown old.

Inside the gallery we visited a single floor. Modern sculpture—Daddo being a passionate classicist—came under fire immediately. 'What's that then? A toilet brush or an artichoke? If that's art then I'm the Queen Mother!'

Only when we reached the classical collection did Daddo grow content. This was a man whose taste in art ran to two-metre-tall marble statues of Bacchus and his wife Ariadne, their children held aloft on finely muscled shoulders. Daddo's views on what constituted art had been formed in the thirties. He was frank, too. Although, when he read my first novel with its sex, stripping and drug use, he mulled over it for days. His verdict, and I know he had worked hard to arrive at it, was 'The punctuation is excellent'.

Outside the gallery, we crossed the road to eat lousy but expensive sandwiches and salad in a café and drink espresso. The weather compensated for the café's culinary failings and the late summer sun softened us so we could relax into conversation or just as easily sit in silence. The Botanical Gardens unfolded, verdant and enticing, on one side of the café. Just over the rise lay Woolloomooloo Bay . . . I could almost smell its gun-metal blue waters.

Daddo had unwittingly created an opportunity for me, an opportunity I had been seeking for weeks. I had to unburden myself, I had to tell him what I'd recently learnt.

'I've had some sad news,' I announced.

'Oh?' He did not seem alarmed by my grave tone.

As I prepared myself I played with the remains of my salad: limp lettuce, dry grated carrot and the ubiquitous tinned beetroot.

'I found my natural father last year.'

I jumped right in, hardly stumbling over the word 'father'. 'Natural' was the term we always used for the other parents—two sets of them—whose genes Jackie and I carried. I preferred, however, to think of him as my 'other father' since our relationship seemed anything but natural.

'I tracked him down when I was living in New York,' I told him.

'Oh?' Daddo repeated, and it was an 'Oh?' of simple encouragement.

'I had only his name and the name of his old university.' Daddo was nodding as though he himself had always known this story and I was telling it for my own sake. 'I wrote a silly letter to the university and thought that would make an end to it. I didn't expect to hear a word.'

Daddo smiled, giving me space to tell my story. I wasn't the first of us to pull such a caper; my sister, Jackie, had been reunited with her natural mother when the adoption laws changed and this other mother was now a regular at family gatherings.

I studied Daddo for his reaction. All year round he was tanned from the hours he spent working in his garden and sitting in the armchair in the sun-filled corner of his bedroom. His beautiful, long-fingered hands were covered in sun spots and—despite the hard work they had known—were soft-skinned, his nails clean and well cut.

'Amazingly, my . . . er, Gus was living in the university town again, years after he studied there. He worked as a barrister. He was quite well known in the area.' I did not tell Daddo that he, Gus, was a character and that—as he presented himself—scandal, intrigue and glamour always surrounded him. 'My strange letter was given straight to him and he just phoned me one day.'

Daddo was silent, lingering over his coffee, which he liked to drink cold.

I was at pains not to use the word 'father' when talking of this other father, but it was difficult to tell the story without it. I remain conscious of how easily the word can lose its meaning.

'His reaction, Gus' reaction, was extraordinary. He was excited, he was wildly excited. He had never had a child.'

Daddo had the first hint of tears in his eyes now, but he was smiling, too.

'I liked him Daddo, we got on immediately. We wrote letters to each other and spoke on the phone. Eventually I went to meet him in Toronto. We spent one day together.'

Daddo did not ask me about Gus' appearance and I did not tell him that as I stood head and shoulders taller than Daddo, so Gus towered above me. He just sat there, smiling softly, but my face was stony. I hesitated to share my delight in the knowledge that through Gus I had apparently inherited native-Canadian, French and Cossack blood.

'I didn't know how to tell you this . . . I didn't want to upset you.'

What I did not say was that because of what had happened, what had just happened, I could tell him then. He took one of my cold hands in his and waited.

'I wrote to him to tell him that my novel would be published. To wish him a happy Christmas. I demanded to know why he'd stopped writing to me. I think I already knew there was something wrong . . .' I hesitated, still bewildered by this news of Gus. 'His brother wrote back telling me I'd never see him again . . . it was just over a year since we'd met.'

I had resolved not to cry over this other father in front of Daddo but he, George, wept for both of us. Tears spurted from his eyes and he absently swabbed his face with an oversized handkerchief and blew his nose.

For a moment I forgot my own role in the story and was sitting watching Daddo's pain. For a moment I thought he was going to ask the only question my friends had asked when I told them the story. Why?

'I don't understand how a father could abandon a child, even an adult child . . . especially an adult child.' Daddo's voice was hoarse. 'How could he have chosen not to be part of your life?'

Daddo's reaction to my story struck me at the time as being

oddly personal, heartfelt, and so much more complex than the reactions to which I had become accustomed. I would only begin to understand why when he was gone. By then it was too late to comfort him in turn, to share his grief as he had shared mine. Although it would be four years before we would learn of Daddo's cancer and another year after that before he would die, already he and I shared an unspoken knowledge of his mortality, of our finite time together.

What we also shared—although I did not know it that day—was something I've come to think of as 'father shame'.

In the Aare

———◆◆◆———

DADDO'S FATHER ERNST was a long lean man who laboured through the night on a flimsy camp-bed on which he could not sleep. The bed fitted him no better than his present circumstances and he would leap from it at first light. Fine swimmer's muscles rippled in his back as he pulled on a pair of old shorts and a shirt, slipped on his leather sandals. He did not bother to flatten his unruly, sleep-tousled hair before leaving the tiny attic apartment in which his mother and sister were still asleep.

The German shepherd was always awaiting him, down there on *Brungasse*, just outside his door. No matter what time he arose, Helga was there to greet Ernst, to nudge her huge warm head into his thigh, to butt her wet black nose at his empty hands. Ernst did not know who owned the dog or who fed her, but she had already declared herself to him; she was his and he—if he was anybody's—was hers. Together the two would stride out through the cobbled streets and twisting arcades of Bern's old town towards the Aare.

Bern, in Ernst's opinion, was as sleepy and self-satisfied as an overfed cat. Curled in on itself there in the sharp bend of the River Aare, Bern barely stirred to scratch itself. It was 1917 and he had been back from London only a few months but it already felt like so much longer. Over there in England—at King George's Court—Ernst reckoned things really moved. He had left high on the acclaim he'd won for masterminding the King's Butterfly Ball. The banquets over which Ernst had presided were notorious for

1

running on into the next day and early twentieth-century London was both shocked and seduced by them.

One of the staff from the royal household had discovered Ernst in the fine dining carriage of the Trans-Continental Express, over which he had presided, and had determined to have him in the Court's employ. Ernst liked to boast that his restaurant could pass through four different countries in one day. His clients, the passengers on the elegantly appointed train, might commence their meal in Italy and finish it in France.

Death, however, had always brought Ernst home. His own father's death, years earlier, had seen Ernst out of college and into paid employment quicker than he could have muttered the words 'the future'. When he took his first job in a restaurant Ernst consoled himself with the belief that it was temporary. His younger brother Walter had agreed—once he, Walter, was earning well and could support the family, Ernst would resume his studies to become a journalist. It was, after all, what their father had always wished. Years passed, however, and other opportunities arose for Ernst which proved difficult to resist. Study was deferred again and again.

This time it was Walter's death, at twenty-one years of age, that had brought Ernst home. Walter had worked at his father's old press in a position that had evolved from his father's job. On Walter's first holiday—after he'd been working four years—he had been walking in the mountains when he had heard the crack and ensuing thunder that could mean only one thing in the Alps. When they dug the snow from his body Walter was found in a kneeling position. Ernst had wondered whether his brother had turned to God in the end and vowed that he would not do so himself. Walter had been killed in an avalanche while his urbane brother was serving the King of England.

Ernst had returned to Bern and, at twenty-eight, had moved into his mother's tiny apartment to set about the business of supporting her and his teenaged sister. There had been a job for him as head waiter at *L'Hôtel de Musique*, Bern's most celebrated restaurant. As his father's death had done, so his brother's had forced Ernst to cast aside his ambitions, to once again swallow his dreams. Or so he claimed.

On plunging into the opaque green waters of the Aare Ernst left behind the narrow confines of his life. It was only the exhilaration he found in being a part of such a river, of such a world of the senses, that enabled Ernst to think of the future again. He liked it best—the Aare—when it was flowing fast, when the early summer melt up in the *Berner Oberland* was at its greatest. He'd launch himself into the torrent—water so cold it stopped both breath and brain—and be hurtled off down river. When his head slipped below the water's surface he could hear the pebbles on the river's floor clacking, swirling, whispering to each other. He rode the Aare as far as he dared, part of the mighty natural world. The German shepherd, who would not let Ernst out of her sight, would follow him into the turquoise waters, her great head straining to stay above the water, her frantic eyes searching the man out. Ernst was intrigued by the water's capacity to transform itself so radically, so regularly; snow one moment, water the next, then evaporating to begin the process again. He longed for such a palpable cycle of change in his own life. He longed to move on, to be free.

It was on the banks of the Aare that Ernst resumed his studies. On a rare day off he would lie wrapped in a blanket in the sun reading Roman history in Latin, or ruminating over Goethe. Beside him Helga would sprawl on the grass, her eyes closed, her body watchful. With a book in his hand and the Aare at his feet Ernst knew, once again, what it was to be alive.

Journey

———◆◆◆◆———

TWO YEARS AFTER Daddo dies I travel to Switzerland in search of my dead grandfather, in search of stories untold and of love, long lost. I want to know how Daddo was fathered. I need to know how he came to be the father Jackie and I were so blessed with. I want to know my grandfather, Daddo's father Ernst. I want to know the man who, I suspect, was the reason for Daddo's tears when I told him about Gus. I'm hunting down Ernst Naher, one of my grandfathers and the man Daddo always insisted would have so liked me. From the stories I'd heard I had come to fear that through some quirk of fate I resembled him. On the second leg of my journey I will travel alone to Canada to meet my other father's family, to hunt down the ghost of this other man, this other father who never was. It is May 2000.

I fly north across the world with my sister, Jackie, and her daughter, Freya. When dawn breaks after a dreamless, pressurised night we are over the spine of Europe and mountains stretch before us, all the way from North Africa to France. The peaks are snowcapped and float in a sea of pink dawn clouds. I remember this cloud and ice spectacle from when Jackie and I flew to Switzerland with Daddo in 1984; he had been taking us to meet our Swiss family.

Freya, at sixteen months, lies on the spare seat between Jackie and me. Her head butts her mother's thigh and her fierce little legs and sock-covered feet pummel mine. Throughout the night flight

4

from Singapore my niece pushes and stretches and sighs; she's claiming her space in the world.

I travel with few expectations, clutching not even a handful of insubstantial clues. Behind me is a year's worth of research in libraries and dusty archival offices in Australia and reams of correspondence with similar institutions in Switzerland and Ireland. There's a year of trawling through Daddo's papers, and his own father's papers, documents so ancient they threaten to dissolve in my hands before I can fully grasp their meaning.

Behind me, also, is a series of conversations with Daddo that I taped at Lodge Road, during the year before his death. They are a testament to his humility but leave his own story, and that of his parents, infuriatingly sketchy. For my searching, my probing, my endeavour, all I have to show for my efforts so far are questions, more questions and an imagined life for my grandparents that I myself have conjured.

My interest is in fathers and for this I make no apology. On this journey I'm searching for three of them: for George, the man who raised me, the father I loved; for Gus, the man whose genes I carry but whom I never had the opportunity to love; and for George's father Ernst, who cast an indelible shadow of tragedy over his son's life. I'm searching, also, for an elusive truth: why did one man choose so wholeheartedly to father while the other two did not?

L'Hôtel de Musique

WHEN DADDO'S MOTHER, Emma Braun, arrived in Bern she was twenty-six years old, carried all her possessions in a small embroidered bag and had her life savings tucked inside the top of one of her black leather boots. She was not yet married and, according to her sisters, was no man's fool. She took a modest room near the station late in the day and retired early. A woman of poise and style uncharacteristic in one so young and from such a humble background, Emma was accustomed to making her own decisions and being treated with respect.

Emma had grown up one of six sisters in the village of Wil in canton St Gallen in Switzerland's east. Of her three brothers only one had survived to adulthood. Her father, Johann, had died when she was twelve. Despite the fact that he had been an engineer with the great Braun Bauveri, he died leaving his wife few assets but an abundance of children. Emma's mother, Maria, was not easily daunted and took in laundry to support her children, instilling in her daughter a connoisseur's appreciation of fine, well-laundered linen.

Emma had left her home town aged only sixteen and had travelled to Milan alone. There had been a rumour in her village that the Milanese paid good money for Swiss maids and kitchen-hands and Emma already spoke Italian. Determined, she had been able to instil enough confidence in her mother to extract the precious train fare. One way only, mind you; Emma was expected to make good.

In Milan Emma walked the streets of the city agape. Never had she seen such riches, such fine architecture and such elegantly attired people. In her long black woollen skirt and white cotton blouse she felt like a peasant girl straight off the farm; she made herself stand taller, straighter, nonetheless. Emma followed her instincts and they did not betray her—they led her to a wealthy quarter in which the grand houses advertised the standing of their inhabitants. She followed four small children and the young woman Emma guessed was their governess to the doors of a stately mansion at which she presented herself.

The lady of the house grilled her on her skills and intentions. Emma told the woman plainly of how she had helped her mother raise her siblings, of how she had worked alongside her mother at the laundry and had eventually taken over the cooking as it proved something for which she had an aptitude. What's more, Emma insisted, she had studied hard and won good grades in school. She spoke French, Italian, German and Swiss-German. There was a position open in the kitchen.

For the first and last time, Emma Braun accepted work—there in the kitchen—without enquiring about the salary. From what she had seen of Milan, and from what she saw of the house and of the style in which the family lived, she knew that the potential to learn there was greater, even, than the potential to earn. Indeed, within days of arriving in Milan she had given herself a culinary re-education. In the bright, light-filled kitchen of the great house in Milan she learned and mastered the art of risotto and would favour the Milanese style of the dish—cooked with stock, browned chopped onion, *grana* cheese and saffron—throughout her long life.

After two years in the house the governess announced her impending marriage to a poor yet promising clerk. Despite her evident talents in the kitchen, Emma was an obvious choice for the woman's replacement; already she was assisting the governess in tutoring the children in French and German.

As governess to the children of one of Milan's oldest families, Emma Braun suddenly stepped out in the world. She escorted the children to parks, museums and galleries, and set about learning what she could of the art and architecture of the city. In Milan Emma taught herself to live on little sleep so she could sit up at night reading books from the house's library on Renaissance and Baroque art and on the construction of the Gothic *Duomo*.

When the lady of the house fell ill Emma was instructed to go to a certain shop off the *Via Montenapoleone* to choose herself a fine dress on the family's account. In the short term she would be accompanying the two elder children to the opera—at the celebrated *Scala*—with their father. When she sat there behind the children in the private box decorated with the family's own heraldic colours, Emma struggled to even picture her mother's solid house by the railway tracks at the end of *Sentistrasse* in Wil.

On the rare occasion Emma had time to herself she'd dash off to *Il Duomo* and pay a few coins so she could ascend to the rooftop promenade. On a clear day she could look north and see the Alps. The sight of them, bluish on the horizon, helped her to remember who she was and from where she came.

The outbreak of the First World War brought Emma reluctantly home. In Wil her mother was still running her laundry and caring for children. When Maria's own were grown there were grandchildren, nieces and nephews to play at her feet as she ironed baskets of snow-white linen. Emma worked alongside her mother for a time but Milan had given her a taste of the world and Wil soon felt claustrophobic to her. She decided to move to nearby Bern.

There, Emma Braun was interested in one thing only. She was determined to find work in the kitchen of a sophisticated Bernese restaurant. She had enjoyed working with the children in Milan but food was her passion.

Like Ernst, she rose early and walked the streets of the capital while they were bathed in the fresh light of day. She wandered the arcades of the old town with their low ceilings, their dark, exposed beams and found little to inspire her. Emma peered through the glass fronts of simple cafés, at neat, white-clothed tables and clean, modest decor. There were restaurants decorated with traditional Swiss craft work—hand-carved wooden furniture, painted in bright colours and adorned with Alpine flowers—and Emma did not bother to enquire within.

As the afternoon was easing into dusk, Emma made her way back towards her hotel. Her feet felt bruised and she cursed the city's quaint but impractical cobblestones. She would bathe, eat the fruit she had bought at the street markets earlier and then go out into the city at night—artificial light would give the restaurants a whole other air, might lend them some gaiety. Surely it was the war, Emma told herself, out there beyond the Alps, that gave Bern its air of sobriety.

The sight of a grand, elegant building made Emma stop short. It was three storeys tall and the ground and first floors boasted rows of arched windows. The balcony off the first floor was all curling iron, some of it painted gold. Decorating the eaves were ornate stone carvings. Emma hardly dared hope . . . The sign proclaimed the place *L'Hôtel de Musique*. She skirted the building and at its rear she could see into a magnificent restaurant.

Fine silver and crystal gleamed on the damask tablecloths, reflecting the light of chandeliers overhead. Emma smoothed her hair and straightened her skirt; this was the place. From the upstairs windows a tuba sounded, then a violin; an orchestra was testing its voice. Emma noted each detail—the moulded ceilings, the mirrored walls, the Renaissance-style paintings, the fresh flowers—and approved. She thought of Milan, yes, but she also imagined Paris, Vienna.

Emma bowled into the great, gleaming kitchens at *de Musique* and presented herself to the head chef; she had no trouble identifying him because his uniform was the whitest, his hat the tallest. He was in conversation with the head waiter, running through the menu for the evening and describing each of his dishes with flourish.

When the chef paused for breath Emma leaped in. She could offer him the benefit of her time spent working in the kitchen in one of the greatest houses in Milan. She could infuse his menu with sophisticated Lombardian cuisine. Emma announced that she knew the tastes of Milan's high society and of its international visitors, too. She had frequented *La Scala* and understood its clientele. Her large brown eyes were alight as she addressed the two tall men. For a moment she broke her speech to laugh, told them not to imagine she was a grand lady herself, no, she was a worker, but she understood taste, sophistication.

The chef didn't grace Emma with a reply, just turned back to Ernst, the head waiter, to describe one of the veal dishes that would appear on the menu that evening. Once again, Emma waited for a break and resumed her pitch. This time she described to them each of the styles of *scaloppine* in which she excelled and, for just a moment, she thought she had won the chef. It was not the chef she had captivated, however, it was the head waiter.

Ernst's eyes strayed to the insistent young woman even when the chef was speaking on. He lingered over her creamy skin, her full breast, the way she held her head high and did not look away when one of the two men met her eye. Her confidence, her self-conviction, were in her voice, in the way she held her body, and Ernst felt his own body stirring, imagined the others might hear the racing of his pulse. As the chef continued to recount the menu for the evening and Emma went on proffering her own suggestions, Ernst found himself unable to avert his gaze.

It was only when Ernst spoke, asked the chef whether he was perhaps intimidated by the bright young woman, that Emma knew she had won. She watched the way the chef puffed his chest and laughed at Ernst's suggestion. Actually, the chef announced, he would be interested in giving this woman the opportunity to show them if she was really as good as she thought she was.

Emma turned to Ernst and put out her hand. She introduced herself and there was laughter in her voice. When the head waiter took her hand he held it for just a moment longer than necessary. Emma could not help admiring Ernst's bearing.

Later Emma was given one of the maids' rooms in the attic and from it she could look out over the terracotta rooftops of Bern's old town. Without even questioning Emma, Ernst would have known by this that she was new to the city; the room she had taken there in the restaurant announced it. He would have guessed that there was nobody for her in Bern, nobody but him.

Before he had spent even a moment alone with her, Ernst told Emma later, he could see them together.

Ernst was tall and slim and his brown eyes were almond-shaped beneath his high brow. Immaculately coiffed and completely out of place among the other waiters, Ernst did not see Emma's ambition. He swore he did not notice, as the other men did, that she wore her determination as another woman would wear a brooch—cool and shiny for all the world to see. What Ernst saw and admired was the strength in Emma's body and the intelligence in her eyes. His whole being—or so it seemed to him—craved these things.

Emma, for her part, knew only that she had an ally in the head waiter. She preferred not even to think about the way the man's gaze made her nervous, left her cheeks burning bright red like a young girl's.

Radiance

———◆◆◆———

I WATCH THE OLD sixteen-millimetre film of my adoptive parents' wedding and for a moment imagine George and Pauline happy together. In November 1959, George Naher—dashing entrepreneur and proprietor of the Hotel Belvedere of Bayswater Road in Sydney's Kings Cross—married one of the receptionists, Pauline Edwards. He was forty, she twenty-nine.

The Belvedere had been established some twenty years before Pauline came along. Emma, my adoptive grandmother, first took the lease on the large stately home and its grounds back in 1938. With the exception of the war years—when George was fighting in the Pacific and the building was commandeered for official purposes—mother and son had always managed it together. First as a guest house and then as a private hotel with five-star dining-room, the name Belvedere had become synonymous with fine European service and lavish hospitality. Its *belle époque* style was as uncharacteristic of Anglo, post-war Sydney as was its standard of excellence.

Pauline came from something altogether more austere, although her bloodline was patrician; she would gesture towards her aquiline nose as though this in itself were proof. Her British grandfather had served in the Black Watch and been awarded the Victoria Cross. Her father had fought for Australia in the First World War and died—some time after his return to Sydney—of injuries sustained at the front. Only a couple of years later her mother had died, leaving Pauline an orphan and the youngest of three sisters. As a young teenager she was already supporting herself and had to cut short her schooling to take on more paid work.

When Jackie and I were children ourselves, Pauline would regale us with vignettes from her own childhood. Her mother would not permit her or her sisters long hair, she told us. Cherishing the thought of it, Pauline would pin plaits made of string to her close-cropped curls and sit at the dining table, tossing the braids over first one shoulder then the other. She had been a hockey player, although only small and slender, and her shins had taken a hammering during her teenage years from which they would never recover. In a spelling bee at Dover Heights Public School Pauline had been the only child who could spell the name of the Babylonian King Nebuchadnezzar. She remembered her mother as the most wonderful of women; to me she sounded quite the martyr. These are the stories I remember her telling us.

Pauline took education where she could get it and became a proficient secretary and receptionist. She sewed her own clothes— late into the night, after she'd worked her two or three jobs of the day—and her slim body displayed her chic handiwork well. When she went to work at The Belvedere in the fifties it was only natural that she would attract the attention of the bachelor proprietor, George. The bright, beautifully dressed young woman would have complemented his charm and management skills admirably.

There are other stories about their courtship, naturally, and from where I sit—half a century later—I would not like to place one over another. There were other women interested in George, I am told. Indeed, one was rumoured to have sat outside his quarters in the hotel one evening with a gun across her lap, so fiercely did she wish to guard him from her rival—the bright, glamorous Pauline.

The title on the wedding film, 'D-Day at Belvedere', smacks of Daddo's particular style of humour. But which party was victorious, the groom or his slender bride?

As an adult, I cannot trust myself to view the film through eyes that lack prejudice, so I invite a close friend to sit by me and help interpret faces, expressions and gestures. She is the same friend who—in the absence of a motherly mother—ushered me to my own wedding, saw me frocked and coiffed and buoyed up by champagne and talk beforehand.

The opening sequence, in scratchy, faded black-and-white, is shot from the dark entrance of St Canice's Church, Kings Cross. The contrast of dark and light in the old film is curious, but for me it is no starker than the difference between the demeanour of the bride and that of the groom.

George, my Daddo, is plump-faced and beaming in his top hat and Morning Suit. My friend says she remembers Daddo smiling with the same warmth, the same radiance, when he welcomed her to his home only eighteen months before he died. He is greeting the guests, giving directions to the camera operator and awaiting his bride with a broad, open smile that can only reflect the state of his heart.

In the film Pauline arrives in a vintage black Mercedes, one of the hotel's cars, although her bedsit adjacent to the church is only metres from The Belvedere. She emerges from the dark car into the light wearing a finely ruched gown designed to emphasise her eighteen-inch waist. Gloves rise from her wrists to her elbows; they are white but appear dull beside the translucent skin of her upper arms. She, with no parents of her own, is accompanied by a man of the community whom she has known since childhood. Pauline's angular face remains fixed in a nervous smile. I see none of her own family at the service and remember being told that they were not invited.

Cut to the newlyweds emerging from the church. He radiates joy, smiling so fiercely one wonders that his face does not split. She, cool, pale in the bright November sunshine, keeps her face fixed in its earlier expression. My friend and I watch as confetti falls around the bride and gasp as Pauline pushes back her veil in what appears a thoroughly staged gesture.

For a moment I glimpse Pauline through the gaggle of guests outside the church; she is standing alone . . . at the centre of the crowd yet so clearly an outsider.

Cut now to the reception in the hotel's beautiful grounds, all viewed through dappled light, obscured by random patches of darkness. George is smiling even harder; Pauline's expression—masking or revealing—has not shifted. Through the ballet of moving guests we see snatches of the finely tended garden, of the Belvedere statues that are more familiar to me than most of the faces in the crowd. One of the waiters—a handsome young Mediterranean-looking man—sings to the camera and behind him is a band, comprising piano accordion, cello and guitar. The film, alas, is silent.

George and Pauline are standing behind their three-tiered wedding cake. Daddo's familiar, freckled hand is over hers on the knife's handle. Together they plunge the steel into the pristine icing and he turns to kiss her. For a moment, only the briefest of moments, she smiles and looks younger than her twenty-nine years. Perhaps she has remembered that beside her is a man who clearly adores her.

A Woman of Vision

DADDO'S FATHER ERNST took to calling for Emma on Sunday mornings after she had attended the day's first mass. He had been baptised a Protestant but had long called himself atheist. In Bern it was summer and the days were long and they both took pleasure in being out on the streets of the capital early, before the day had assumed its warmth. While the city was quiet, Ernst, Emma and the German shepherd Helga would walk the streets together. He, at Emma's request, would recount the city's history in which he was an expert. Emma had a talent for filing information away and remembered almost every word he told her. In years to come Emma would surprise her son with snippets of Bernese history from the golden days of her courtship—'George, did you know that nearly two thousand years ago the Celts built a fort where Bern now lies? Did you know that there was once a Burgundian royal court there?'. Ernst was flattered by Emma's attention and Emma, or so she said later, had found a companion from whom she could learn.

Emma came to love the facades of the *Zunfthausen*, the guild-houses, with their finely wrought figures advertising their members' skills. Their magnificent frescoes imbued their tradesmen with an heroic quality. It was the humour and honesty of the figures Emma enjoyed—the monkey with stone pick and gauge for the stone masons and bricklayers—and she would stand and gaze up at them until Ernst tired and moved off down *Kramgasse*

16

without her. He, by contrast, felt ambivalent towards these effigies. Ernst was not the sort of man to be impressed by toil, by labour, he told Emma. His interest, and he would have wanted her to be absolutely clear about this, was in the life of the mind, was in learning and the intellect.

They were both visitors in the other's domain, Emma and Ernst, or this is how he chose to see it—Ernst in her world of service, of fine restaurants, and Emma in his land of the mind and of learning. Ernst, however, who had worked in hospitality for some years now, had unwittingly become more than a visitor in Emma's world; he was now a long-term inmate.

Emma borrowed books from Ernst which she read late into the night, long after she'd finished her evening shift. The girl she'd been sharing her attic room with had long since moved out, complaining she could not sleep with Emma's candle alight so late into the night. The management had turned a blind eye to this peculiarity and had left the second bed in Emma's room empty. They had already learned that Emma genuinely had something to offer them, just as she'd promised.

Like Ernst, Emma distinguished herself quickly at *de Musique*. When the second chef walked out in a fury—having been accused of drinking the cooking brandy and then fumbling a waitress' breasts—Emma was there to take his position at the stove.

During their first outings together, Ernst sat on the riverbank, the cool waters of the Aare tantalising him, distracting him. He was there with Emma, wanted to be there on the grass with her, but also desperately wanted to swim. He finally confessed this need to her, calling his condition 'calenture'. He could not, he explained, sit by a large body of water without an ache in his bones that compelled him to immerse himself. Emma was so intrigued by the word, by the notion of it, that she encouraged him to swim. She would, Emma claimed, sit happily on the riverbank and read.

The first time Ernst swam when they were at the Aare together, Emma demurely averted her gaze as Ernst strode towards the water in his bathing suit, the dog at his heels. Later, when she saw him returning, walking upstream towards her, she could not help noting that he was a man of some stature. While his bathing suit covered him from knee to elbow, wet it revealed as much as it concealed. Apart from noticing Ernst's manliness, there by the river, Emma found herself inexplicably moved by his friendship with the dog. Emma later told her sister that something in her would soften when she watched the dog, Helga, leap into the torrent behind Ernst.

One of these Sunday mornings by the Aare Emma told Ernst of the plan she was hatching. It was the blueprint for her next move. She'd been approached by the *maître d'* of the Burgdorf Casino, who had heard about her through his cousin who also worked at *de Musique*. Burgdorf was a wealthy town only a half hour from Bern by train. The man had told her he was moving on to a bigger job in Bern and that he wanted to offer Emma—of whom he had heard such impressive things—the lease.

Emma was not the sort of woman to feel flattered, no, she was the sort of woman to reach out for an opportunity with both hands. After her first meeting with the man from Burgdorf she was already planning what she would say to Ernst—that the place was a perfect beginning . . . for an industrious *pair*. The current proprietor had advised that she would need a male partner in her venture.

Ernst felt flattered, intrigued and then somewhat put out in quick succession. In Switzerland, in 1917, women would not get the vote for another sixty years. Men made the decisions, men took the initiative. Emma anticipated Ernst's apprehension and prepared a dozen arguments to counter each one of his.

By the time they had to leave the riverbank to change for work it had been decided. Ernst took Emma's arm in his. She, full of plans, of schemes, of ideas for her own business, allowed him to.

The Baby Factory

I, THE ADOPTED CHILD, in the absence of hard facts, of detail, have imagined so much. For years I shaded the outline of my own story with colours that I could not even name. Gradually, as pieces turned up from here, from there, the story began to take on its own life.

Here's a fact: Pauline and George tried for years to have their own child, but suffered miscarriage after heartbreaking miscarriage. Eventually, after so many hopes raised and dashed, they decided to adopt. First they brought home Jackie, and then they made their plans for me.

Here's another: Jackie's other mother had cared for the other women's babies during her confinement at the place I once dubbed 'the baby factory'. These were the babies held in limbo before the courts approved their adoption. These were the babies whose own mothers would never know the pain of their cries or the privilege of caring for them. The baby factory was actually Waitara Babies' Home, and I was there, too.

I used to imagine my pregnant mother, the woman who was preparing to 'relinquish' me, helping to care for other women's babies in the weeks before I was born. I could picture her—my other mother's name is Jane and she was twenty-two years of age—with long, slender legs and a large, taut belly out in front of her. I could see her with those other babies, easy and capable, yet all the while knowing that she would never hold me. For her and for women like her I cannot imagine a greater torture.

19

I would try to imagine my birth, although not yet a mother myself, and I would see the cool detachment of the medical staff, the way disapproval furrowed the brows of the doctor and made his lips curl. I would be lying if I said I could imagine how my other mother felt when—after a long sad labour—I, her baby, was wrestled from her body and taken away. I could never say that I understood.

I would try to imagine my own bewilderment, a baby's bewilderment. I would try to imagine the confusion of being returned to the Waitara Babies' Home with all those pregnant women, with the other babies whose cries I had already heard from within Jane's womb. I, tiny baby, was back at the Home but the warm body I knew—my own larger body—was absent. The voice I'd heard soothing the crying babies and the other pregnant women, singing and shushing and whispering words of love, was gone. I was, in turn, cared for by pregnant women, their big bellies pushing me away from their bodies, even when they tried to hold me close. Their big bellies putting another baby between them and me.

Perhaps my other mother had returned to the family property out west and to her parents' well-meaning attempts to behave as though nothing had happened. I tried to imagine my other grandparents' efforts to go on regarding their daughter as the same little girl they'd farewelled when she'd left for the city and university, and for the love affair that would result in me.

Here's another fact: the nuns at the baby factory, in their attempts to reassure my other mother about the home to which her daughter was going, had described a long, sweeping driveway and music floating out across carefully tended gardens. They had told her of the way the staff had formed a guard of honour to welcome the first baby—my sister Jackie—when she had been adopted two years earlier.

Curiously, I struggled to imagine the appearance of George, my Daddo, and my adoptive mother, Pauline, by my cot at the baby factory. I could say that when they arrived, when they first held me, I knew I was going home, but I will not. I cannot. Nothing is that simple.

After Jane gave birth to me—gave me up and gave me away—I imagined her slipping back into university life. Perhaps she was determined to study and do nothing else. Some kindly family friends invited Jane to lunch, oblivious of her recent trauma. Perhaps she, Jane, saw this invitation as the moment she would leave the past—and me—behind and step out into the world again. This is how my other mother came, quite innocently, to be invited to The Belvedere and to happen upon her baby's new home. This, also, is a fact.

She had heard of Daddo's hotel, The Belvedere, but had never been there. By the sixties it was something of a local icon. Sydney people who didn't know it assumed the Kings Cross hotel terribly grand. It was, after all, favoured by actresses, astronauts and politicians. I would imagine that she, the young woman who had given me away, thought that this might be the moment she'd begin to live again. I would imagine that it seemed possible, when she arrived, that the outing could give her the kick-start her life needed. Perhaps the blend of elegance, luscious food and good, warm hospitality would lift her. I would imagine her being driven down the sweeping driveway and hearing music floating out across the finely tended gardens. There would have been a familiarity to the place, as though she'd dreamed of it already. In a flower garden outside the reception, a small girl with plump, dimpled cheeks placed snails on the back of a supine Great Dane.

Jane and her friends were, I imagined, ushered into the restaurant from which they could still see the garden, the little girl and the large, gentle dog. The news, it might have seemed, was trumpeted across to her table. First one of her friends made an enquiry of a waiter: 'Has the new baby arrived yet?'. Then the restaurant manager with her dark hair swept up onto her head came to the table to chat to her guests and to proudly confirm it. She, the cousin of the proprietor, was to be the godmother.

The restaurant, I imagined, must have suddenly seemed full of it. Full of the news of my arrival. Outside in the garden was the first of the adoptive girls; more precious than gold yet in the care of a gentle dog. George and Pauline, Jane learned, had recently adopted their second girl, had brought her home to the adoring staff, to the doting grandmother, Emma, to the proud godmother, Leny, and to the warm smelly dogs who were primed to guard her.

This is the part of my not-entirely-imagined story that cuts me every time. This is the part of the story where Jane had to sit there and listen. This is where she had to experience the buzz and excitement of the homecoming. This is where she had to listen to the talk of the bravery of the couple for adopting—who knows what problems they might have been bringing into their home?—and where she had to hear about the other woman, surely a martyr, who had taken on somebody else's unwanted child.

Meanwhile, behind the scenes, I, the baby, might have stirred in my cot. Perhaps Jane's voice or her nervous laugh floated across the gardens and into the penthouse apartment where I was sleeping? Surely, even months after our separation, I still carried the imprint of my other mother's voice, of her laugh, of her own particular warmth and smell?

The Kiss

———◆◆◆———

I T WAS NOT UNTIL January that my grandparents, Emma and Ernst—who were not yet even Daddo's parents—could schedule a day off together on which they could both visit Burgdorf and the casino that Emma hoped would be their future. For her, increasingly frustrated by what she perceived as the limited scope of the kitchens at *de Musique* and hungry to plan her own menus, the move was a foregone conclusion. The Christmas season at *de Musique*—despite the rest of Europe being at war—had been busy and determinedly festive. Ernst later insisted that he found it just a little obscene; so many young men lying dead on bloodied European soil all around them and Switzerland celebrating Christmas, regardless. He kept his concerns about taking a lease on a restaurant at such a time to himself; his feelings for Emma compelled him to act against his better judgment. What's more, living in Bern in such close quarters with his mother and sister made Burgdorf all the more attractive to him.

On the day Emma and Ernst took the train to Burgdorf from Bern, snow lay deep on the ground outside the city and enveloped them in its forgiving softness, wrapped them in a pleasant cocoon inside their heated compartment. As the train moved away from Bern Ernst felt lighter, even tapped one of his feet on the floor at the pleasure of escape, of anticipation. Emma remained serious, deep in contemplation of her plans and largely oblivious to Ernst and the snow-covered fields rolling by outside.

Emma dealt with the issue of money there and then. Did not hesitate to ask Ernst what he needed for his mother and to quickly factor this, along with what she had always sent to her own mother, into her calculations. Ernst was embarrassed to talk money with Emma but was already in her power. When she named the figure they would need to earn in order to pay the rent and help support their families, Ernst balked. A picture-postcard image of an old timber farmhouse bowing under the weight of thick snow flashed by and at that moment he resolved to leave the details to Emma. He was preoccupied by the thought of kissing her, there in the warm privacy of their compartment. He watched her handsome face, her fine dark eyes, and marvelled at his good fortune.

When the conductor walked through their carriage announcing that they were arriving in Burgdorf, the two rose in unison, both eager, uncertain. Ernst saw just a flicker of anxiety on Emma's face and seized the moment to place his arm around her shoulders, to tell her with a firm voice that everything would turn out for the best. Out on the platform, the town of Burgdorf up on the hill before them, Ernst and Emma made a striking couple, their faces aglow with hope and the smell of the future.

They walked in silence through the quiet, near-deserted streets, first passing houses surrounded by large gardens and fields, their feet sinking deep into the snow at each step. Ernst glanced down at the lace-up black leather boots Emma always wore and wondered whether they were already soaked through. She was not the sort of woman who would mention such a thing and he was not the type of man to fuss in concern. A horse and carriage glided by, the rails making a shushing sound in the bluish snow, but this was the only sign of life. Emma and Ernst's prospective clients were nowhere to be seen.

The town of Burgdorf was perched high on a rocky outcrop in the Emme Valley, with the railway station down on the valley floor below. At one end of the rise the castle towered over both the town and the river plains. At the opposite end of the town the Protestant church reached heavenwards, its steeple rising even taller than the highest turret of the castle. Emma had already ascertained that the town had a Catholic Church. At the bottom of *Kirchbuhl*, she admired the *Hotel zum Stadthaus* on one corner, and Ernst gazed with some longing at the Langlois & Co Bookshop across the road. Further up *Kirchbuhl* Emma noted Herr Marti-Walchli's butchery, boasting the latest sausage-making apparatus.

The sight of the Casino halted them both in their tracks; an elegant, imposing building in a row of fine buildings. On the ground floor five arched windows stood in a row, each bordered by ornate columns and delicate carvings. On the first floor this pattern was echoed, but the arches were taller and grander, with windows reaching from floor to high ceiling.

Ernst described the man who received them, the outgoing proprietor, as 'keen as a shiny new coin' and asked Emma how it was that the position he was going to in Bern was still open to him after a delay of some months. The proprietor was apologetic; first about the snow on the pavement outside and then about the fact that he had not been able to arrange a carriage to meet them at the station. What's more, neither the dining room nor the kitchen were clean as his woman had not yet arrived from her farm outside the town.

Emma barely heard the man, so pressing was her need to scrutinise the dining room, to stand in the kitchen and inhale the place. Ernst stood back and watched the way Emma's nose twitched at the smell of stale cigarette smoke and spilled beer. Her expectations were dashed and then quickly disregarded as she saw the place first for what it was and then for what it might be. The dining room was crude compared to that to which she was accustomed. On the walls the wooden panelling was dark and unappealing and there was no plasterwork to speak of. The room was dominated by a tall stove, its naked pipes twisting in ugly knots just below the ceiling. With white tablecloths, gleaming silver and candles on the tables, it might—or so Emma imagined—become something quite other.

The proprietor led them upstairs to the concert hall; it compensated for what the dining room lacked with its stucco around the balcony and proscenium arch and high, detailed ceilings. The concert hall—managed by the *Liederkranz*, or Choir

Association, that owned the Casino—was the heart of the place and the restaurant more of an afterthought.

The inspection of the rest of the Casino was a mere formality. The proprietor treated them to a tour of the cellar, the larder, the guest amenities, the smaller rooms on the second floor that could be used for private dining or for meetings, and the broad sweep of terrace out the back that looked down over bare trees towards the valley.

Beneath the eaves he presented Emma and Ernst with the large bright room that was, he said, to be their own. As the man flung back the door with a flourish, Emma flushed, colour rising high on her cheeks. It was a spacious, simple room, running right across the building with a stove and small dining area in one corner and a large, high bed in another. Its windows looked out towards the Emme on one side and across *Kirchbuhl* towards a gracious building, on the other. The proprietor prattled on about the room's warmth in winter, about the way the morning sun came streaming in through the windows and about how he would often be woken by the sound of musicians rehearsing in the concert hall below.

Emma later told her sister Alma of her intense embarrassment when the man had enquired about their wedding plans and had chatted on, not even registering their failure to reply. Emma was too mortified to speak and Ernst had moved off on his own to gaze out across the valley. The man went on to propose a small toast to his future and their own.

Ernst regained his tongue and turned down the offer of the drink, a gesture so out of character Emma was quite sure that she had ruined everything.

He guided Emma from the Casino, extricating them smoothly. Emma appeared to have misplaced her powers of speech. Neither of them spoke as they retraced their steps through the snow and by now Emma's toes were achingly cold in her wet boots. Her step had grown heavy.

Ernst steered Emma down *Kirchbuhl*, into *Hohengasse* and up a narrow path, up dozens of steps towards the castle. The linden trees in the park were bare and snow lay deep on the ground. The couple moved towards the low stone barrier that formed part of the castle's high, thick wall. A sharp bend in the Emme lay before them. Ernst cleared his throat and Emma gazed out at the snow that seemed to cushion the forest. She longed to be as anonymous and shrouded as any one of those trees. The frozen river was sky blue.

As Emma started to apologise, Ernst identified an excellent swimming spot at the river's bend. She had never thought to ask about the accommodation . . . it hadn't even occurred to her. Ernst must understand that she had never, not for a moment, led the proprietor to believe that they were engaged. How could she have?

She went on apologising, her voice taut with emotion. Ernst tried to silence her, to indicate that none of that mattered but she was unstoppable, so great was her embarrassment. In exasperation Ernst drew Emma towards him. With Burgdorf Castle behind him and the Emmental before him, he kissed her and immediately felt the shock of it, the surprise in her body.

When Emma finally broke away from him she spoke of taking a room in the town as though the kiss had not happened. Ernst would naturally live on the premises in the bright room atop the Casino. Naturally.

Perhaps Ernst took her hands then, or kneeled in the snow. When he proposed his voice held nothing of the panic, of the shame that Emma's had.

It wasn't what she had intended, Emma rushed on, she didn't mean to orchestrate this, to embarrass him into such a position. Ernst only hushed her. Asked her to answer yes or no.

Emma looked away, looked out to the valley and the forest. When she looked back to Ernst he must have seen that she had decided but he could not tell which way. To cover his nervousness, and because he feared he might never have the opportunity again, he bent down to kiss her once more. When she did not resist, when she met his kiss with her whole body, Ernst knew her answer.

The Womerah and the
Belvedere Ghost

———◆◆◆———

I HAD BEEN TRYING to cut a deal for one of my clients with a film producer—it was the late nineties and I was working in Sydney as a literary agent—when, in true Sydney style, the woman quizzed me about my background. I told her I was a Belvedere child and she flushed beneath her navy beret; she and her ex-husband, the tycoon, had frequented the place. 'We adored it.' The word 'adored' went on and on. 'It was just like something from the set of a Baz Luhrmann film!' Immediately I pictured the Capulets' mansion from Luhrmann's *William Shakespeare's Romeo + Juliet* and knew just what she meant.

One Melbourne journalist who regularly stayed at The Belvedere as a young boy confessed with illicit pleasure that it was there that he saw his first naked woman, an actress who was having an affair with his father. Another journalist described the staff as so well-trained no request was too outlandish. His friends had once called room service for an oyster sandwich; it was promptly delivered without comment.

The house named Belvedere—which means 'beautiful outlook'—once stood on part of the Thomas West Estate. The land, in keeping with the concept of *terra nullius,* was granted to a free settler, Thomas West, in 1810. On it he established a flour mill, the first in the colony. The site had long been the home of the Womerah people, who had camped for centuries among the forests of mahogany and blackbutt. Brush wallabies, bandicoots and possums were in ample supply and aquatic birds flourished in the swamp.

No doubt the Wests, like other colonists, saw what they wished to see. The beautiful view from the house named Belvedere—it was high up on the hill—was real enough but the sense of idyll the name conjured was not. Rushcutter's Bay, down below, was indeed full of rushes and in the early days of the colony parties of convicts were dispatched to cut them for the thatched roofs of the settlement's houses. In 1788, two white rush-cutters were speared to death, allegedly in retaliation for the rape of some of the Womerah women. This marked one of the first fatal attacks made on whites in the history of the colony.

The area continued to be inhabited by the Womerah for decades until the Wests' subdivisions—rows of terraced houses and the Darlinghurst Public School—meant they could no longer survive in the area. The Womerah continued to return for their annual 'dole' payments of blankets and food on the Queen's birthday; on this auspicious day they were expected to perform corroborees.

For Daddo, a bastardisation of the grand house's history became an integral part of the hotel's character and provided it with its very own ghost. The story is here beside me on paper, the page speckled brown with time and typed out on one of Daddo's old manual typewriters. It is unsigned but I know that he wrote it.

Belvedere Hotel. Family Ghost.

One wing of the 'Belvedere Hotel' consists of part of the original mansion which stood on the site, and which was built for Obed West, one of the early flower [sic] millers of the colony. His mill stood beside a creek [now a storm-water channel] which ran through the low-lying land where The Stadium is now situated.

Legend has it that Obed West had a beautiful young daughter, Millie, who fell in love with the cook employed by her father.

They used to meet under the willow by the old mill stream. Obed, a wealthy man, disapproved of this association and forbade his daughter to have anything to do with the cook. They defied him and continued to meet in secret.

Finally they made plans to elope one night, but through the treachery of another servant they were discovered by Obed. He immediately dismissed the cook and ordered his daughter to be kept locked in her room. When she died some time later from a broken heart Obed decreed that her room be always locked and never used again by anyone. On hearing of her death the cook committed suicide.

- The Ghost -

Millie's room is never used as a guest-room in the hotel. If you go in there at night and sit in the darkness you will hear, after a time, a faint knocking on the closed door. Then the door will slowly open and the eerie ghostlike figure of a cook, in a tall cap, will materialize. There will be the soft music of 'Down by the Old Mill Stream' in the distance. The figure calls gently, 'Millie, Millie'. There is no answer. The music fades and the figure disappears from view.

Daddo always referred to the Hollywood film company as Metro-Goldwyn-Naher, not Mayer, and it's clear from this story that he harboured secret aspirations in that area. It's difficult to imagine that West would have had a chef with a tall hat as described in the story; indeed, it's difficult to imagine that he had a chef at all. The house itself, as far as my search shows, was never inhabited by so much as a single member of the esteemed West family.

As a writer, I delight at the extent of fabrication in the story of the Belvedere ghost. Was Daddo imagining a future in which he would be the father of teenaged girls, a future in which hot-blooded chefs needed keeping in check? Or was he writing his own, preferred version of the family history?

To the Castle

The premise under which Emma and Ernst were lured to the Casino was a lie. I learn this in the office of the town archivist. In the minutes of an extraordinary general meeting held by the Casino's owners, the *Liederkranz*, I discover that the proprietor— who had recommended the business to Emma and Ernst—was leaving because he'd managed to accumulate a debt of nearly 1000 francs during the last three months of 1917. In March 1918 the *Liederkranz* agreed that prospective managers of the restaurant should be adequately informed. It was stipulated that Emma and Ernst must not be misled. They were deemed appropriate candidates for the lease not because of their skills in the industry but because Ernst's business and journalistic studies—even incomplete—would give him the prospect of earning a living elsewhere.

Astonishingly, my search reveals that the Burgdorf town archives hold the glass negatives of the two earliest photographs of Daddo, both taken by Louis Bechstein. One is dated May 1920 and shows a bare, pale-chested baby with chubby face and neck so dark that one suspects the use of tan boot polish. The other is a luminous image of mother and son, taken in 1922. In it Emma gazes in wonder at her son, George, and he, bony-kneed in a white smock, looks dreamily ahead. There is no family portrait, no image of Ernst for me to gaze at and wonder.

It is the same precious, mother–son image that we used two years ago at Daddo's funeral. I marvel that a photo taken in a Swiss town in 1922 could survive two migrations and most of a century. Nothing of Ernst had that sort of longevity. Perhaps I, his adopted granddaughter, can change that.

When I take the train from Bern to Burgdorf in June 2000, it's already balmy by 9 am. The journey is so brief—only twenty-odd minutes—I am quite unprepared for my arrival when the moment comes. The railway station, unlike many I've seen on my travels around Switzerland, is modern and without charm. I want so many things of the town in which Daddo was born.

As I climb the hill from the station it's so hot I find myself gliding from one pool of shade to another. At the top of the hill, in the Catholic church, I see the font in which Daddo, as baby George, was christened and the ledger that records the event. His godfather— who didn't bother to travel from Bern for the ceremony—was the composer Feruccio Busoni. Later, in an old family album, I find affectionate postcards from Busoni to my grandmother, Emma. The handwriting is showily artistic and the image on the cards is of Busoni himself, seated at his piano, his head flung back in a dramatic flourish. There's not a musical bone in the Naher family and I wonder whether Busoni—who died when Daddo was only five— ever so much as laid eyes on his godson. Years later in Sydney we visit on Busoni yet another honour; we name a family cat after the man.

I am looking for ghosts, for memories, for some sort of proof. I do not even know the dates of Emma and Ernst's stay in Burgdorf. At times I find myself pondering the very truth of my grandfather's existence. Ernst's story is as absent from this period as Emma's is present.

At the local *Gemeindehaus*—where good Burgdorf citizens have registered their arrivals and departures for centuries—a clerk leads me underground, installs me in a dusty vault. A friend has already made a preliminary visit for me and in the company of the archivist conducted a search that produced no trace of the Nahers. I am faced with three walls of floor-to-ceiling shelving; hundreds of leather-bound ledgers—the size and weight of great flagstones—with no clue as to the order in which they have been arranged. I have only one day in Burgdorf.

I stand back and petition the family ghost to guide me now. It has, after all, looked over my shoulder most evenings during my journey as I've written up my notes. I step forward, pull out a single ledger from the middle of a low shelf and turn to the index. Ernst's name is inscribed on the page marked N. I have found them.

In the ledger Daddo's father is Georg Ernst and Daddo himself is Johann Georg; this reversal of Christian names proves not uncommon. I am all too conscious that Emma and Ernst once gazed at the same page I'm scrutinising, once watched an official inscribe their names in that barely legible Gothic script, his pen moving back and forth between the page and the ink pot. Here, Ernst is called *Wirt*, restaurateur.

Below the *Gemeindehaus*, on *Kirchbuhl*, rises Burgdorf Casino. Aside from two tall lights out the front and a blocky fourth floor addition, archival photos show that from the outside the building is just as it was when Emma and Ernst first saw it. Although it is closed until the evening, to simply stand before the building in which Daddo was born is a powerful experience for me. Travelling with my niece Freya—aged one and a quarter—has made it easy to imagine Daddo at sixteen months of age, negotiating the steps with careful concentration, arse first.

Further down *Kirchbuhl*, the *Hotel zum Stadthaus*, the Langlois & Co. Bookshop and the *Confiserie* all still exist. I stop for coffee and sit in the cool of the stone arcade in front of a window of exquisite cakes and chocolates. The street before me is cobbled and each building well preserved. The archival photos I study tell me that superficially little has changed here in the old town since 1918. At the *Confiserie* I buy *Burgdorfer Leckerli* for Jackie—a hard gingerbread biscuit which the family dog in Sydney, Bono, would condescend to eat only once it had been soaked in milky tea.

When I enter the Casino later in the day I see that the traditional interior—all that dark wooden panelling—has been replaced by a blend of minimalism and art nouveau. It's functional and sparse and the warmth that must once have imbued the restaurant has vanished with almost as little trace as Ernst. The terrace, which looks down over the Emme Valley—now industrial as well as rural—is the only space that has not been significantly altered. The atmosphere in the surprising, blinding heat of late afternoon resembles nothing I think of as the Naher style—'*la touche*', as Daddo used to call it.

All that remains is to walk up to the castle, now occupied by courts of law and a museum. I rest in a pleasant garden beneath linden trees, the castle towering above me, its wall falling away below. Down on the valley floor a bend in the Emme provides bathers with a small stony beach on the edge of a pine forest. The water there is an opaque, dreamy pale blue. Like my grandfather, Ernst, before me, I too experience calenture; I too crave immersion in a soothing, embracing body of water.

The Danes

My EARLIEST CHILDHOOD memory is of a smell, not an image. It's the warm, comforting, doggish smell of the two Great Danes, Helga and Spatzi, who lived in The Belvedere's gardens. I would lie on them, ride them, cuddle them and sleep on them. My face had to be right up against them, buried in their warm, soft fur that I was forever finding in my mouth. With the Danes I knew safety.

Leny, whom I called Aunty, but who was really Emma's niece and my godmother, used to tell Jackie and me that if we swallowed dogs' hair we'd never grow. We didn't care, we just wanted to be with the dogs. We wanted to be on the dogs and lying right beside the dogs. When I was an older child I imagined that I'd been raised by dogs, by these two Danes in a whimsical garden behind a high wall in Sydney's Kings Cross.

The garden in which Jackie and I lolled with the dogs was just outside The Belvedere's reception; apparently Daddo, Pauline and the office staff could watch us there. As a child I imagined it was the dogs who looked after us, not our parents.

It was also the dogs' duty to keep away the undesirables; we were on the road once known as the 'dirty half-mile'. The dogs were the size of ponies so when one of them came upon a drunk curled up in the garden, it didn't even need to bare its teeth to provoke a reaction. The Danes claimed a few trouser seats in their day.

It was not unusual for guests to pull in off Bayswater Road and have a Dane's head thrust in through the driver's window. To a small child it seemed their heads were big enough to fill a car.

I remember collecting snails in that garden; I loved touching their feelers and watching the poor things shrink back into their shells. Jackie and I would have been dressed in matching velvet frocks so short they revealed all of my chunky Monette thighs—I'd inherited them from my other father, Gus Monette—with white socks pulled up to our knees and patent leather shoes on our feet. We were show children but we were in the garden with the dogs and snails, nonetheless.

We threw toys from a high balcony into the garden and some-times snails, too. Jackie and I liked the waiters—smiling, doting young European men—who would retrieve our toys and return them to us in the flat. It was great sport, standing on the balcony, waiting until we knew the waiter had returned to his station in the restaurant beside the garden and then hurling the toys over, one by one, again.

In the boiler room we snuggled into great mounds of sunlight-smelling clean linen. In that room at any moment I might have been clasped to the bosom of my nanna Emma, or of Chiarina, a Swiss-Italian woman and one of the hotel's longest-serving staff. In the boiler room the table—when it wasn't being used for folding linen—was where the family sat and ate. Winston, Emma's bulldog, had his own place at the table and sat beside her on his own low stool. When Winston wasn't in the boiler room he was chained up outside; he was so strong—a compact square of sinew, muscle and face folds—that he'd regularly pull the gas pipes right out of the wall.

The chef would find little fist marks in slabs of finest sirloin and would complain to Daddo that I'd been in the cool room again. I was crazy for raw meat and would embark on commando raids into the fridge when the chef was busy elsewhere. With both hands and all my strong fingers I'd claw chunks of meat from the steaks and stuff them into my little mouth. I must have been raised by dogs, after all.

The only thing I remember about my parents' penthouse apart-ment was that a possum used to visit. It would scuttle across the balcony and into the dining room during my afternoon sleep. Of course I was only pretending to be asleep and was really waiting for the possum. As the story goes the possum would scamper into the flat and up onto the polished mahogany dining table where it would help itself to the fruit in the bowl. As evidence it left scratches on the table's polished surface. In my mind's eye the scratches are great gouges like those a wolf or bear would leave behind. Possums, however, are nocturnal—such is the flawed nature of memory—which means this visitor could not have come during the day and I would never have seen it myself. If we'd kept that dining table I'd be able to verify at least one of these stories from my early childhood.

I confess, and with some guilt, that I remember nothing of George or Pauline—my adoptive parents—from the first years of my life, from those days at The Belvedere. It was all dogs, to me, dogs and a chorus of Swiss women with their ample bosoms and boundless warmth and laughter.

Amour

◆━◆━◆

M Y GRANDPARENTS, EMMA and Ernst, were married in Bern in March 1918. The civil ceremony was attended by the bride's mother, Maria, and the groom's sister, Elsa. Maria had taken the train from St Gallen although she could ill afford the time away. Emma's sisters later explained that their mother had been uncertain about the match; her daughter was, after all, marrying outside the Catholic faith. Ernst's mother, Elise, invented a cold and sat out the ceremony in her tiny apartment nearby. Perhaps the moment Elise Naher set eyes on Emma Braun she knew that the last remaining Naher man was lost to her.

Emma wore an exquisite dress made of navy lace as fine as the tracery of snowflakes on glass. The dress, which she had worn to *La Scala* in Milan, was her most cherished possession. Falling to her ankles and tapering to a point at the back of each hand, it suited Emma well. The pale skin at her full breast took on the lustre of marble beside the midnight-blue lace. Ernst wore the three-piece English woollen suit he'd used while officiating at functions in King George's court. In his waistcoat pocket—the one closest to his heart—was his father's watch. It was engraved with my own initials which are the same as Daddo's—GN—for the first Georg Naher registered in Frauenfeld, Canton Thurgau, in 1832.

They were a handsome couple and Emma's mother wept when she first saw them there together at the church. Maria later told one of Emma's sisters that she feared it was a love match.

The newlyweds were to have retreated to Emma's attic room at dusk but the chef had engineered a different fate for them. He had chosen the previous night—perhaps in his ire over losing Emma—to take Ernst out drinking. Come the wedding day evening the chef was still too ill to look at food. The bride would have to step in and cook; the show must go on. The groom was reported to be looking weary himself although he swore he never experienced hangovers. He retired in the late afternoon with only the bridal frock—shimmering on its hanger in the evening breeze—for company. One can only speculate as to whether Emma woke her new husband when she finally climbed the stairs to her attic room, late on the night of her wedding day.

Almost immediately upon the newlyweds' arrival in Burgdorf the dreaded Spanish influenza gripped the town. By the time they were settled in the large, airy room atop the Casino the town's people—all 9500 of them—were virtually confined to their homes. This flu saw all public venues closed indefinitely and came fast on the heels of what had been a winter of privation. The previous year's crop had been so poor that there had been only twenty-five kilos of potatoes per head for the winter season.

That summer the town's annual *Solennitaet* procession was cancelled and even as the autumn drew to a close visits to the cinema and Casino were still officially forbidden. It was not until the end of December that the citizens of Burgdorf were permitted, once again, to attend church.

The country itself was in turmoil. A general strike took place in November as Kaiser Wilhelm abdicated and the German Republic was proclaimed. The Swiss socialists tried to imitate the success of the Bolsheviks and for three days the country was paralysed. The army was called in and soon it controlled Switzerland. By the time the strike collapsed, however, the country was on the brink of civil war. The Russians were blamed for the strike and relations with the USSR were severed until 1945. Some say that the real losers were not the socialists but the radicals, a group with whom Ernst had felt intellectually aligned.

Ernst and Emma would have barely known each other when Ernst—because his own restaurant was not permitted to open—was forced to return to his position as head waiter at *de Musique*. A man of pride, this return to his former position and to the small camp-bed at his mother's came as an extraordinary blow. He could no longer be bothered to rise early and walk the streets of the city with the devoted dog. Emma remained in influenza-ravaged Burgdorf and lent her hand to any paying task that presented itself: she worked in the kitchen at the *Confiserie*; toiled making sausages at the delicatessen; and emptied chamber pots at the *Hotel zum Stadthaus*. Her knuckles were raw from scrubbing grease from her new kitchen at the Casino but she took pleasure in every moment she spent readying the restaurant. With careful spending on linen, silver and crystal Emma prepared for the opening.

When they met on Emma's errands to Bern, or when Ernst visited her briefly in Burgdorf, she would tell him 'Soon, soon darling, soon'. Ernst, inexplicably, found himself at something of a loss when Emma was not beside him . . . he had grown accustomed to being driven by her energy, by her personality. When he was not working, Ernst was drinking; Emma later confided to her sister that even when he was entirely sober, she could still smell the wine fumes on his skin. Once, in a moment of intimacy, she asked him how it was that wine had become his best friend. Her words surprised both of them and the subject was not mentioned again for some time.

Emma started advertising the new restaurant at the Casino in the depths of winter, early 1919. They had arrived almost a year earlier. Despite her determined optimism Emma was struggling with fatigue and nausea and repeatedly postponed the moment she would tell her husband she was pregnant. The commitment of the lease, Emma maintained, already weighed so heavily on him.

Come the beginning of February, Ernst returned to Burgdorf to take his place beside his wife for the restaurant's opening. The morning he arrived at the Casino Emma took one look at him—at the dark circles under his eyes and the slack, pale skin at his once-firm jaw—and felt a new and different responsibility land on her shoulders. It occurred to her, only briefly, that she was somehow to blame.

On the evening Emma and Ernst opened their restaurant a small crowd arrived from the quiet streets as miraculously as an immaculate conception. These were the people Emma had come to know and respect over the months she had worked at bit jobs in the stricken town; the good citizens of Burgdorf had come to support her and encourage her husband.

Emma danced between the dining room and the kitchen that night while Ernst inhabited the space behind the great mahogany bar. Ernst soon struck up conversations with the male guests; an academic here, a town official there, a journalist with his glamorous female companion there. He dressed well, groomed himself exquisitely, and this night Ernst looked exceptional. He wore his dark chestnut hair swept from his high forehead down to the nape of his neck. His starched white shirt with its winged collar gleamed like the new snow that was falling outside. Over the shirt he wore a fine black moleskin waistcoat, its back panel the softest silk. A white linen apron was tied at his waist and at his throat nestled a maroon silk bow-tie.

Alone in the kitchen, Emma still managed to keep a close eye on the dining room. She would have been aware of her husband's argument with the official over the ethics of compulsory military service and was keeping a close eye on the young couple in the corner. The woman was so young and her neckline plunged so dramatically.

By 11 pm the last of Emma and Ernst's guests had left, extolling the virtues of the food, the service and the rarefied atmosphere. When they were all gone, Emma told her husband that next time their guests would come for the food and hospitality, not out of duty. By *de Musique*'s standards, this was an early night, but for Emma—already four months pregnant—the evening had been a test of endurance.

When Emma emerged from the kitchen for the final load of dirty glasses her husband was opening a bottle of claret. She sank onto one of the hard bistro chairs. Ernst watched her and his pleasure changed to concern. In their time together at *de Musique* Emma had never sat down on the job.

Perhaps he came to sit beside her, to hold her red hands in his. Or perhaps from across the room, from the safety of his bar, he demanded to know what was wrong with her. Whichever way it happened, Emma would have hesitated and drawn breath, steeling herself before finally sharing her news. They had not, in their short time together, discussed the prospect of children. The silence in the room, after the noise of the evening, was not entirely welcome.

'We'll call him George, after my young brother,' Ernst announced after a lengthy pause, then poured Emma a glass of wine she could not drink. 'We'll name our boy George.'

Ernst's brother, George, the boy after whom Daddo was to be named, had died when he was only six. Not for a moment did it occur to Ernst that Emma would bear him a daughter.

I do not know whether Ernst embraced Emma then, drew her to him and buried his face in her hair, her bosom. Indeed, I wonder whether this moment—the announcement of Daddo's conception—marked the beginning of the end.

The End Starts Here

———◆◆◆◆———

. . . beauty alone does not save it . . . If beauty and architectural significance or even sentiment counted, then the Belvedere Private Hotel . . . would still be standing.

The Belvedere was a gracious old white-painted Victorian mansion with wisteria-twined balconies and shady courtyards, camphor laurels and marble statues, a fountain, and even a family ghost. It stood in an acre of gardens amongst Moreton Bay figs, palms and creamy-flowered magnolias, and inside were chandeliers and Persian rugs. The atmosphere was New Orleans belle époque and the hotel's personal service was in keeping with the traditions of the grand old European hotels. From its butter and oil kitchen came traditional French cuisine. The famous and the celebrated stayed there—Sir Eugene Goossens, Yehudi Menuhin, Maurice Chevalier, Joern Utzon, Alan Shepherd, Margot Fonteyn, Sir Francis Chichester, Sir Paul Hasluck. In the middle of brash and brazen Kings Cross it was for years an enclave of solitude and old world values that refused to capitulate to the demands of progress. But anachronisms like the Belvedere have no place in the future of Kings Cross.

Rennie Ellis on the final page of the book, *Kings Cross Sydney*, by Wesley Stacey and Rennie Ellis.

WHEN THE BULLDOZERS came down the drive to demolish The

Belvedere my grandmother Emma, whom I called Nanna, was still sweeping out the kitchens. She was nearly eighty. It was 1969 and she had first taken the lease on the place in 1938.

The land on which the hotel and its grounds stood had been resumed by the Department of Main Roads to build the Kings Cross tunnel and expressway. All that exists of The Belvedere now are the trees: Moreton Bay figs and a flame tree from the front garden and the peppercorns from out back. They stand sentinel on either side of the expressway, two swathes of greenery in a tangle of roads and high rise. My old dog, Bono, and I pass the peppercorn trees every day on our morning walk. I imagine he shares the Naher dogs' collective memory of those trees in the same way he shares their collective hatred of drunks.

The traffic up the Cross had been heavy for so long that they'd been talking about building a tunnel since before the Second World War. During the war years there was ongoing discussion of a tunnel under the Cross; for one thing it would make an excellent air raid shelter.

I couldn't say whether the loss of the hotel was a blessing or a curse; The Belvedere had been everything to the family . . . it *was* the family. Emma had already been fretting that the place had grown too big, so successful that it was too much for Daddo, Pauline and Emma's niece, Leny. Perhaps she didn't want Daddo to raise us as she'd raised him, always off to the side while she was working. An old friend once accused Daddo of not knowing what normal family life was. Hurt, Daddo rejected this suggestion point-blank. He had always been around his mother as a small child, he insisted, was always sitting there at the table as she shelled the peas, was always beside her as she worked.

I know they fought the decision, employed the best silks to challenge the resumption. Daddo claimed that the expressway was to have run in a straight line from William Street to Rushcutter's Bay, easily avoiding The Belvedere. William Street was to have been a grand boulevard linking the city to the eastern suburbs. Whoever owned the land at the top of William Street proved too powerful, however, or too adept in petitioning council. At the last minute it was agreed that the expressway would veer to the right, straight through The Belvedere and the gardens that were my early childhood.

The Belvedere was so loved in the community that its demise merited a requiem mass at St Canice's, the Catholic church across the road. In holding the mass, the priests were honouring all The Belvedere represented: family endeavour; embracing hospitality; indeed, nothing less than sanctuary. Perhaps the priests, who had become close family friends, saw the magnitude of the loss for the family. Within the year they'd be gathered again, burying Emma.

The Belvedere was all my family knew; Emma, Leny and Daddo. What other life, they must have wondered, could possibly await them out there? Leny had a house in Edgecliff but was rarely there—with her husband John and daughter Angela—while The Belvedere lived on. Emma had taken her own small apartment not far from The Belvedere but she still went to the hotel every day to lend a hand, even when she was frail and ill. At the end of the day she'd sneak off to the bus stop; she was a working woman, she would say, and she would take the bus.

I can see her, my nanna, Emma, known to her clients as Madame Naher and to her close friends as Aunty. She's just short of eighty and she has moved into the empty dining room, staring defiantly out at the bulldozers on the drive and willing them away so she can finish her sweeping. Over her dead body would the bulldozers start their work before she'd finished hers; before she'd put the place in order one last time.

Birthing

EMMA'S FIRST CONTRACTION came on as she was cooking lunch. It was a Friday and there was a large group of businessmen in the restaurant whom she would have wished to impress. Her sister, Alma, had come from Wil two weeks earlier to assist at the birth and in the restaurant. By the time Emma's labour commenced, however, Alma had not yet cooked a meal alone.

Business had been building steadily since January and in March the *Liederkranz* had recommenced its programme of concerts and performances in the theatre upstairs. There had been plays mounted by visiting theatre groups, a week of entertainment by a magician and a single performance by a singer. On the evening of Friday 13 June 1919, *Im Schwyzerkusli* was billed to sing at 8 pm. A choral group, it would perform the Swiss folk songs that Daddo—even after he'd lived in Australia for decades—adored.

The first contraction came when Emma was moving a great vat of soup from the back of the stove to the front. The weather was far too hot for soup but she'd gained a reputation for it and her customers would frown in disappointment if it was absent from the menu. She later said that lifting the soup had brought the baby on. It was cauli-flower soup; a vegetable Daddo relished throughout his life. The second contraction came during the preparation of the *Rösti*—just as Emma was flipping the cake of grated potato, cheese and ham—and this, too, would become one of Daddo's favourite dishes. By the time Emma was whipping the cream for the chocolate mousse she was prepared for the next onslaught. She told neither Alma nor Ernst; she was determined to cook the dinner herself as well.

Instead of taking a short break in the afternoon—as Emma had been encouraged to do since her sister arrived—she worked right through. She later told her sister that it helped endure the pain, standing, working. Had she sat and waited, or had she lain down, there would have been nothing to distract her.

The evening menu comprised various dried, cured meats with *cornichons*; a herb soup; salmon with hollandaise sauce; roast beef with vegetables; ribs with sauerkraut; veal schnitzel Burgdorf (a recipe Emma had adapted from a Milanese dish); chicory salad; hazelnut cake; fruit; cheese; and small pastries. Later in the evening, after the performance, she planned to offer more cold sliced meats with potato salad.

Emma had already cooked the first and main courses before her waters broke on the scrubbed kitchen floor. This situation posed a wonderful dilemma. It wasn't that she was leaving the dinner undone, because she'd already prepared the desserts during the afternoon. No, the dilemma concerned how she could leave the kitchen and go upstairs to her room without her guests seeing her. As there was only one exit from the kitchen, and this was into the dining room, there was nothing for it but to give birth right there. The two women, Emma and Alma, set about preparing a corner of the kitchen with cloths and hot water for the birth, all the while chastising the man who had designed the place for not thinking to give the kitchen a second exit.

George—my Daddo—emerged quietly and without fuss, Emma squatting in a corner and her sister rushing to serve the desserts. He timed his first cries for the moment the guests were leaving their tables and moving upstairs for the performance.

The first Ernst knew about his son were the wails he heard once the dining room had finally fallen silent. Instead of joy he experienced a sharp pang of hurt; Emma had not even seen fit to inform him that their baby was on its way. When he entered the kitchen, his wife had already washed her tiny son in the sink, had wrapped him in dishcloths and was cleaning the floor with the boy clasped to her breast.

Daddo always had the most impeccable sense of timing—nothing, I repeat nothing, would interfere with the preparation and serving of a meal.

LOSS

IT WAS PAULINE WHO found the house at Lodge Road—to which we moved from The Belvedere—and Daddo who had to be persuaded. It clung to the edge of the slope in an impressive act of defiance. Emma thought it ostentatious but she didn't have to live there.

Daddo covered the balustrades on the balconies that wrapped around the house with chicken-wire lest Jackie, five, or I, three, should fall to a certain death. Below the house was Middle Harbour, impossibly quiet, the hush of bushland on the opposite shore showing only a smattering of houses. Sir Edward Hallstrom, the refrigerator magnate, lived on the point; there he had his small private zoo for albino kangaroos. Jackie and I would stare across the bay at the white shapes on the point, hardly able to reconcile these ghostly, hopping forms with kangaroos. Roy Luxton next door—whom we came to call Uncle Roy—told us that he used to watch emus swimming across the bay from the point, their long necks rising from the water like periscopes. Middle Harbour was known then, as it is now, as 'a breeding ground for sharks'.

This was our first and only stint living as a nuclear family, as opposed to the large, extended family we were part of at The Belvedere. It was an attempt at ordinary family life. Daddo slowly transformed the house into a whimsical gesture to The Belvedere, eventually filling the house with 'Belvederia', but in those early days he struggled to recreate the hotel's emotional landscape. For the first time in his life—with the exception of his years fighting for Australia in the Pacific—he was not part of an establishment whose main purpose was to offer exquisite hospitality to strangers.

Daddo managed some real estate around the site of The Belvedere, a handful of inner-city terraces that had been considered slum dwellings when he was a boy and that he had bought cheaply. These provided an income, but following the sale of The Belevedere, he was looking for the focus of the rest of his life.

To say that things were difficult between my parents is an understatement but this is my preferred usage. Things had already been unravelling at the hotel where the staff and extended family acted as both a buffer and a braking agent. Pauline seemed to find life at Lodge Road exhausting. A housekeeper was employed but still things were too difficult. Some days she'd rise, get to the top of the stairs and turn around to go back to bed. She just couldn't face it. She was not well; I have never known her to be well. Later, as older children and teenagers, Jackie and I were very conscious of what would and would not affect Pauline's blood pressure. In those early days at Lodge Road, Daddo—adrift from the only world he knew—was not at his best. He could demonstrate extraordinary bursts of temper, of ill humour, just like his father had before him.

I remember the fights, although I was too young to understand the substance of them. To me the long hallway into my parents' bedroom represented a battlefield. Thirty years later when we strip the house back to its bare bones before finally leaving it, the hallway still feels like the domestic equivalent of the Bermuda Triangle. Mine was the tiny, dark bedroom beside that hallway. I heard it all.

Across the harbour in Woollahra, Emma also laboured under poor health. Her apartment, too, although modern, had something of The Belvedere's style. I remember only small, snapshot images of the place; it was dark and cool inside, decorated in rich, deep reds and greens and it had a smell—a blend of perfume and furniture polish—that was pure Nanna. Under the silky pillows of the gold velvet sofa she hid lollies. After Nanna's embraces and the search for lollies, Jackie and I would go to a low drawer in the dark wooden cabinet where Nanna kept a set of plastic farm animals with which we'd play on one of her soft Persian carpets.

She called me 'the professor', because I always asked why and because I wore the most serious of expressions on my young child's face. I don't remember Nanna ever being irritated by my whys, even during that period—after The Belvedere's closure—when she had grown ill and weak. Jackie and I were her 'little girls'. In her own tongue, we were *das Maidli*.

I remember being taken to see Nanna before she died. She was lying in her bed, smiling at us, and the flat seemed quiet beyond all imagining. I remember this visit not because it was the last time I saw her, but because she was in bed.

The three albums filled with condolence cards are the most tangible of the many proofs that my nanna, Emma Naher, was loved. That her son, Daddo, could not bear to let her go is a more subtle truth. I do not remember him crying, or mourning her formally, or specific events around her actual death. What I know, however, is that within the family she did not die. I say this because most of my knowledge of her is indirect and comes from the anecdotes Daddo, Leny and Pauline repeated throughout my life.

Emma's portrait—in which she looks stern and amused in equal measures—watched me whenever I sat on the formal blue sofa, during my childhood. It watches me here in my home in Darlinghurst, too. Daddo kept his mother alive for his daughters in much the same way Jackie keeps Daddo alive for her daughter, Freya: with daily stories, with the regular sharing of memories and with a fierce love that will not diminish.

Firemen

JUST AS I ONCE imagined I was raised by dogs, Daddo claimed to have been raised by firemen. During the first four years of his life—there in the Casino in Burgdorf—his parents were as occupied by their business as mine would be by The Belvedere.

'The firemen looked after me,' he said, without any appreciation of how odd this might sound. For Daddo it was the firemen, for Jackie and me it was the dogs. In both cases there were grandmothers, too, and heaps of crisp, laundered linen in which a baby could lie comfortably.

Regulations deemed that firemen must be on hand at premises where the public gathered regularly in large numbers. There was concern—in conservative Burgdorf—that the excitement generated by the performances in the concert hall above the restaurant might cause people to stampede. Burgdorf officials were exceptionally cautious after they had lost so much of their town in the great fire of 1865.

Emma was nothing if not sensible and it bothered her to see those two bored firemen standing around idle. Before her wonderful idea—to turn them into honorary godfathers to her little boy—the firemen had sat in her restaurant playing cards day and night. Emma believed in the therapeutic effect of hard work and hatched a plan for these two able-bodied yet under-occupied fellows. It would benefit all of them.

I said to Daddo, 'Surely when you were a baby Nanna looked

after you?' and he went on to say 'yes, of course', but I could see that he was not sure. I'm not sure either. I entertained a fleeting image of Daddo as a tiny baby, asleep in a bucket marked WATER.

Alma, Emma's sister, remained in Burgdorf, helping in the restaurant. In the absence of the firemen and of her sister, Alma would take her turn with her tiny nephew George. The restaurant, under the capable hands and inspired direction of Emma Braun Naher, flourished. With Alma to hand, Emma suggested Ernst return to *de Musique* in Bern from time to time; they needed him so badly at this old restaurant that they would make it worth his while. Ernst and Emma both agreed they could use the extra income, but Ernst felt wounded that his wife seemed to cope so well without him.

Alma later let slip that Emma and Ernst fought in Burgdorf. One worked too hard and one too little and neither was satisfied with the situation. Emma liked to work, it was who she was. Ernst tolerated the work and sometimes enjoyed the clients. That was all. Life, he would insist, should provide for both the body and the mind. A life without books, without talk and debate, was no life. There was no agreement between them; Ernst was as stubborn as Emma was strong. When he was there in Burgdorf Ernst got sucked into the vortex created by Emma's endeavour, drawn into her plans and exotic menus and changes to the decor. For days they would work together—they could make an excellent team when they put their minds to it—and then something would give and Ernst would start to slide.

The baby, George, slept in a basket in the kitchen or was dandled on the knee of one or other of the firemen. His mother worked and his father remained cool and aloof. Ernst's only experience with children had been with his own siblings. His favourite brother, little George, had died of tuberculosis when the boy was only six. Ernst's other brother, Walter, died at twenty-one. Elsa was the only girl but was fourteen years younger than Ernst. She arrived soon after little George's death and four months later their father died. Ernst, stricken with the double loss, never gave her a chance.

They would stay together, Emma and Ernst, because that's what one did. Anyway, before the second pregnancy there was still some passion, some spark. Emma and George formed the family's nucleus and Ernst orbited them. When Emma saw the signs—they appeared regularly enough to be clearly recognisable—that flagged Ernst's drinking binges, she'd pack up the baby and take him by train to her mother's house in Wil. For a few days the firemen would sit idle and Emma would work even harder, her baby elsewhere and Ernst unreachable. Only when the next set of signs appeared—a sudden, quiet sobriety and softness in Ernst—would Emma set out on the train again to bring her baby home.

Taken

The first Jackie and I knew about it was when Pauline came to collect us from school and the car was crammed full of bags, spilling clothes and toiletries. I remember walking towards the black Mercedes and seeing her old hair dryer—the sort that comes down over your head like a hat—sitting at the rear of the car. She hadn't told us anything yet and she didn't need to; I knew that something was very wrong. I was five years old.

Later Daddo told us that the first he knew of it was when he arrived home after a long day of meetings in town. The black Mercedes was gone, the house at Lodge Road had been cleared of all manner of portable items and we girls were gone too. There was a solicitor's letter under the door. It told Daddo, simply, that his daughters were safe.

She took us to a two-bedroomed apartment in Manly. The rooms were cold and bare and the wind beat relentlessly against the windows. Outside the water looked grey and the surf big and angry. There were ugly blue chenille covers on the two beds in the room Jackie and I were to share. The apartment in Manly was austere after the pageant that had been The Belvedere, after the sun-filled house that cascaded down the slope at Lodge Road.

I remember almost nothing of that time in Manly and have not since been able to warm to the place. Jackie claims that I have blocked out all the painful memories from my childhood but I reckon plenty remain in my awareness.

I do remember the day—it seemed like months and months after Pauline had taken us—that we saw Daddo again. I have a clear image of the three of us, of Daddo, Jackie and me, clinging to each other on the beach front at Manly, crying. He was wearing a skivvy and a soft, pale, sand-coloured suede jacket, the one I now wear, and this was the first time I saw Daddo cry. The dying pine trees and scavenging seagulls were witness to the spectacle.

When we were older Pauline would remind us that she left him for our sake, for 'you girls'. What did she mean? we asked. 'You were afraid of him,' was her claim. I do not believe it. I almost believed it then, living in her house, but I do not believe it now.

He served her with the divorce papers. It was Easter 1975. She insisted she was devastated. How could he do this to her?

The Great Masked Ball

In Bern, Ernst sat up late, drinking with the chef in the kitchens at *de Musique*, working on a scheme to win his wife back. He would not compete with her, had no desire to work as hard as her, but could bring to their business, to their lives, another, a different, element: dreaming.

After hours at *de Musique* Ernst made notes that became the blueprint for Burgdorf's first masked ball. As a means of wooing his wife to the idea—and also the town's good citizens—he composed a teasing dialogue designed to run in the *Burgdorfer Tagblatt* in the months preceding the ball.

On the pages of the local newspaper, those who would be attending—characters as diverse as Mata Hari, Maybloom, Titus and Orpheus—would correspond in a series of brief postcards on the nature of the evening. They would speculate about the wine, the food, the music and exactly where in the concert hall or restaurant their amorous encounters would take place. Emma, when Ernst presented her with his script, was enchanted, remembered—for at least as long as it took her to conceive a second child—why she had thrown in her lot with Ernst in the first place.

When Ernst inspected his work each day as it appeared in the *Tagblatt*, he read, also, of the events taking place in Ireland. On 10 January 1922, the front page of the *Burgdorfer Tagblatt* announced that *Dáil Eireann* had voted to accept the treaty between England and Ireland. Ernst also read that the first

57

President of the Irish Free State, Eamon de Valera—of whom he had become something of an admirer—had resigned. Throughout the early months of that year the Burgdorf paper prominently covered the Civil War in Ireland and Ernst became an avid follower of the trials of the new Free State. While working at George V's court had been the most exciting time of his life, he told Emma, it had made him a confirmed republican.

On the night of the ball, some three months later, Ernst wore the costume of a magician: a long black cape, a top hat and white gloves with his tuxedo. Emma, whose role would be played out behind the scenes and who was not well in her pregnancy, refused a costume.

Emma and Ernst had decorated the concert hall and restaurant with coloured lanterns and garlands of paper flowers to celebrate springtime, which was almost upon them. When the lanterns were illumined and casting their golden light onto the other decorations the dark rooms took on a magical, otherworldly feel just as Ernst had imagined they would. The two orchestras that played in the concert hall offered both modern and traditional music and a string quartet performed in the restaurant.

Ernst stood in the foyer, greeting each of his guests as befitted their character—there were hunters, soldiers, queens . . . even a couple of exotic birds—while Emma and her sister toiled in the kitchen to create the advertised spring feast. As more guests arrived and the Casino's rooms echoed with music and laughter, Ernst felt his former confidence and well-being return to him. He was as much conductor as magician, guiding the finely dressed folk to the bar, to the tables of food and onto the dance floor.

Behind their masks the Burgdorfers felt anonymous and somehow liberated. Many danced with an abandon they'd never before experienced and others found themselves laughing with neighbours they'd feuded with and drinking toasts with strangers. When Ernst heard his clients commenting in delight that the scene was more of Paris or Vienna than Burgdorf, he felt himself the magician his clothes proclaimed him to be. Indeed, in subsequent reports on the ball the *Tagblatt* pronounced that Emma and Ernst had created nothing short of *Märchenland*, fairyland.

The morning after the ball Emma rose to begin clearing the debris, leaving her husband to sleep on. When she was on her hands and knees scraping the tattered shreds of their decorations from the corners of her restaurant, the bleeding started.

My Father's Shoes

—◆◆◆◆—

DURING THE MONTHS and years after Pauline took us from Lodge Road, Daddo rattled about the large house and garden alone; he had bought the place as a family home.

'Like a hermit,' he said of the period, 'I lived like a hermit.' At fifty-three he had even less experience of living alone than his mother had and at first he felt something akin to embarrassment at being there on his own and abandoned. The sudden, unfamiliar quiet in his life came as a tremendous shock. Over a period of three years he had lost his business, his mother, his marriage and his daughters. A lesser man would not have survived.

He consulted lawyers, consulted the men of the community he held in high esteem. What should he do about getting his daughters back? What *could* he do? Nothing, he was told repeatedly. He could and should do nothing. In the early seventies a man alone had no chance of winning custody of two small girls from their mother. So high was his regard for these men's opinions that he took their advice. I'd like the opportunity to talk to each one of them in turn, now. As Pauline told us again and again, he did not fight for us. But that moment, then, when he was at his lowest, was the only time he failed us.

At Lodge Road he continued to work, slowly, towards creating an echo of the dream that was The Belvedere. With his mother's auction-bought antiques and his own innovation and whimsy, he slowly brought the simple house to life. The neighbours—aghast, delighted—watched him place classical marble statues in his garden.

He said he lived as a hermit; this is most certainly an exaggeration. Daddo was not capable of such a thing, he was a man who felt compelled to reach out. During those bleak, solitary years he continued to manage some real estate to earn his living, but commenced what would become the work of the rest of his life. He stepped up his volunteer work for the charity Legacy and for the Lions Club. He trebled his commitment to the elderly and needy in the local Swiss community.

Leny and a friend, a long-time former Belvedere employee, tried to look after him. He was a man well-versed in the domestic arts from his experience running and working in hotels, but nonetheless these two women would come to the house once a week to fuss over his laundry and housework and to tend the large garden he already cared for so well. Daddo, indignant, would protest that he could manage, that he was more than capable of looking after himself. The fact was they enjoyed their Wednesdays together; these days of shared domestic pottering provided them all with an oasis of community.

During this period Daddo's shoes took on a curious shape. Each of them became mysteriously bent, their toes pointing heavenwards, deep creases in their middle. When somebody commented on it Leny identified the problem immediately. 'He spends hours on his knees,' she announced. 'He is alone and sad; he spends his quiet time in prayer.'

Last of the Nahers

———◆━◆◆◆━◆———

I TRAVEL TO FRAUENFELD, the city in Canton Thurgau—in Switzerland's east—where the Naher family is registered. I already have a family extract from Frauenfeld documenting the generations of Nahers back to 1832. The town official insists he can tell me little more but I am compelled to visit the Naher place of origin, nonetheless. I am troubled, for one, by Daddo's brother, Maxli, and by his failure to appear on family documents.

The official has agreed to meet me but only after assurances from my friend, who acts as go-between, that I know I'm adopted. He makes it clear that should I not already know this story, he does not wish to be the one to tell me. I reassure him in person; not only have I met both natural parents but I'm presently en route to Canada to meet my other father's brothers.

Swiss records—despite the fact that in my family's case they are spread across the world—are predictably organised. In Frauenfeld I scan the original papers, from which the family extract was made, in search of Maxli, Emma's second son. No Maxli. I find myself asking, awkwardly, whether there is any way the child's birth could have failed to have been recorded. I hesitate to ask at what age a miscarried foetus must be registered. According to Frauenfeld, Maxli never existed. I remain protective of Daddo's recollection that he once had a brother; while I have no facts with which to fight Maxli's absence, I do not completely accept it.

The official is pleased to create a paper trail for me; each married son acquires his own record and his own new document in the files, while each married daughter of the line effectively disappears from the family's records and is transcribed onto her husband's register elsewhere. As Jackie and I have both married foreigners without a Swiss *heimat Ort*, we remain registered in Frauenfeld, our wedding certificates having been duly forwarded to the Canton by the Swiss Consulate in Sydney, just as Daddo's once was. According to Swiss law, if I come to Frauenfeld penniless and destitute the city will be obliged to feed me.

I learn that the first Naher registered in Frauenfeld in 1832 went by the name of Georg Johann, just like Daddo. He is my great-grandfather Georg Friedrich's father, or my father's father's father's father. There is no document to precede Georg Johann. His father could have come from outer Mongolia—which would account for Ernst's almond-shaped eyes—or been there in Frauenfeld since 1291, the time of Wilhelm Tell and Switzerland's confederation.

My final question is both the most poignant and the most difficult to answer. Am I really the last of the Nahers? Was Daddo the last Naher in the bloodline? The paper trail leading to my great-great-grandfather is direct. It is not far-reaching and chaotic like the trail we create in trying to trace the fate of each one of his descendants.

We follow the fates of each of my great-great-grandfather's sons—all six of them—and of their six sons in turn. Five children died in infancy and another six never reached adulthood. Others married but failed to reproduce, though probably not for lack of trying. The first of them, Georg Johann, married twice. Of his sons, two married twice and one three times. A grandson also married twice. One of Georg Johann's sons married his half-brother's ex-wife, after she'd borne her first husband a child out of wedlock who died aged five. When I try to draw a family tree it looks more like a shrub; it's broad and far-reaching at the top and very narrow at the bottom, making it squat. Its foliage is in eastern Switzerland where its roots should be and its tiny root base is here in Sydney. Daddo, born in Switzerland, raised in Ireland, married and buried in Australia, is the last Naher of the bloodline.

On the register, below the record of Daddo's marriage, appear the names of his two daughters, Jackie and me. 'Naher, Jacqueline (adopted)', followed first by her natural mother's name and then by George and Pauline's names and the date of her adoption. 'Naher, Gabrielle (adopted)', followed by Jane's name, then George and Pauline's and another date. Prominent under both our names and succinct histories are the words '<u>Not citizen of Frauenfeld</u>'. Had we been Daddo's natural daughters, citizenship would have been a given. Some years after our adoptions were recorded the Swiss changed the law and Daddo petitioned Frauenfeld successfully on Jackie's and my behalf.

For my part I am bemused. Not by the fact that my adoption rendered me bureaucratically lost in Switzerland for at least half my life. Nor by the strange disappearance of Daddo's brother. No, I am bemused by the curious fact that the Naher family continues only as a result of the injection of new, non-Naher male genes.

In my mind's eye I stand my fathers—natural and adoptive—side by side. One is six feet four and over 200 pounds of bone and muscle, to use Monette terminology; he died young and alone. The other, at five feet five, comes only to my shoulder, has skinny legs and the face of a wizened monk; he lived a long, full life.

The Quality of your Biscuit

AS A YOUNG CHILD I understood that being a good Swiss girl depended on the quality of your biscuit. There were, of course, dozens of different Swiss biscuits but one of them—an object of exquisite culinary simplicity—was 'it' as far as I was concerned. This was a chunky yellow biscuit, traditionally cut into stars, Christmas trees and the ubiquitous Swiss cross. It was a buttery biscuit, so plain you could eat a dozen before you got sick. Before the biscuits went into the oven they were painted with egg yolk to give them a glossy golden sheen.

Jackie and I begged Leny, cajoled her and the others who comprised the chorus of Swiss women, for these secret recipes. We could hardly endure the wait for the special events at which the lovely morsels were offered and longed to possess ourselves the knowledge that would bring an infinite supply of biscuits. Despite years of nagging, no member of the chorus ever committed one of the recipes to paper. They'd been handed down from mother to daughter, from aunt to niece, from grandmother to granddaughter over decades of communal baking. Jackie and I, in living with Pauline, had fallen out of the loop.

Wearing our brightly coloured smock-shirts embroidered with *Edelweiss*, Jackie and I attended First of August picnics to celebrate Swiss National Day with Daddo. We'd cram into his two-tone Kingswood station-wagon for the drive out west and often we children rode in the back with the baskets of food and eskies, facing the cars behind us.

The First of August picnics were primarily about eating, and the chorus of Swiss women went to great efforts in the preceding days and weeks in order to present elaborate banquets on the day. Leny was the consummate biscuit-maker and her sandwiches were exceptional, too; they were elaborate adventures in eating and might contain anything, even tongue. There were plum and apricot tarts with the fruit laid out in delicate patterns and the simple yet delicious *Kugelhopf*.

There were Swiss sausages: *Bratwurst* and *Weisswurst*, from Iseli, the celebrated Swiss butcher in Ashfield. There were *Fleishkäse* and *Landjäger* and great slabs of Swiss cheese, bigger than my head. Wheels of cheese were cut in half and suspended over a flame and the melted cheese that dripped onto cooked potatoes and gherkins was called *Raclette*.

Later, when the sun slipped down in the sky and the kookaburras started calling, an oompapa band—German or Austrian— would set up in the barn and we children would take our positions atop the teetering bales of hay to watch the dancing. From where we lay, itching from the hay against our skin, the spectacle below was like so many brightly coloured umbrellas, twirling and pirouetting in time with the music. There was whooping and yodelling and laughter. When I was very young I wondered whether this was sex.

Once the sun had set the bonfire was lit. Branches and discarded timber formed a tower as tall as a house by the muddy dam, or so it seemed. It had to be high because when it was alight we wanted them to see it from Switzerland. At 'home' they'd be lighting bonfires on mountaintops, not on the dusty slope on the edge of a dam. I imagined a ring of bonfires visible from alp to alp across Switzerland and from country to country around the world. If I had been just that little bit taller, with eyesight just that little bit keener, I was sure I'd have seen the *auslander* Swiss' bonfire in New Zealand.

Jackie and I were given coloured paper lanterns with the red and white of the Swiss flag on them or the more intricate detail of the cantonal flags. One year we struck off across the field to the makeshift dunnies with our paper lanterns to light the way. These toilet blocks were just holes in the ground surrounded by carefully constructed screens of hessian sacking. The structure was highly flammable, or so we discovered one evening when first the sides of our lanterns caught alight and then the walls of the bush dunny.

If we stayed really late at the picnic—at the risk of angering Pauline—there'd be singing. The local yodellers did not confine themselves to yodelling, they sang, too. Their melodious folk-songs seemed as beautiful as the alpine fields they described. At times these songs brought tears to Daddo's eyes. The land they evoked—a picturesque, peaceful country—was a place of dreams, not reality. It was a land of cuckoo clocks, cows and fine chocolate, from which all dark things had been deleted by distance.

Not only did Jackie and I lack the recipes for the coveted Swiss biscuits, but we did not speak the language like the other Swiss-Australian children. We were Swiss but we were not Swiss. I longed, not to be Swiss, but to *belong*.

Maxli

<hr />

I FIND NO HARD evidence of Maxli's existence in Frauenfeld or Burgdorf, but I do not stop believing in him. The women of the family whispered about a miscarriage—a slow, aching falling away—that came in the wake of the Great Masked Ball. Was this the end of the pregnancy that should have resulted in the birth of Maxli? Or was there, perhaps, a third pregnancy in Dublin and a baby born who quickly died? I doubt that I will ever know.

As the family story goes, on the day after the Great Masked Ball in March 1922, Emma started to bleed. I cannot imagine her afraid but her every action speaks it. Carefully she climbed the stairs to lie on the bed beside her sleeping husband. For days she lay on the tall bed, staring down the Emme Valley and hardly daring to move. She would do anything to keep the baby—the one she would call Maria or Max—inside her.

Only three weeks after the ball, Alma and a friend took over the lease of the restaurant. Emma had packed her husband off to Bern—she preferred to cope with her women's business alone. Ernst, wounded, bewildered that this had come after the glory of his masked ball, had left without argument, a diminished man. For Emma to have transferred the restaurant's lease—the signing of which had thrown her into marriage with Ernst—she must have been profoundly shaken. I do not know whether it was days or weeks that she lay on her bed holding her belly, praying that her baby would remain inside her. George was with his grandmother again and downstairs Alma and her accomplice were making a hash of running Emma's restaurant.

It was not until August that the minutes of a *Liederkranz* meeting noted that Mr Naher had announced the family's intention to quit the Casino and the transfer of the lease to his wife's sister. Reason: his wife's ill health. Ernst was the master of potent euphemism.

Once she had finally miscarried and she knew there was nothing left inside her to hold, against her doctor's orders Emma started to visit her kitchen again. Already the two new lessees—Alma and her friend—were in heated conflict.

In Burgdorf, Emma was fretting for her son who was still in Wil—and for the baby she had lost—and trying to endure the shame of what looked like a failed marriage. In Bern, Ernst read of the emergence of the Irish Free State with keen interest, with something Emma would later describe as zeal. One day, Emma travelled to Bern to try to reconcile with Ernst. She had told her sister that their only option was a new beginning; she was going to persuade her husband that they must try again and that he must plan the next move, he must choose their destination.

Ernst and Emma met outside *de Musique* before Ernst's evening shift and walked to the river together in silence. They sat at the place where Emma had first spoken of Burgdorf, the joy in each other's company drained from them. It was here Ernst started to speak of Dublin. Dublin, he insisted, Dublin was where they would start afresh.

In the days and weeks that followed Emma grew resigned to her fate . . . She visited her mother and son in Wil and travelled across Switzerland for final goodbyes with her sisters. One of her nieces clearly recalled Emma's visit. On her arrival she had given the children a few coins, telling them to go out and buy themselves a treat. Emma had serious business with her sister and, even to a young girl, she seemed like a woman with the worries of the world on her shoulders. Perhaps she was making arrangements for her little boy in the event that something should happen to her, over there, across the Irish Sea.

Emma and Ernst invited the townsfolk to the restaurant for a farewell drink and the jazz band Lyra played above the solemn, hushed voices of the crowd.

When Emma and Ernst finally took their leave of the town, the citizens of Burgdorf showered the couple with praise and gifts. Emma later admitted that her friends in the town confessed their fears for her. 'Why Dublin?' they pleaded. 'Why Ireland when there was a civil war there?' Emma, wishing to hide the bare bones of her marriage, grasped for a reason and found one.

'Opportunity,' she pronounced. 'The gentry are fleeing and there's room for the industrious to make good.' In Dublin, they would be able to afford their own hotel, she confided, while in Switzerland they could afford only to lease a restaurant. Dublin, she went on to tell them, was the second city of Georgian Britain and would appreciate their fine Swiss skills in hospitality.

The townsfolk smiled and nodded. Behind Emma and Ernst's back they asked each other, 'Do they not read the newspaper?' The *Tagblatt* was still regularly reporting on the fighting and the murders of the Irish Civil War.

The Second Sunday Ghost

<hr>

MY CHILDHOOD—ONCE Lodge Road and The Belvedere were firmly behind me—involved having a father only every second Sunday and for half the school holidays. This is what the courts decided for us and was the norm at the time; I doubt the arrangement suited any of us. It was too much contact for Pauline's liking and she was always tormented—grilling Jackie and me—about what we did with Daddo and whom we saw and of what we spoke. For Jackie, who had already bonded closely with Daddo before Pauline took us from him, these token visits were far from adequate. Second Sundays barely gave Daddo the chance to get used to having us, let alone the opportunity to feel he was fathering us.

How did I fare, in all of this, the youngest who had never developed her own relationship with her father before being taken from him? I was afraid of something, then, I know that much. Every second Monday, the day after our Daddo Sunday, I was ill.

Those second Sundays developed their own rhythm and routine. Pauline had moved us from Manly to leafy Castlecrag, only two bays from the house at Lodge Road. When Daddo's car appeared in the driveway there, Jackie and I would be out the door before he'd even cut the engine. We didn't want them to have to face each other.

On the way to Lodge Road we'd stop for a milkshake served in a tall aluminium beaker of silver or red. Daddo ordered banana and Jackie chocolate. Years later, when Daddo was having radiotherapy, Jackie and I coaxed him back to strength with takeaway banana milkshakes that we carried to his hospital bed with such hope. I can't remember whether I had a regular flavour back then, but already I would have had knots in my stomach. Already I would have been anticipating stomach cramps, later that night.

At Lodge Road we felt neither at home nor like visitors. Jackie and I would wander around, commenting on things new or changed in the house and making surreptitious visits to view the contents of the chocolate cupboard. We'd play ping-pong and Daddo would take great delight in 'sloshing' us, to the disapproval of the chorus of Swiss women. They thought he should let us win sometimes.

Later we'd go to my godmother Leny's, whom we called Aunty. She lived not far from the site of the former Belvedere and at her place things were somehow easier. Spatzi, the youngest of the Belvedere Danes, was living out his dotage there and we still tried to lie on him, even though we had grown big and he frail. In Leny's house we found the familiar magic—the sun-dried linen comfort—of The Belvedere boiler room.

Leny had bought us some special clothes—comfortable, easy dresses and a poncho each—that we would wear at her house. That way we didn't have to worry about dirtying the clothes Pauline dressed us in. In Leny's clothes we could roll in the grass with Spatzi down at Cooper Park and share ice-cream with him, although he was always given one of his own. In Leny's clothes we could forget Castlecrag's very existence for a few hours.

Second Sunday afternoons comprised visits to the Museum, the Art Gallery or to Luna Park, where Daddo would go on all the most terrifying rides with us. He would take us to mass in the evenings and I'd feign illness in the hope of being allowed to stay in the car. In truth this quiet time in church was harder for Daddo than for me—he'd sit between Jackie and me, knowing he would soon take us to a home that was not his own—and tears would roll down his cheeks.

After mass we'd return to Lodge Road and Daddo would cook us one of his famous omelettes. Into his 'ommies' would go all manner of exotic ingredients or just the common baked bean, but they would be prepared with the same gusto. Daddo flipped the half-moon omelettes high over the stove and would serve them to us with a flourish, often with a perfect half eggshell sitting on top. A visitor from New Zealand once filmed him making an ommie, such was his fabled prowess.

I see now that these days were packed full of distraction. They were crammed with activity that gave little or no time for the three of us—a father lost to his daughters and two sad, confused girls—to sit and talk. Even the car trips from one house to the other had their own agenda. It was in the car that we would hear, in weekly instalments, about the ghost.

It was not the Belvedere ghost of which we demanded an account but the more distinguished Dublin ghost. Second Sunday after second Sunday, Jackie would insist Daddo provide yet another instalment of 'the ghost'; sometimes she'd ask for two or three in a day. The story of the ghost goes something like this.

When Emma, Ernst and George arrived in Dublin, in 1923, they moved into Count Plunkett's house in Fitzwilliam Square. It was to be their first hotel. They arrived at the end of the Civil War but the unrest was still a part of Dubliners' lives, had not yet been relegated to history. The city was scarred from the fighting and killings and most households had suffered substantial loss. Dubliners still spoke of the Black and Tans with ill-concealed hatred, with fear. The hotel, according to Daddo, was haunted by the ghost of Plunkett's son.

Count Plunkett came from a grand Irish Catholic family and was a staunch republican. A politician himself, his sons were actively involved in the Easter Rising of 1916. One of his sons, the eldest, had been killed. The distraught family had left their Dublin home just prior to my grandparents' arrival. When Emma and Ernst moved into the house in Fitzwilliam Square, grim reminders of the family's history remained. There were bloodstains on one of the walls that Emma scrubbed for days but that reappeared when the weather changed. In the cellar below the house they found shackles. The Nahers speculated. Had Plunkett's son been executed in the house? Had the chains been used to confine him, or other members of the family?

When Emma and Ernst finally opened The Swiss Private Hotel, the ghost of Count Plunkett's eldest son—as the story goes—still wandered the house's high-ceilinged rooms. The ghost, apparently, had his likes, dislikes and habits. He took an interest in the very young, in the children and babies who slept in what had once been his childhood home. Daddo says he clearly remembers the ghostly form of a soldier leaning over him when he was in his bed. On the occasions Emma babysat for her guests she'd regularly enter the room of a crying baby to find the same figure of the soldier bending over the baby's crib. The ghost would also appear to priests who stayed at the hotel, and liked to extinguish their candles when they read the Bible in their rooms at night.

I was fascinated by ghosts and was an avid believer, but that story—which Daddo expanded on week after week—irritated me as much as it intrigued me. Jackie, who always rode in the front seat beside Daddo, would be begging for more as I was pleading with him to stop. There was a beginning and a middle but, infuriatingly, there was no end.

The irony of my reaction, in light of my present mission, is not lost on me—I, the ghost's greatest critic, have devoted months and years of my life to reviving his story and the story around it.

Flight of the
White Butterflies

EMMA AND ERNST HAD already purchased their train and steamer tickets to Dublin and packed all their effects before an official end to the Civil War was declared on 24 May 1923. The Civil War seemed to have been mercifully brief; it had erupted just after the signing of the Anglo-Irish Treaty in January 1922. The truce, although not unexpected, came as a huge relief to Emma; later she admitted that she had feared they would be sailing to their deaths. She told all those who'd been so anxious for them that this was the good omen for which she'd been praying. If she had been a practising Catholic before, the truce made her positively devout.

As Emma, Ernst and George travelled west across Europe, Mount Etna was erupting, spewing molten lava across great swathes of Sicily. There was an economic crisis in Germany, and Russia had announced a boycott of Swiss merchandise. Against this backdrop the newly formed Irish Free State looked a promising prospect, even to Emma.

Daddo's recollection of their brief stay in London was of the smell of coal smoke. The ornate stone buildings on Pall Mall were dark with coal dust and the sky seemed always to be shrouded in it. Already Burgdorf was remembered as a place of boundless blue skies. This first impression of London etched itself so firmly upon the child who became Daddo that it clouded each one of his subsequent visits to the city. On his final trip to London—as a man in his sixties—he reported with considerable indignation that somebody had gollied on his suitcase while it was in Left Luggage at Victoria Station. The act of a stranger spitting on his suitcase epitomised everything Daddo had ever felt about the place. It would take a great leap of faith for him to accept my decision to live in London, years later.

Ireland, by comparison, seemed calm and civilised to Emma and George: the Davis Cup was in competition at the Fitzwilliam Club; there were advertisements in the paper for a 'Cinderella Dance'; and dockworkers argued about the name of a new import for the zoo—was it a dromedary or a camel?—or might they perhaps settle on cameldary? As summer approached one innovative company was advertising ice-cream bricks guaranteed to remain intact for nearly three hours, or just long enough to get the treat home.

When Emma, Ernst and George arrived in Dublin on 23 June 1923, the only reference to the Civil War in the *Irish Times* was news of a hunger strike in Kilmainham Gaol. Heartened by this semblance of peace, Emma quickly lost herself in the columns of newsprint advertising auctions and house clearances. Already she was imagining the fine Irish antiques that had been left behind by the departing English with which she would furnish her hotel. Ernst, by contrast, was a little crestfallen that all the 'excitement' was over.

George's first impression of Dublin was olfactory; he claimed it smelled of horse manure.

Oblivious to the fact that he spoke with an accent too English for the republican trap driver, Ernst commanded the man to drive them from the docks to The Shelbourne Hotel. Not only was The Shelbourne Dublin's finest, but the drafting of the Free State's first constitution had taken place there. Emma, in her more personable Swiss accent, countered the order, requesting only a modest hotel but in the best area.

Emma later speculated that she got her way only because the driver's brother worked at the Fitzwilliam Private Hotel, which is where they ended up. At one end of elegant Upper Fitzwilliam Street was the women's confinement hospital and at the other end a view of the mist-shrouded Dublin Mountains. Ernst reportedly squinted at the horizon in scorn before going to great lengths to impress upon his son that those were hills, not mountains.

Further west, across the Atlantic, another curious epic journey was happening in conjunction with that of Emma and Ernst. A mass migration of white butterflies was departing Florida. Reported to be heading south, the cause of the creatures' spectacular flight was unknown. To me, nearly a century later, my grandparents' move to the westernmost country in Europe appears both as dramatic and as lacking in logic or reason. Like the flight of the butterflies, that of Emma and Ernst looks heroically doomed.

Chosen

———◆◆◆———

I AM ADOPTED, AS IS my sister Jackie. To her I am irrevocably bound by love, not blood. We both insist that we've always known. My oldest friend, however, disputes this second fundamental truth. She distinctly remembers the day her mother told her and her sisters the story. We were already ensconced at Castlecrag by that time so I must have been at least six. My friend insists that she and her sisters were informed the same day Jackie and I were to be told ourselves.

Whenever it was that we were officially told, I know the how of it. We were informed that above all else we were special. We, unlike children who arrived under more ordinary circumstances, had been 'chosen'. As a young girl I imagined Daddo and Pauline going to a baby showroom where they walked from cot to cot, staring down at each tiny face and discussing one's virtues over another's. Later I learned that this was not the way it had been done. It had been the nuns who made the decision, based on the available information about both sets of parents. George and Pauline had brown eyes, so they would be given a baby who was likely to have brown eyes. George and Pauline had dark hair, so their babies should have dark hair. My other mother's eyes, incidentally, are blue, as are the eyes of her daughter—my half-sister, Ella—whom she chose to keep.

Later I learn that because of the Nahers' influence with the nuns, whom they entertained at The Belvedere, they were privy to more information about my natural parents than other

78

adopting couples would have been. They knew my mother's name, and the name of her mother, and had been told that my father was a French Canadian. Apparently they had been promised a child of 'excellent stock'.

I cannot remember a time in my childhood when I was not self-conscious of my height, my broad shoulders and my big-boned heaviness. Quite simply, I was certain I knew nobody as big as me and longed to be one of the petites who blended with the crowd. Jackie, by contrast, seemed less obtrusive; prettily dimpled, well proportioned and clearly attractive to the opposite sex.

From around the age of eight I see that in every photograph I'm stooping forward, my shoulders slumped, my head hanging down in an attempt to appear smaller. After my first date—to Manly Beach during the day—the boy escorted me back to the house at Castlecrag. He and I sat downstairs chatting and Pauline sat upstairs, entertaining her guests. She was laughing about 'the long and the short of it all'. The boy and I sat, stricken, silent; he came only to my shoulder.

When Jackie and I were children and young teenagers we regularly discussed our adoption with Pauline. Daddo, however, seemed to periodically forget that we were adopted and would absently make comments like 'I don't know where you got your height from', as he looked at the two of us standing side by side in a photograph. Most of the early information I gleaned about my adoption, therefore, came from Pauline.

I was not yet a teenager when I had the circumstances of my conception down pat. My other father was a visiting French Canadian professor of literature. This clearly accounted for the fact that I was an avid reader of the French classics and aspired to speak French fluently and live in Paris one day. My other mother, I was told, was a country girl in Sydney for the first time and one of his students. One can imagine the rest easily, or some of it. They fell in love—it was 1966—and soon conceived a child. Now here's where the story twists and takes on its air of tragedy. He, the visiting French Canadian Prof. Lit., wanted to get married, wanted to play happy families with my other mother and for them to raise me together. She, however, would not have him, and nor would she have the child who was me. Scene ends with his return to Canada, heartbroken and dreaming of the day his love-child from Australia would come to claim him. I, the love-child, also dreamed of that day.

Across a Smaller Sea

<hr />

AT ZURICH AIRPORT Jackie, my niece Freya, and I are to go our separate ways. I to Dublin and Jackie and Freya to London. They will join me in a week's time. When I wave them through the security check towards their flight I feel a pang of anxiety. Freya seems so small to be travelling across continents, across oceans like this. Daddo was not much older—and was perhaps smaller than the robust Freya—when he left Switzerland with his parents for a journey of a far greater magnitude across the Irish Sea.

Down at my own gate I wait to board the flight to Dublin in the company of a Swiss oompapa band. If Daddo were with me he'd be cracking jokes with these men and admiring their sensible green uniforms, their pillbox hats, the shine on their heavy shoes. I watch the men and smile when one of them catches my eye; I regret the loss of *Schwyzer Deutsch* during those years at Castlecrag. By five I spoke fluent Swiss-German—which I had learned from the chorus of Swiss women in The Belvedere boiler room—but after years of Anglo-Australian homogeneity in Pauline's house, the language slowly bled from my consciousness. My regret for the loss of the language masks a far greater regret for the loss—at age five—of Daddo.

The plane flies northwest across Switzerland and below me I see the benefits of a political system that leaves nothing to chance. For every tract of farmland there is a swathe of verdant wooded land, giving me flashes of forest and field all the way to the French border. Once over France the green spaces and forests disappear and in their place is a grid of field after endless field of cultivated land. The coastline, where we cross to the Channel, is merely a line of pebbly sand and then pale blue water deepening to granite.

England offers yet more farmland, more grids and roads and urban conglomerations, so that when the plane reaches the Irish Sea, the dark, white-capped water is both shocking and unexpectedly welcome. The sea is deep green, its surface heaving and pitching. The Irish coast, when we reach it, is all jagged cliffs and grassy verges. Here to the west is Hibernia, the place the Romans saw as the land of eternal winter. When the plane screams to a halt on the runway—on rich Irish soil—the Swiss oompapas applaud the pilot and I wish that their shiny brass horns were not confined in the cargo hold.

The skies overhead are coal grey as I sit in the bus that moves slowly through thick traffic into Dublin. Outside, pebble-covered semi-detached houses defy me in my attempts to romanticise the city. In the taxi from the bus station the driver comments on the splendid weather and I listen for a note of irony in his voice. There is none. I've been in Ireland for only an hour but already I know that the summer clothes I've brought with me—including two bathing costumes—are woefully inappropriate. For all my travelling, my two passports and complicated bloodline, I feel utterly Australian.

We take a nondescript bridge across the Liffey and below us the water at low tide is a gravelly grey. The river is bleak and unwelcoming and I cannot imagine it beckoning my grandfather Ernst or me.

I direct the driver to the room I've booked just around the corner from Fitzwilliam Square and he takes me for a regular visitor or an expat. I explain that I've been studying the city for months. He wants to know whether I have family in Ireland and I tell him no, but that my grandparents emigrated from Switzerland in 1923 and stayed a few years. His dumbfounded reaction to this news sets the tone for many subsequent Dublin conversations. Why, in god's name, would anybody have migrated from Switzerland to Dublin in 1923?

In my simple room that overlooks a lane way, I unpack, do some yoga and shower before venturing out. I've been planning this visit for so long, have dreamed it so many times, that I'm almost frightened to begin. I do not want to rush things. I want to see and experience the family's sacred sites in my own good time.

Despite my best intentions I rush to Fitzwilliam Square. In my diary is a single photograph from my grandparents' time in Dublin and as I enter the square and walk, gazing up at the tall Georgian houses, I hold it in my hand. I am hoping that some detail in it will match something I see. In the photograph a small boy sits at the top of three stone steps. Behind him, a large, square-paned window which drops all the way to the ground reveals a dining table swathed in white linen. On the table sits a vase containing real flowers and there are white linen napkins, folded into jaunty sails. Lace curtains are carefully draped to draw the passerby to the quiet elegance of the table and its comforts. The walls, the stone steps, the flagstones and the iron balustrade are all grey, dark and sombre, and provide a stark contrast to the crispy whites of the dining room; *Edelweiss* in post-Civil War Dublin.

The building is Emma and Ernst's hotel and the boy is George, aged only five but already himself. He is the same age I was when I was taken from him. A large, pale ball sits on his thighs. His shorts reveal square knees and pale, slender calves with socks rising to mid-calf above buckle-up black shoes.

George is only young but the eyes that look out at the world from below his cheeky curl of dark hair are already knowing. The child is alone and appears somehow self-contained. This is how it was with Daddo throughout his life, a solitary figure, even when he was surrounded by people.

I walk the square in hope but cannot match the details. The steel railings are generic and so are the flagstones. No small, solitary child sits outside his house to help complete the image. Blue plaques tell me that William Butler Yeats once lived here and his brother Jack, the painter, there. There is no plaque for the people who inhabited the story of 'The Ghost'; no plaque for George Noble, Count Plunkett, nor for his son Joseph, the poet–hero of the Easter Rising.

Other

———◆◆◆———

I HAVE NEVER FITTED IN. I have never felt like an integral part of a group nor like one of the crowd. Jackie and I attended the same school for our entire school lives—a convent overlooking Sydney Harbour—and even after thirteen years I never felt that sense of belonging that for many is synonymous with their school days.

Nobody else in my class was adopted. Nobody else—up until I reached high school—had parents who were divorced. Even from the early years of high school only three other girls' parents had divorced; one of the girls, a friend of mine, had been so ashamed that she only told me of the divorce years after the fact.

Pauline bought herself a white Triumph Stag which came with a removable hard roof and a soft black top that folded down behind the back seat. She had a special hat and scarf and a pair of driving gloves, but the car was always breaking down which detracted from its glamour. She favoured clothes that made a statement: muu-muus in the seventies; a calf-length yellow leather coat in the eighties; and always, but always, furs and expensive jewellery.

The bush that skirted the headland on which Castlecrag sat became my refuge and my best friend and I would spend school holidays and weekends exploring it. Reading became my other great escape and was ostensibly encouraged in the house at Castlecrag. As a young teenager I read voraciously: French classics, Russian classics, contemporary American fiction, encyclopaedias and just about anything else I could lay my hands on. Pauline would stand outside my room demanding I come out and talk to her. 'I'm nearly finished the book,' I'd reply, pleading to be left alone. When I was finished there'd be another book, and yet another.

Whether it was the scant knowledge of my other father that drew me to books or literature itself that inspired my father-dreaming, I could not say. However it happened, literature became bound up with the imaginary world in which I would one day be reunited with my other father.

Jackie sought her escapes, too. She would sit in her bedroom with a novel on her knees, a textbook on the desk before her; when Pauline burst in on her, Jackie would claim she was studying and must be left alone. She was the sort of girl who rode horses and—or so it seemed to me—always had a boyfriend. Of the two of us, she hankered after Daddo, the father she had already so adored when we had been taken from him. I, as the younger child, felt my loyalties torn. Perhaps this, also, encouraged my other-father-dreaming.

Onwards

———◆———

FROM THE FITZWILLIAM Private Hotel—strategically located between Merrion and Fitzwilliam Squares—Emma, Ernst and George ventured out to explore their new home. In Dublin they would design a whole new way of living for themselves, or this is what Emma later said she had hoped for.

Ernst was drawn to St Stephen's Green for its association with the Easter Rising as well as for its Georgian elegance which, he was the first to admit, was in such contrast to its immediate history. The Shelbourne Hotel was located there, as was Earl Iveagh's Belvedere College. Emma, for her part, preferred what she saw as the more exclusive environs of the Merrion and Fitzwilliam precincts. Her aim was to run the best hotel on one of the city's most elegant squares, not to set up alongside The Shelbourne where their more modest venture would surely pale by comparison.

On the first working day after Emma and Ernst's arrival the Irish Free State Army paraded on the streets of the city to the accompaniment of brass bands. Emma, Ernst and George, done out in their finest clothing to make a favourable impression on prospective landlords, were thwarted at every turn in their attempts to cross the city. Ernst railed against his wife's single-mindedness; she rushed everything. Viewing such a parade, according to Ernst, was to participate in Irish history and support the miracle of the Irish Free State.

The cabbie who had driven them to the Fitzwilliam Hotel had made curt enquiries about their motives for migrating to Dublin as though this line of questioning was as much a part of his job as driving the horse. When Emma told him with false confidence that they'd come to open a hotel the cabbie had laughed at them. Surely they didn't expect him to believe that, he insisted. Ernst, indignant, announced that just in case the cabbie had missed the fact, the Civil War was over. Their driver had only raised one eyebrow and whistled. 'Is that what you heard then?' he muttered, before giving them a few sober words of warning for which he said there'd be no additional charge. Truce or no truce, soldiers still raided private homes late at night and at whim. Free State soldiers and Sinn Feiners alike were being shot dead in their beds or at their break-fast tables with their children looking on, just as always. Emma watched the way the man turned to look coolly at her little boy; whenever she told her Dublin stories she described this moment as pivotal. At this moment, she said, she tasted blood in her mouth.

Emma, Ernst and George walked along Baggott Street, moving against the crowds who'd gathered to watch the soldiers march. Despite Ernst's insistence that the Free State would go from strength to strength and that signing away the north had been necessary, he noted that there was no euphoria on Dublin's streets that day. The people wore such guarded expressions that they might have been holding masks to their faces just like those the citizens of Burgdorf had worn to the ball.

On the way to St Stephen's Green Ernst admired the number and quality of the city's public houses, clearly seeking an excuse to sample one. In Dublin, Emma feared there were more opportuni-ties for her husband to drink, and more willing and literate companions than there had been in Bern or Burgdorf. She would have to shoulder as much of the burden of the business as ever, but without the support of her sister in the kitchen and her mother with the boy. Just as she had played alongside her working mother, her son George would play alongside her.

As though with a view to making up to George for all future loss, Emma went to great lengths to ensure that her boy was well entertained during their early days in Dublin. On the first Friday she took him to the harbour to view the futuristic hydroplane which cut through the water at an incredible speed. A sleek timber vessel, when the hydroplane moved it was simply a dazzling swoosh on the green of the bay. The boat's name, *Onwards IV*, perplexed Emma. She and George, who spoke only Swiss-German together, repeated the word to each other in wonder. 'What could it mean?' they speculated. 'Is it something to do with Neptune, god of the sea?' Later, when George told his father about the boat he explained the curious name and what he and his mother had surmised. Ernst's laughter at his wife's whimsy and at the standard of her English wounded George.

Ireland became a place of wonder, mystery and the new for the young George. Back in Switzerland the citizens in the eastern canton of Graubunden—afraid to welcome both the railway and the car—had conceded to open only a single road to the automobile. In Dublin, by contrast, automobiles were extremely popular despite their evident danger. The *Irish Times* was always reporting the latest accident; a car falling into a ditch here, knocking down a pedestrian there.

As during the year of Emma and Ernst's move to Burgdorf, their arrival in Dublin was marred by strikes in the city's docks. Unemployment, already at 32 000, was climbing by the staggering figure of 1000 men per week.

In addition to her scrutiny of the classifieds for an appropriate rental property, Emma kept a close eye on alternative homes for herself and her boy. On the last day of June, migrant ships jockeyed for position off Ellis Island in New York Harbour; immigrant quotas set by the US Government for each nationality could have been reached as early as two days into July. Ernst made it clear to his wife that the USA had never been an option for them—the government, after all, had implemented prohibition. From lush Dublin he mourned the loss of good champagne as cases of it were being ceremoniously lowered into the sea three miles off the US coastline.

Emma also read the reports from the impossibly distant Commonwealth of Australia. They had, she noted, proclaimed that the House of Representatives would reconvene in a place called Canberra. The capitol would be built on a site of 'almost virgin bush' where the climate was said to be perfect. The British Government announced it would be sending a weekly airship to Australia carrying two hundred passengers and tons of mail.

The family's project to find suitable premises became Emma's alone; it was easier this way. By mid-July Emma was no closer to signing a lease than she'd been on the day of their arrival. There was a marked scarcity of quality rental property, despite the fact that the gentry were fleeing their grand Dublin residences for England.

On a day the mercury was tipped to rise above seventy-five, Emma took one look at her swollen, blistered feet and allowed herself to be led astray. She, Ernst and George left the city by train in the cool of the morning and watched the wide mouth of Dublin Harbour open to the sea. At Sandymount, George played in a pretty cove as his mother stood on the water's edge, the bliss of cool salt water on her naked feet. Ernst preferred to swim with the men over the rise and later reported that the Irishmen dived naked off the rocks and glided out into the deeps. Emma quickly surmised that in the Forty Foot Pool Ernst had found yet another distraction from the business and from his son.

It was not until August and the first day of the celebrated Dublin Horse Show that Emma read about the property of which she had dreamed. The leasehold on a Fitzwilliam Square house was advertised; best offer over three hundred pounds was sought. The owners, apparently, had already vacated. Ernst had departed early for the Horse Show—at which he insisted he would make some crucial contacts—but this did not stop Emma setting out to make the enquiries herself. By the time Ernst returned that evening—sullen on a mix of champagne and Guinness—Emma had negotiated the lease and handed over a significant chunk of the cash she had sewn into her petticoats. On receiving the news, Ernst turned on his heel and went out to find a pub. Emma, he claimed, clearly did not need him.

On the day Emma, Ernst and George moved into the fine Georgian terrace that was to become The Swiss Private Hotel,

Eamon de Valera was arrested in Ennis while giving the first speech of his new election campaign. Emma heard this news while she was unpacking tea chests late at night. She knew it did not bode well but chose, at this moment, to repeat the new English word she'd been toying with over the last few weeks. Onwards, she told herself, walking the four flights of steps from the attic to the basement to check on her sleeping boy yet again. Onwards.

Sanctuary

———◆—◆—◆———

DADDO MADE HIS home an idyllic place, a more tangible escape than the one I imagined my other father might bring. During the summer holidays at Lodge Road, I'd awaken to the bell-like music of halyards, or the chocolate-box strains of Swiss folk music. It was a place where classical marble statues and cuckoo clocks held a similar status, a house in which a meat pie in front of the television might be enjoyed with the same enthusiasm as a fine five-course meal.

Jackie and I spent December at Castlecrag with Pauline and January at Lodge Road, which meant we were with Daddo during the sleepiest, dreamiest month of the year. When Daddo's part of the holiday commenced the summer shimmered before us, a mirage of endless promise. As it drew to a close we mourned both the heat haze and the end of our time with him.

Mine was the blue room at the top of the stairs. It was a large, cool room with a wall of windows facing the harbour and crazy, turquoise wallpaper covered in writhing blue-green flowers, the curtains similarly patterned. It was not my true childhood bedroom, not the room decorated for me, the one chosen by George and Pauline. That room was smaller and darker, with circus wallpaper, an animal train picture on the wall and only a sliver of window. Eventually it became Daddo's office and he hung his certificates alongside the elephants and lions on the circus wallpaper and put his own trinkets beside my old toys that had been left behind. Across

91

the hallway, Jackie's bedroom had ballerina wallpaper and, by contrast, seemed light-filled and airy; the prize of the eldest child.

The beds in Daddo's house were made up with crisp white linen that was bright with sunshine from the washing-line. At the end of a hot summer's day the sheets felt firm and cool against sunburned skin. When Jackie and I first arrived for the summer there'd be neatly folded towels at the foot of the bed, just like in a hotel. The bedside table would hold a vase of freshly cut jasmine from Daddo's garden.

Each day without fail the table was already laid for breakfast when I rose. Some mornings, Daddo would be in his armchair reading the newspaper. His enormous square reading glasses made his eyes more intense, more questioning, and his clothes for round the house always showed evidence of his travails in the garden or kitchen. Most days, though, I'd go outside, padding on bare feet through the dew-damp garden or along warming sandstone paths to find him.

Some days he'd be in his workroom beneath the garage, from which coloured light would filter through the holes in the fancy brickwork. This was Daddo's domain and smelled of paint and sawdust and of damp, stored documents containing the family's past. Its shelves were alive with gadgets and widgets and tools and light bulbs and curious pieces of carved wood. He reckoned that one day all these things would find their proper use.

Other days he'd be in the garden somewhere, kneeling at a flower-bed, plucking at onion weed.

'Hello Gubs,' he'd say. 'How did you sleep?'

I always slept well there, even with possums dancing over my head. Daddo would smell of soil and by 7 am he might already have filled two or three large green garbage bags with weeds and garden refuse. During the hottest summer months he worked in the garden early in the morning and spent the day inside at his desk, or out on the road visiting frail war widows in his work for Legacy.

Jackie and I worked alongside Daddo, gardening at his side, learning what was a weed and how to pull it. Summers were full of house-painting; the three of us labouring for hours over the complicated, curling, fussy wrought iron that acted as a fringe on the balconies and on the overhanging roof at the house's front entrance.

There were the sailing days that gleamed and pulsed, each one with its own distinct colour, its own markings. Daddo had been keen for us to learn to sail, as he had never done himself. He had always imagined that one day he'd buy a yacht, a big two-master with plenty of woodwork and brass to polish, and we'd sail around Australia together.

When Daddo bought us a simple sailing dinghy the pattern of my days at Lodge Road changed. I'd take to the harbour on my own for hours on end, would disappear around Hallstrom Point mid-morning and head for the open reaches of the harbour, out where the ferries crossed between Manly and Circular Quay. I'd take a few dollars with me to buy a drink and a sandwich at Balmoral Beach and wouldn't return home until the water was turning violet in the dusk. During the days when I was first learning the harbour, I was still deemed too young to go to the movies alone.

Without fail—as though he'd been watching all day—Daddo would appear at the waterfront as the boat drew level with the house and would be there to help me haul the thing from the bay. Together we'd wash the salt water from the boat and its rigging and hang the sail to dry. Once I was dry and warm, having spent as many as eight hours in the water and the sun, Daddo would prepare us a meal which he, Jackie and I shared, accompanied by a glass of wine.

Now that I determine the rhythm of my own days and work for myself, I understand the discipline and motivation that were so much a part of Daddo's life. Now I fill my days creating otherworlds on paper, just as Daddo once did in the flesh with The Belvedere and with the sanctuary that was Lodge Road.

The Monkey and the
Model Railway

———◆◆◆———

ONE DAY I ASKED Daddo what he really remembered about his time
in Dublin. I wanted to try to separate the stories that had been told
and shaped within the family from his own, personal memories.

'Of course Mum and Dad were working all the time,' he told me.

There had been a monkey, he remembered. A naughty, mischievous
monkey owned by one of the guests had somehow fallen into Daddo's
care. When the monkey had arrived Daddo was only a small boy, aged
five or six, and clearly no match for the wily primate. The maid, who
had been given some responsibility for caring for the young George,
would lend her larger hand to the task of trying to keep the monkey
in check, but to no avail; the cheerful creature had run amok. Daddo
clearly remembered the monkey stealing a tube of toothpaste and
squeezing it until it was empty while scampering along one of the
Georgian balustrades. The creature had eventually escaped through an
upstairs window—which the maid may or may not have left open
intentionally—and across the rooftops, never to be seen again.

Daddo recalled caring for a kitten in the back garden of the
Fitzwilliam Square house and from the sweet, boyish expression
that came over him as he talked I knew his connection with the
animal had been special. Jackie's cat, Oscar, always chose Daddo's
lap above all others and seemed blissful when Daddo would beat
out a familiar rhythm on his back.

'They'd lock me in the garden in the centre of the square,' he told
me as though this was the most normal thing for such a young boy.

'There was a friendly gardener and other children to play with.'

He had once fallen from the very same balustrade the monkey had made its own, down two flights of stairs and into a basket of linen the maid had fortuitously left in the wrong place. Daddo showed me an invisible scar below his chin and told me dentists always commented on the crack in his jaw. He scratched his fluffy grey hair and commented absently that he didn't know whether his brother Maxli had been with them in Dublin or not. I prodded him for detail . . . how old was the child when he died? Daddo only pulled at his ear and said, 'It's terrible that I can't remember'.

'I was given a wonderful model train set, it had been made in Germany,' Daddo had a look of remembering and of sadness in his eyes. 'The workmanship was really something . . . it was the best train set I've ever seen. Dad had bought it from a German student who needed the money to get home.'

Daddo had given Jackie and me train sets when we were young girls but we never responded to them with the enthusiasm he had anticipated. He enjoyed the train sets himself, nonetheless.

'Dad didn't want me to have that train set,' Daddo told me. 'He thought I was too young and wouldn't be able to look after it. Mum persuaded him to give it to me anyway.'

Daddo went on to recount the way he had it set up in the back garden and how he had constructed a station and a village and a forest. The neighbourhood children had come in to play with the set and sometimes they'd ask to borrow a carriage and take it home. It had never even occurred to the young George to say no and one by one the carriages disappeared just as Ernst had predicted they would. Daddo clearly still thought the loss of the train a shame—it had, after all, been the best set he'd ever seen—but the other boys had wanted their turn too.

Once I admired Daddo's African walnut desk, the one he worked at for all those years at The Belvedere. Without a thought he said, 'You have it'. It didn't matter that in giving it to me he would no longer have it, the important thing was that in giving it away it would give me pleasure. I would not take it then, but I work at it now.

Good, Honest Work

OF COURSE HE WASN'T perfect. I have to remind myself of that; Daddo was not perfect. Those who knew him when he was a younger man—when he was running The Belvedere—claimed he had a shocking temper. Most of the people who knew him at that time, however, loved him throughout his long life. If I know anything about Daddo during the Belvedere days I know that he was an exacting taskmaster, that his best was likely to be ten times better than another bloke's.

At Lodge Road the emphasis was on diligence, on industry and on doing for others. While Daddo wanted to do everything and more for Jackie and me, he took immense pleasure in seeing us working by his side. At Castlecrag when things needed doing it was Jackie and I who were expected to do them.

Daddo expected us to behave well, to pull our weight without being asked, to treat each other and others with kindness and to do our simple best at school without too much fuss. These expectations weighed heavily on us and on our visits to him we fretted that we just weren't getting it right. But we wanted to, we so wanted to. There was an unspoken agreement between us that his example of hard work and community-mindedness was indeed worth striving for.

His first choice for me—for both Jackie and me—would have been hospitality, and after that just about any small business in which I could roll up my sleeves, sweat and make my mark.

Writing, even journalism, was not on his map. Although I've come to recognise that my own ambitions were worlds away from Daddo's, his principles apply to the life I lead now as easily as they would have to the life he might have chosen for me.

As a teenager my compulsive reading seemed somehow un-Swiss. Daddo read, but only on a need-to-know basis, which meant newspapers and current affairs magazines. To say that he was intimidated by literature, by academia, would be too extreme, but he was most certainly wary of such things. When Jackie and I were teenagers Daddo regularly railed against long-haired university professors—along with trade unionists—whom he regarded as the true blight on our community.

He always hoped that there would be Nahers in the Sydney hotel scene once again. Neither Jackie nor I were interested; we'd experienced enough catering at home to know that this wasn't where our futures lay. With our good academic records the world was wide open to both of us and it would almost certainly hold a university education. Daddo didn't think we needed it. When Jackie took up her place in an arts/law degree he fretted, worried, but could not help feeling a quiet pride, despite himself.

Like many Australians of his generation, he took a hard-line attitude to the welfare system, to 'dole bludgers' and to what he saw as the pitiful helplessness of Australia's indigenous people. There was work out there, he claimed, for anyone who wanted it. He would have rather scrubbed toilets for an honest income than taken handouts. As far as he was concerned no work was too menial and in toil there was dignity. Yet despite these attitudes he devoted nearly half his life to working for the community and to doing for those who could not do for themselves. He was on call all day and well into the night for the war widows in his area and we regularly received calls from elderly women who wanted 'Legatee Naher' to come and change a light bulb for them or to help them understand a bill or a notice from the council. He'd visit them in nursing homes where for the most part they sat and stared into space in a stupefied daze. He felt immense compassion for them.

Within the Swiss community he worked to ensure that systems were established that would act as a safety net for the entire community: he helped coordinate visits to the lonely and sick; he worked on events such as children's community Christmas parties and 'oldies' gatherings; and helped pack elaborate Christmas hampers for the elderly and infirm. In the Lions Club he was an inspired fundraiser and applied his good humour and creative energy to themed dinners and fairs. When there was food left over from one of the many functions for which he catered he took it to the Matthew Talbot Hostel down at Woolloomooloo—to the homeless men—and enjoyed his banter with the 'poor coots' down there. The concern he felt for others was a simple fact of his life; when I quizzed him about it he shrugged and said, 'There but for the grace of God go I'. He returned to the former family church—St Canice's in Elizabeth Bay—to cook for the homeless on Sunday mornings up until only a few months before he died.

Mother and Son

————◆◆◆————

As WINTER DREW IN on the tall house in Fitzwilliam Square the pattern of my grandparents' days became established. This was Daddo's childhood and it would change little, even when they crossed the world and started all over again. The Swiss Private Hotel had opened its doors to the public in September and by November there was at least one guest in residence every single night. By December Emma was confident enough to start furnishing the place in the style to which she aspired.

Emma, Ernst and George all slept downstairs in the basement; Emma and Ernst were in the room traditionally occupied by the housekeeper and George in the narrow pantry that lay between their room and the kitchen. George's room was dark and crowded with great earthenware jars of food, and dead rabbits, chickens and pheasants hanging from the ceiling. His small cot lay beneath a high window which connected the pantry to his parents' room; on the few occasions on which he was truly afraid at night he could call out to his mother for reassurance.

On the ground floor was the main reception hall with a cloak rail, a bevelled-glass oil lamp hanging from the ceiling and great doors opening into the guests' dining room and sitting room. Higher up, on the first, second and third floors, were the guests' bedrooms, some of which were large enough to accommodate a couple of armchairs, a writing table and a small dining table at which a guest might elect to dine in private.

At the foot of the long, narrow garden lay the old stables which, at the time of Emma and Ernst's arrival, sprawled in considerable disrepair. Emma dreamed of repairing the old building and installing additional guest rooms while Ernst thought he might one day keep a horse. For the time being the rooms upstairs, where the household's groom had once lived, were occupied by packing cases and the occasional shady, non-paying visitor.

In the house in Fitzwilliam Square there was hope. The couple saw Dublin in 1923 as a place of breathtaking opportunity, a place in which Emma's industry and Ernst's distinctive style might just make an impression. Emma wrote to her mother, telling her she felt this way both despite, and because of, the political scene. It was also, she hoped, a place in which her husband might learn to look forward, might learn to leave behind dashed hopes and family loss and reach out to grasp the new. Emma longed for him to embrace the hope that was sometimes so fierce in herself that it could override the fatigue she had felt since the loss of her second baby.

Emma rose at dawn each day in the biting cold of the stone-floored basement. Before either her husband or her boy had stirred in their beds she had already fired up the kitchen stove and placed the large vats of water on the hot plates to heat. She always looked in on her son before leaving for the markets . . . was full of inexplicable fear for the boy. If George—in his dark corridor with those dead rabbits hanging from the ceiling—woke and called for her when she was gone she hoped her husband would hear, would respond.

Each night, after they had served their clients dinner, Ernst went out to one of the public houses on Baggott or Leeson Streets. He always found someone with whom he could discuss the evils of imperialism and maintained he was forging crucial connections. All Emma saw of these connections were odd, nervous fellows who'd heard that there was a safe place to sleep above the stables at the back of the hotel.

Emma revelled in the first light of dawn and, although Ernst no longer shared this time of day with her, in Dublin it was no different. She often elected to walk to the markets—five miles as the crow flies—and took pleasure in experimenting with different routes.

Without fail, however, she always crossed the Liffey at Ha'penny Bridge and paused atop its arc to consider the grey swirling waters of the river in which she prayed her husband would never swim. Emma could imagine her husband being sucked down and away from her in the dark, swirling currents. She could picture him struggling to claw his way out of the water and finding no purchase on the river's hard, grey walls.

She missed the softness of the forests that ran right down to the rivers' edges in Bern and Burgdorf, however, she also admired Dublin's architecture and the ambition it denoted. She regularly told her small son that she could see him attending Belvedere, the Catholic college on St Stephen's Green; she imagined him as a tall man, like his father, climbing the steps below the masterly figure of the supine stone lion who guarded the entrance.

Emma enjoyed her shopping, liked the banter of the fruit and vegetable market near Ormond Quay and took pleasure in visiting the meat market where the alleys were often thick with blood. When she had time she'd visit other markets, seeking the fine Irish linen, the gold-framed oil paintings—all abandoned by the departing British and the Anglo-Irish—with which she was slowly furnishing her hotel. A shrewd yet enthusiastic buyer, Emma had a keen eye for quality and for the original. In years to come at The Belvedere in Sydney, Daddo would dread the arrival of the Lawson's van the day after the auctions. What, he would beseech the driver, could his mother have possibly bought this time?

When Emma returned to The Swiss Private Hotel she would smile to see the dining tables partially laid for breakfast. Each day she allowed herself to hope that it was Ernst who was up making the necessary preparations for the day ahead. But in the kitchen it was usually her son who greeted her, not her husband. George, aged only five, treated the laying of the breakfast tables as though it were a game. Wearing a thick red sweater that hung almost to the hem of his long nightshirt, a pair of woolly blue socks and a tea towel for an apron, George practised the routine he'd memorised from the times he'd laid the breakfast tables with his father.

Each day George tried to wake Ernst. His efforts were at best met with some mumbled excuses after which his father would turn away and start to snore; at worst they were met with a torrent of abuse in *Schwyzer Deutsch*. Regardless of the way his father treated him, George was always at pains to protect Ernst and never revealed to his mother the extent of his father's daily malady. During the warmer months of the year Ernst would stagger from his bed, gather his swimming things and George would silently walk his father to the tram. Ernst claimed that the water down at Sandymount, at the Forty Foot Pool, was the only thing that roused him. George never stopped hoping for an invitation to join him.

The quiet hours of the morning were precious to George and Emma. There was time for him to practise the folding of linen napkins into the shape a Dane—Joern Utzon—would later use for an opera house in Sydney. There was time to help his mother boil eggs, brew the tea the Irish so enjoyed, and serve jam and toast. There was time for the two of them to talk, to chatter endlessly about how best to care for the guests. When it was just the two of them, the warm glow that came over Emma's face helped George forget his father's indifference.

In my Father's House

I, TOO, WANTED fathering and returned to live in Daddo's house at Lodge Road when I was seventeen. Jackie and I had been gone for twelve long years and Daddo had lived in the big house alone for most of that time. Later, when Jackie asked him how he had endured it for so long he said, simply, 'I always knew you'd come'.

The coming was not easy, nor the leaving. Jackie and Pauline had a fight over Jackie's boyfriend—their screaming matches had been getting louder and more frequent—and my sister just packed her bags and drove away. She was already in her second year of university and easily of an age to leave home.

Pauline's constant illness had placed a huge emotional burden on my shoulders, and on Jackie's, and I longed to be free of it. Within a fortnight of Jackie's departure, I too had left the house at Castlecrag for Lodge Road. I had found my way home.

Going to live with Daddo seemed—at the time—like the first adult choice I had ever made. In hindsight I see that moving to Lodge Road was a step towards being parented, a return to childhood.

Jackie and I took over the bottom of the house, which was to be our domain. I moved into the Cardinal's Room, so named for the religious man who had once slept there. It sported gold flock wallpaper, mustard-coloured carpet and wrought iron on the wall around the bed and hanging from the ceiling. At night I'd look up at the hanging wrought iron and imagine its trajectory should it

103

fall. If it had fallen straight down it would probably have pierced my heart.

Although I accepted that I had made the only possible decision, my limbs were heavy with guilt. At the convent school I had attended since kindergarten, mothers were held in the highest esteem and should therefore be loved, honoured and obeyed. I had transgressed this fundamental. One of the mothers phoned to chastise me. 'When are you going back to her?' she demanded self-righteously. 'How could you do this to her after all she's done for you?'

Early mornings at Lodge Road saw me mindlessly ploughing up and down the old salt-water pool down by the harbour—it was calming—before retreating to my room to study for my final exams. Jackie was at university and worked odd hours at two jobs, one in a bar and another in a restaurant. Daddo would be out getting about his business but often he'd come home at lunch-time, bringing a quiche or a barbecued chicken for us to share. This was his first opportunity to worry about the solitary hours I spent at my desk, a worry that would be a constant in the dynamic of our relationship. Daddo understood industry, not study. His work was about reaching out.

Later in the afternoon I'd take a break and we'd sit on the balcony together, drinking coffee and watching the sunset change the colour of the water on the bay. Somewhere there'd be kookaburras laughing at dusk and from across the harbour the sound of a dog's bark or a siren or some music. This is when Daddo would start to say things like, 'Haven't you studied enough today? Why don't we go and see a film? Let's go out for Chinese'. I'd sit and agonise, tempted, torn. Eventually I'd say no, I can't, I have to keep studying. Then I'd return to my desk with a new, iron resolve, determined to make good progress because I'd turned down a trip to the movies.

Going to live with Daddo was also a step towards moving right away. During my years at Castlecrag, those years in Pauline's house, I had dreamed of escape overseas. Although escape was no longer an imperative, I had already set my life's course. As soon as my exams were finished I would be gone. Daddo, Jackie and I were to fly to Switzerland together for Christmas and then travel by train around Europe for a couple of weeks. Daddo wanted to show us the Europe he had come to know when, as a young man, he was sent 'home' to study.

I planned to stay away for at least a year. I had always imagined that I would need to travel far to be free, to become the person both my genes and my upbringing had destined me for.

His Secret Garden

THEY USED TO LOCK him in the garden in the middle of Fitzwilliam Square when he was as young as five. Most of the year George wore short pants with long woollen socks. In winter he wore a thick overcoat to his knees and a woollen peaked cap that left his ears to flap cold and free. To him—to Daddo as well as to the five-year-old boy who became Daddo—that was just the way it was and there was no point fussing about it.

Daddo said it was mostly the maid who left him there, in the seemingly vast garden. She was supposed to be looking after him but took every opportunity to go off and visit her boyfriend. No matter how I phrased the questions Daddo maintained he didn't mind. He liked spending time with the maid—she'd sing to him and tell him about the make-believe world of her own childhood—but he especially liked her when she returned from visiting her man. She was softer then, Daddo said, affectionate and tender towards him.

I peer through the tall iron bars of the gate into Fitzwilliam Park— the only private park remaining in Dublin—and stifle a sob. There are ancient trees and a mossy path leading into the central lawn and tennis court, but the gate is locked and I cannot stand in the centre of the park and peer out. To a five-year-old this would have been a vast garden and George would have looked small and alone, standing all the way in there on the grass, or on a leafy path beneath one of the Square's plane or beech trees. I feel a curious desire to protect him from the hurt of that abandonment, to hold his hand as he wanders

106

the great garden, his dark eyes wide with fear and wonder. I nursed Daddo right up until the end and even two years after his death the intense protectiveness I felt for him then still burns bright in me.

Daddo told me that the only other person who spent as much time in the Square as he did was the elderly gardener. Even when there were other children in the Square Daddo gravitated to the gardener's side. He liked to watch the man turning the soil, bending towards the earth to plant the delicate seeds that would erupt into sweet peas, lupins, poppies and stocks in the spring. He liked to watch the man's capable hands and listen to his low voice as he patiently explained to George exactly what he was doing and why. The gardener talked plant lore as easily as Emma spoke the language of the stove.

Anyway, the other children said George was different, said his parents had funny accents and that his mother worked like a scullery maid. Not so many years earlier it had been shameful to be associated with hotels, Emma explained to her son, even with a hotel as grand as The Shelbourne. The upper class might have been departing in boatloads from Dunleary, but they were still in evidence around Fitzwilliam Square.

There were other children, thin and barefoot, who crept along the street following their black-shawled mothers. George knew them because Emma would bring them into the kitchen for a bowl of soup even as she was serving the paying guests upstairs. Offering food to the needy was something on which Emma and Ernst were in accord, although they approached it from quite different perspectives. She gave away food because, she said, it hurt her to see so much need. He endorsed this practice because, he said, he approved of thwarting capitalism.

At the house in Fitzwilliam Square Daddo had his first pet and in the garden he tended his first flowers. It was only a matter of time, he said, before he and the gardener were working side by side, only a matter of time before the garden and its seasons became as much his concern as the laying of the breakfast tables. Daddo said his mother would make tutting noises at the soil on his knees and at his cuffs when the maid returned him from the garden, but he knew she wasn't unhappy. He said he once heard his parents arguing about his friendship with the gardener. Ernst, apparently, was appalled that his son squatted in the soil but Emma was adamant that it did him no harm. She accused Ernst of hypocrisy; he supported socialism intellectually but when it came to practice, digging in the earth was too good for his son. If he was so unhappy about the way his son occupied himself then he, Ernst, should take the time to be a real father to the boy.

Daddo told me that the gardener was a hard worker, was in the Square just after dawn and only gone at dusk, but that he always had time to notice a new bud and point it out to George. The man took immense pleasure in the birds that danced on the park's manicured lawns and nested in its evergreen oaks and lime trees. George, aged five, was amazed by the way the man would talk to a small boy and solicit his opinions on the behaviour of birds or on the positioning of a row of bulbs.

This gentle gardener helped shape the way Daddo saw the world and this helps me forgive the maid and my grandparents for leaving such a small boy all alone. The gardener told George that the other children's fathers, while of a good class and standing, were cut of a different cloth; their hands worked only at shuffling dull, dry paper. He said theirs was a world of talk, of barter and of great things that the eyes could not see. His own work and the work of George's mother, the gardener explained, concerned the business of making something from nothing. People like them took a few simple ingredients and nurtured them, fashioned them into a feast for the senses. It was, the gardener emphasised, good, honest work.

Märchenland

◆━◆◆◆━◆

ON THE WAY TO MASS with Daddo at St Patrick's on Sunday evenings—back when we were still young children—we'd reach the crest of a particular hill in the car and see before us a magical spectacle of light and dark. This was the harbour by night and the lights of the city all around it. We called it fairyland, but the real fairyland was the world Daddo had created himself.

To get to Daddo's house you leave the main road behind at Cremorne Junction and you follow the contours of the land downhill, towards the harbour. Each time you have a choice, you take the turning that leads you closer to the water.

Daddo's house is the one with the lacy iron hanging from the roof of the garage; above it is a string of coloured fairy lights. Take the uneven sandstone path beside the garage. There's an old iron gate, it's all curlicues and swirls. You'll soon find yourself walking alongside the Inclinator track, it's on your right. The Inclinator is a small carriage on a greasy track that will carry three people down to the house and is particularly useful for hauling bags of groceries. Beyond the Inclinator track you'll see the first of the statues, one of the classical marble statues that came from The Belvedere.

The statue up here, in the top garden, is of the Virgin Mary. That's what I think, anyway. She wears a scarf covering her hair and such a beatific expression on her downcast face that it could be no one else. Daddo insists that she's just a peasant girl. Age and the elements have turned her white marble a little green. And she's lopsided, she's sinking into the lawn on top of Daddo's wine cellar. I enjoy the fact that the Virgin Mary is falling, slow motion, into the wine cellar.

Keep walking down the path. The next in this cascade of gardens is middle station. *Mittelstation.* Here, built into a dark stone wall, is the entrance to the wine cellar. It used to be our neighbour Roy Luxton's air raid shelter. Uncle Roy was a bit of a character; when they cleared out his garage years after his death they found a couple of unexploded shells. He was a gentle soul who spent much of his time in the garden. Once he fell from a ledge between his garden and Daddo's; the only thing that saved him were his baggy old shorts that caught on a rock and left him hanging upside down, exposing his capacious, old man's underpants.

Beyond the fancy wrought iron gate, back at middle station, lie the remains of hundreds of bottles of wine. They came across from The Belvedere at the beginning of the seventies. The elements got to the wine quicker than Daddo could and inundations over the years spoiled two-thirds of the hoard. The wine cellar remained locked when Jackie and I were children, but from time to time we'd timidly follow Daddo inside. We'd been raised on stories about the carpet snake that lived in the cellar at The Belvedere; it was said to keep the waiters honest. There were always a few centimetres of water on this cellar's floor and as a child I imagined a cold, slimy creature lurking just beneath the surface.

At middle station you'll find the cheese tree. You won't be able to miss it. Its branches reach across to shelter the whole terrace, reach out to grab at your hair as you're passing in the Inclinator. From time to time an owl comes to perch in its branches. It seemed like the most natural thing for Daddo's garden to have a cheese tree. He is Swiss, after all. He used to point out the tiny cheeses—the tree's fruit covered in waxy orange skin—when they first appeared each season. I never saw one of these cheeses grow any bigger than a five-cent coin but I always believed it was only a matter of time. The connection between the tiny cheeses on the tree and the big yellow cheeses on our kitchen table, however, remained a delicious mystery to me.

Continue on down the sandstone path, to where it broadens into wider steps, the ones on which Jackie and I were photographed on my first day of school. That was the beginning of our last year here as a nuclear family. Don't forget to look to your right at the foot of the steps, you don't want to miss the marble eagle with the shiny brown eyes that guards the foot of the Inclinator.

Stroll across to the pond, onto the small bridge. From here you might glimpse our ancient goldfish; we have never known how many of them there are. Across the bridge is another of the Belvedere statues, a small boy with curly hair. He's chubby and naked. At The Belvedere he was at the centre of the garden in which Jackie and I farmed snails.

Turn back towards the house now and walk past the orange tree down to the tiled courtyard outside the front door. To your left is a two-tiered fountain that never spurts. Behind it is another statue, another chubby, semi-naked boy, but with wings. This one is modest; his torso and abdomen are draped with cloth. If you get down on your knees and look up the boy's skirt you'll see his tiny penis, snails are attracted to it. Behind the fountain is a fish tank containing an old train set with a backdrop of the Swiss Alps. This is one of the sets Daddo gave Jackie and me when we were small children. Perhaps if we'd spent our childhoods at Lodge Road we would have known the local children and these carriages, too, might have been slowly disseminated across the neighbourhood.

Above the front door is a Bacchanalian relief which was unobtrusive until Daddo painted the cherubs pink and their wine flasks gold. Below the relief is the heavy iron cast of Foo. He's just a nose with a forehead and two hands. He used to peer into a garden at The Belvedere from one of the hotel's high walls.

By now Daddo will be standing at the front door waiting to greet you. Even if you're a distant acquaintance and he isn't expecting your visit, he'll be beaming at you. He'll be saying, 'Well what have I done to deserve this?' and 'Come on in, mate. Let me just whip up a little something. Can't I at least offer you an ommie?'.

As you walk through the front door you will notice the wall of windows facing the bay but will only be distracted by the view momentarily. It's difficult to get past the set of lamps, blue porcelain, and the clock. They stand taller than me and are in the Viennese style, or is it Turkish? They're ornate all right, very ornate. Two tall lamps and a clock that never works for long but which can be encouraged to chime, occasionally. Passed down from generation to generation is the precious knowledge that there's only one other set in the world, in Buckingham Palace. Antique dealers, however, will tell you they've heard that one before.

Don't do the view just yet. Turn and look into the room, towards the fireplace. Walk towards it on the Persian carpet, the one decorated with forests, wild animals. It's hollow underneath, isn't it? That's because when Daddo had the terrazzo done—with marble from The Belvedere—he had a fountain installed. The plumbing's there, but I never saw it working, not in thirty years.

You can walk through the arches now towards the windows, towards the harbour. There is Daddo's battered desk, made of African walnut and coated in years of grime from the cigarettes smoked in the hotel and in his old office. Daddo didn't smoke but the desk was once surrounded by people who did. We had it meticulously restored after Daddo died, but some parts of the desk, its edges on which my arms now rest, are still dark with the oil from my father's skin.

On either side of the windows facing the bay are the Bacchus—the two-metre-tall marble statues of Bacchus and his wife. 'The Bacchus' is how we've always referred to them, as though Bacchus was a family name, Jones or Smith. The Bacchus are solid marble. There's over a metre of red marble plinth with bronze detailing comprising vine leaves and hoofed feet, and draped bronze loincloths for the pair, swathing their hips. Ascending from the bronze cloths, in all their milky white marble glory, are the exquisite torsos of Bacchus and his wife. The two figures are gloriously muscled, he with a washboard stomach and she with delicious curves. They wear vine leaves in their hair and high up on his shoulder sits a young boy, on hers a young girl. The statues disassemble into three pieces, three great chunks of marble, but nonetheless it takes four men to move them. Daddo will tell you that when they came across from The Belvedere to Lodge Road the carriers used elephant straps. I envisage small elephants parading down our steep, twisting garden path, great chunks of marble strapped to their backs, to their sides.

Beyond the Bacchus is the harbour. Its beauty is simple, unfussy by comparison. The pale yachts moored outside appear Spartan framed by the Bacchus and a lacy fringe of wrought iron which hangs overhead.

Move on, out of the house and into the second Inclinator. Daddo will travel with you, just so you know the small cage on its high, narrow track is safe. On the way down in the Inclinator you'll pass another statue; this one is a weather-darkened bronze woman, sitting playing jacks. There's a flag mast on this level. It flies not one flag but three. The normal configuration is the Australian flag at the top, and the Swiss and Bernese on either crossbar.

The area around the swimming pool has been turned into a Grecian court with columns and statues—winged lions—spouting water into the pool. And beyond all of this, again, is the vivid blue-green of the harbour, the simplicity of sky and water and wind.

Although he did not choose Lodge Road himself, it became the physical embodiment of Daddo's dreams.

The Family Ghost as Hero

BY THE END OF MY first full day in Dublin I'm sitting beneath the pale green stuccoed dome of the National Library of Ireland's Reading Room. I have wasted the morning trying unsuccessfully to get my laptop computer to talk to a local internet server and now I am comforted by the solid reliability of leather-bound books and by the librarian's assistants who seek out readers' requests by foot. Give me this century-old library over cyberspace any day.

I am immediately seduced by the Reading Room with its rows of wooden, leather-covered desks, each with its own discrete desk lamp. I am content in the silence of the domed room in which James Joyce's Stephen Daedalus made his speech on Shakespeare. By the end of my first day in Dublin I possess a reader's ticket for the library and a list of books on the enigmatic Plunketts, the family whose eldest son inspired Daddo's story that Jackie and I called 'The Ghost'. Although I do not even know whether my grandparents ever met Count Plunkett, my own family's Dublin story has always seemed irrevocably bound to that of the Plunketts.

Through the Plunketts I am confident I'll be able to piece together the beginning of my grandparents' stay in Dublin. Indeed, I'm so certain about this that calling the Swiss Embassy to check its records is a low priority. Through the Plunketts I will find my grandparents' address and this, finally, will make their Dublin lives tangible.

When I and my fellow readers are politely ejected from the library at closing time I make my way down Kildare Street to the Green. My destination is one of the Lower Baggott Street pubs and I choose a Victorian bar called Toners for my first Dublin Guinness. Although my first week in the city—before Jackie and Freya come from London—will be solitary, I'm determined to get out and experience the place. The pub is packed with office workers and a few older men. I find a place in one of the wooden cubicles at the back of the smoky pub that I will share with one of the resident drinkers—a man of about seventy in a tweed suit and waistcoat—who barely lifts his eyes from the newspaper when I arrive.

My first sip of Guinness gives me an unexpected sense of homecoming and I ponder the possibility that I may have mysteriously inherited the Guinness gene from my grandfather Ernst. I can easily imagine him in the pub. Like the man beside me he'd be well dressed, likely sporting a three-piece suit, hat and glasses. He too would have his nose buried in a newspaper or a book and would only deign to emerge from it if he caught the strains of a suitably erudite conversation nearby.

When I picture Ernst beside me in Toners I am reminded of Brendan Behan's words: 'Dublin to an alcoholic is like a girl's gymnasium to a sex maniac. Its atmosphere generates a drinking mood'.

I finish my Guinness so quickly it's almost a desecration and gather my things to go. I, unlike my grandfather, am ill-at-ease in the bar on my own. Nonetheless, as I walk along Lower Baggott Street I choose another pub for the following evening.

The next day I am at the National Library before it opens and prepared to rush up the marble staircase with the other readers to present my request for books to the librarians. One of the books is *Inside Ireland* by Eilis Dillon. It is only when I hold it in my hands and read its jacket blurb that I learn Dillon is Count Plunkett's granddaughter. Chance or one of the family ghosts has guided me well.

I immediately feel a connection with George Noble Plunkett, born in 1851. He went to school in Nice, back when it was still part of Italy, and there he developed his taste for Renaissance art as my grandmother, Emma, did in Milan. Later the Count studied law at Trinity College and wrote for, edited and owned the journal *Hibernia*. He collected books, pictures and manuscripts, and took an interest in the movement to preserve the Irish language.

Among his friends was Oscar Wilde, with whom he had a long correspondence. Plunkett's wife would subsequently burn all of Wilde's letters during his trial but the Count and the writer, according to Dillon, remained friends to the end. I confess that these links—albeit rather tenuous—thrill me. Perhaps my grandparents associated with the Count after all.

Plunkett's father gave him and his new wife a house just off Fitzwilliam Square at 26 Upper Fitzwilliam Street. I give a very small squeak of discovery when I read this, confident that this is the house in which he and his wife remained. Confident, also, that I have found the address of The Swiss Private Hotel.

I find I'm surprised by this development and can only attribute my surprise to the doubts I've been harbouring. On my arrival in Dublin the only proof I had that the family had been here is the one tiny photograph of Daddo atop a small flight of stone steps, the words *Georgli im Dublin* scrawled on the back. The fact that the Plunketts did indeed live in a house near Fitzwilliam Square— although not in the Square itself as I had believed—seems like evidence of my grandparents' very existence.

I learn that George and Josephine Plunkett were given fine furniture for wedding gifts, fashioned by Dublin craftsmen. Back in my terrace house in Sydney is an immense linen press, so large that each of its six drawers are the size of rowboats; it is one of the items Emma and Ernst brought with them to Sydney from Dublin. Could it be one of the Plunkett wedding gifts?

The Count became Curator of the National Museum and was a man whom both my grandparents would have admired. Catholics in Switzerland had comprised a powerless minority during Emma's girlhood and she would have felt honoured to serve this devout Catholic—one who had risen to such heights in his community—at her table. Ernst would have been more inclined to seek out the Count's company over a glass of claret and endeavour to engage the man in political debate.

As the events of the Easter Rising of 1916 took shape, the Plunkett family's fate was being sealed. At twenty-eight, Joseph Plunkett, the Count's eldest son—whom I believe is the one known to my family as 'the ghost'—was the youngest signatory to *The Proclamation of the Government of the Irish Republic to the People of Ireland*. The Count himself wished to bear arms in the uprising alongside his son but was, alas, deemed too old. Joseph Plunkett was arrested and imprisoned like the other revolutionaries and the Count himself was subsequently gaoled at Kilmainham just like his son.

Before Joseph's scheduled execution the Count was conducted to a high cell overlooking a yard in which his son was forced to stand for hours on end. The two could only gaze at each other. Joseph was weak, recovering from an operation to remove tubercular glands from his neck. The night before the young man's execution—in the presence of soldiers and fixed bayonets—Joseph was married to his fiancée, Grace Gifford, there in the prison.

According to Eilis Dillon, the marriage of our family ghost to his beloved on the eve of his execution was one of the incidents that raised public sympathy for the insurgents.

As closing time approaches I become impatient; I've reached July 1922 in the Plunketts' story and they show no signs of leaving their house. My emotions conflict; I'm frustrated that my own family's Dublin story cannot yet start but concerned at what further tragedy might befall this fascinating family.

The National Library closes before lunch on Saturday and does not reopen until Monday morning. I'm disgruntled when I realise that I'll be left in suspense for the entire weekend. After all these years I am determined to identify the bloodstains my grandmother Emma washed from the wall in Plunkett's former home. Where is the final bloody incident that will, once and for all, authenticate the story of the 'The Ghost'?

Later I walk down Baggott Street, past the pub I have already chosen for my second Guinness, and turn into Pembroke Street to walk towards Fitzwilliam Square. I am nervous, I anticipate disappointment and disillusionment. I am about to touch a family myth. I am about to confront the past head-on.

26 Upper Fitzwilliam Street is a tall, thin, brick terrace house not dissimilar to the others on the street and in the nearby square. Unlike many of the houses in the area it shows no evidence of having been renovated and its red front door and glass-panelled fanlight both look shabby and unloved. There are four floors, including the basement which is below street level. The configuration of window and steps does not correspond with that in the tiny sepia photograph I carry in my diary. It only occurs to me much later that the photograph might have been taken on a flight of steps at the building's rear and that I have only imagined a house with its dining room facing the square. Wind tears at my thin cardigan and penetrates my light, summer trousers. I stand shivering in front of 26 for a long time; some of the glamour falls from my grandparents' lives as I linger.

My Fathers' Tongues

———◆◆◆◆———

WE TRAVELLED TO THE fatherland in 1984—Daddo, Jackie and I—a place of snow and chocolate, of mountains and cuckoo clocks, of order and routine. We rushed around meeting members of our grandmother's family—Emma's family—all over the country, but we contacted nobody from Ernst's.

'One day,' Daddo said, 'I'll explain to you why there are no more Nahers.' One day but not then. Not ever.

I arrived in Switzerland with a working knowledge of Italian, with near-fluent French but with only a smattering of Swiss-German. I knew words in *Schwyzer Deutsch* from my childhood such as belly button, bottom, fart and burp, but could not converse with my adult cousins. Jackie and I were welcomed warmly but the language, or lack thereof, was a hurdle and would remain that way. Even after we had studied German for a few months and could manage a polite conversation, we did not attain the fluency we would have had we grown up in a house in which two languages were spoken.

Daddo still spoke Swiss-German but was clearly rusty. He was short of vocabulary and would make liberal use of '*das Ding*', for 'thing'. A Swiss friend claimed that he was too proud to say when he did not understand, and she would always ensure she repeated important details in English, later.

That visit to Switzerland with Daddo remains a blur of mountains and pretty villages—all glimpsed from train windows—and endless family meals at which Jackie and I communicated in sign language so as not to speak over the top of the conversation taking place in *Schwyzer Deutsch*. As a different form of oral satisfaction, and perhaps because it was the stuff of our childhood at The Belvedere, we gorged ourselves on Swiss pastries, breads, sausages and cheese. Soon the clothes we had brought with us from home were as tight on us as the skin on the pale flesh of the *Bratwurst* we ate with such gusto.

We were a curious trio; Jackie and I were teenagers and Daddo sixty-five. Upon occasion Jackie and I would slip out alone in the evening to savour the sense of truly being at large in the world. If there was tension, it was over reading. Jackie and I were both bookworms and for this reason train travel was paradise. Daddo preferred to observe, to sit back and watch the landscape of his childhood in absolute wonder. How, he asked us, as the train crossed a high bridge over a deep alpine gorge, could we bear to miss such stunning scenery? In Switzerland Daddo's emotions ran close to the surface; the sound of church bells ringing could bring tears to his eyes.

On our final day in Switzerland together in early 1985, Daddo took us to the first-class restaurant at the Zurich *Hauptbahnhof*. When Emma had brought him—aged seventeen—to Switzerland to study, she had treated him to a last supper at a similar establishment at the Lausanne station. Daddo had keen memories of the high standard of service and food, back in 1937, and was eager to lavish upon Jackie and me a similar treat.

We three were exhausted from our travels and the end of the journey came as something of a relief to me. Daddo, however, seemed distressed to be leaving us there on the other side of the world, alone. It was as though he feared that the moment we were separated, some tragedy would strike. When we said goodbye to him after our meal at the Zurich *Hauptbahnhof*, he appeared small, tired and melancholic. I wish I had known then what I know now; that while Daddo was separated from his own parents at the same age as me, the worst sort of loss had befallen him.

Daddo left us in Switzerland to study for the year—just as his mother had once left him—and returned to Australia alone. The house must have seemed even quieter to him then, after it had been filled with teenaged voices and the constant white noise of Triple J on the radio. For the briefest of periods—perhaps six months in total—the house at Lodge Road had been a family home. Daddo must have wondered whether in taking us away he'd ever get us back again. But his was a releasing love, the sort of love that launched me into the world. It was not a grasping, needy love.

Jackie and I stayed with friends outside Zurich and tried to fit in. We studied German at a school in the city and continued our exploration of the Swiss staples—of chocolate, cheese, bread and *charcuterie*. Zurich never suited us, nor we it, with its grey skies and serious working folk with whom we failed to communicate. Even as our German improved the Swiss continued to reply to us in English. Even with our Swiss passports, small Swiss bank accounts and our white skin, we felt ourselves to be utterly foreign. There was a grave regularity to life in Zurich that didn't sit well with what we knew, with what we were accustomed to. We learned, quickly, that Daddo's maverick sense of humour had developed elsewhere. In Switzerland we understood just how much of his character was Aussie larrikin, from his days of service for Australia in Borneo and New Guinea, and how much less of him was good little Swiss boy.

I picked up German easily—having spoken it as a small child—but even as I progressed through the textbooks and leaped into a more advanced class, I dreamed about speaking French, longed for a second language about which I could feel passionate.

Leaving Zurich for Paris was inevitable. It's what I'd always secretly wanted, what I'd fantasised about. I don't know what came first, my obsession with the French language or the information, which I never questioned, that my other father was French Canadian. Swiss-German seemed like baby talk, which is how I first experienced it, with so many nouns having -*li* tacked onto the end so that everything and everyone became diminutive. French, by comparison, seemed sophisticated, seductive and somehow literary.

When I eventually phoned Daddo to tell him I planned to move from Zurich to Paris—that I could easily find a job there and thought I had a good chance of being accepted at the Sorbonne—he told me simply that I must do what I must do. It was as though he'd known this was my destiny but had felt duty-bound to show me what the culture of his birthplace had to offer.

Not once did he refer to what was foremost in my mind; that I would be learning the language of the other father. Jackie says he never saw us as his adopted daughters, that we were just his daughters. He never denied the truth of our origins, but to him my other father—if he ever thought of him—was only one of the many facets that made me who I was.

The Storyteller

When I finally reach him on the phone, the official at the Swiss Embassy in Dublin tells me he has my grandparents' registration card. If I can present him with proof of identification he'll let me have a copy. I travel out across the Grand Canal by bus and along a leafy suburban road flanked by fine Victorian homes. I'm contemplating my day's reading in the library, anxious that the Plunketts did not yet seem poised to leave their Fitzwilliam Street house.

The photocopied document I am given by the Embassy official has a dark slash across it, above the phrase '*parti pour Australie*'. Written with such bold finality, the words on the page make Australia seem like the end of the earth and a place for which people depart and are never heard of again. In faint print, just above those words, is my grandparents' address: 34 Fitzwilliam Square, Dublin. I find myself squinting at the page, frowning, shaking my head and the official asks me whether there's a problem. There must be a mistake, I tell him. My grandparents lived at 26 Upper Fitzwilliam Street. Is it possible that an error has been made? Seventy-five years after the fact there is no way for this official to know. Of course there might have been a mistake, he concedes, but I can tell from his tone of voice that he thinks it unlikely. I, in turn, restrain myself from embarking on the story of 'The Ghost'—as recounted on my second Sunday visits to Daddo—in order to explain why this cannot have been my grandparents' address.

On further scrutiny of the form I learn the date of my grand-parents' arrival in Dublin—19 June 1923—and see that they never bothered to inform the Embassy of their final departure. In 1927, a month or two before my grandparents left for Australia, my grandfather paid his outstanding military tax of just over eight Irish pounds. At the same time, he renewed his passport which he could not have done without paying up in full.

As late as 1930 the Swiss Embassy was pursuing Ernst for unpaid military taxes, a penalty, of sorts, for his absence from Switzerland and for not participating in compulsory military service. Inwardly I cheer my grandfather's avoidance of this tax. I would love to be able to goad Daddo about this; he was an avid believer in compulsory military service, although to my knowl-edge he never served in Switzerland himself. His father, Ernst, was an objector.

On the bus back into central Dublin I ponder the two differ-ent addresses. Perhaps the hotel was in one house and my grand-parents and father lived in another? I start to feel irritated. Am I annoyed with the Swiss for their immaculate records or with Daddo for orchestrating this dilemma? This chapter of the story, featuring the ghost and the Plunkett family, is, after all, one of the most regularly told parts of my family history. It has also become my favourite.

When I finally reach the National Library it is midday and the librarians are all at lunch. Terribly civilised but terribly bloody frus-trating. I decide that it's time to sign on at Trinity College's library. Duly clutching my polite introduction on University of Technology, Sydney, letterhead, I visit the library and receive my reader's ticket. I have visions of working in a grand, ancient library in which every corner resonates with the passions and pursuits of scholars from generations past. The Berkeley Library, however, is as modern and as functional as an airport and only marginally quieter.

I go directly to one of the librarians with what seems to me a ludicrous, hopeless request. I need to know who lived at two different addresses in Dublin from 1923 to 1927. The librarian suggests a set of red directories called Thoms; these are the Dublin directories and the library keeps a near-complete set dating back to well before the period in question. My romantic search is suddenly reduced to flipping through a telephone directory.

I load myself with volumes of the said Thoms Official Directory and try to find myself a quiet desk at which to read; all around me are teenagers cramming for final exams. All the best desks near windows and in private corners have been colonised and are scattered with papers, books, pens, pencils and drink bottles; the colonists are apparently out of the library on smoko. I settle between two students who both stare at large tomes with glazed eyes.

Before me is the Thoms Directory for 1923 in which I easily find the listings for Fitzwilliam Square and surrounds. As I knew it would be, 26 Upper Fitzwilliam Street is in the name of Count George Noble Plunkett, M.P., barrister, and 34 Fitzwilliam Square, where the Swiss claim my grandparents resided, is empty. In 1924, The Swiss Private Hotel has filled the blank beside the listing for 34 Fitzwilliam Square, alongside the name, E. Naher; 26 Upper Fitzwilliam Street remains the home of Count Plunkett.

For a time I stare at the book before me in a daze. The story I grew up on—about the ghost in the Dublin hotel and the Plunkett family—is as fabricated as one of my own novels. Someone, most likely Daddo, took a bit from here and a bit from there to form a fabulous tale. One of the underlying truths of my family—the tale of its brush with history in Dublin—is, quite simply, untrue. And if this is untrue then what else might be, too?

I am not disappointed. If anything, I am delighted. Daddo was pulling our legs—mine and Jackie's—all along. Daddo was a storyteller, just like me . . . just like his father before him. In Dublin I thought I would find Ernst but, as always, I am led back to Daddo. I learn he's invented two ghost stories that each serve to silence the untold story of his father. Ernst, I am coming to see, is the true family ghost. The more I search, it seems, the more obscure he becomes. I am utterly intrigued.

Number 34 is on the south side of Fitzwilliam Square. It's a more stately building than the Count's house and helps shift the tarnish on my grandparents' story. There are no steps, however,

leading up to a front window before which a small boy—
Daddo—might once have sat. The building appears empty and
through the basement windows I can see piles of rubble and
building materials. As it was when my grandparents arrived, the
tall terrace house is awaiting renewal. It's awaiting the arrival of
somebody who'll scrub its walls, who'll stir its ghosts. I climb the
stairs to get a closer look at the heavy, forest-green door. Below
the brass plate with 34 on it is another brass object, the head of a
lion. I enter a narrow lane way that gives me access to the rear of
the property, but my view of the garden in which Daddo once
played is obscured by a pair of great timber gates.

In my room in the evening I read V.S. Pritchett's account of
Dublin in the twenties and keep laying the book aside to consider
my conundrum. I am a storyteller trying to string together what I
have always thought was a sequence of truths. Pritchett, however,
writes that 'Dublin stories float about as light as air with the
telling'. What other, more bloody story does Daddo's fabricated
Dublin ghost story conceal?

A Writer

———◆◆◆———

I WONDER WHETHER IT IS possible to understand, in a short, contained period, the authentic nature of your character? During my nine months in Paris—far from my stalwarts, from Daddo and Jackie—I worked out who I was. Or who I was to be.

During my last years of school I had been drawn to the law as an occupation. I'd been a debater and standing up and speaking for a living seemed like something I could do. Stuffed full of self-righteousness, defending the underdog appealed to me. But there was a doubt, a whispering doubt. I was obsessed with books and was always scribbling. I was more engaged with an imaginary world.

In Paris I found myself a good job as an au pair for the de la Rochefoucauld children. They lived on the first floor of an apartment building on the *rue de Rivoli* and I was given a room on the sixth, just below the eaves. From my wall of windows facing into the courtyard—a couple of cracked panes let in the icy wind—I could look into the lives of dozens of Parisian families. There was no telephone and no television. With its view of the Paris rooftops and the wild sky overhead, and with the rest of the world so very far away, the room was made for a writer.

I studied at the Sorbonne, or pretended to. I was, after all, eighteen and this was my first year out of school, out of Australia and living alone. In reality I was having far too much fun to study seriously and Paris—just out there across the rooftops—was a constant distraction from the French history and grammar I should have worked harder to master.

At Shakespeare & Co. English language bookshop on the Left Bank I saw a note advertising a writing group. Although I was not working on a short story or a novel or a body of poetry—like so many other expats living in the city, laying their notepads, their dreams, their hearts on café tables—I did not hesitate to take the details. I had, after all, written what I imagined were novels, and some poetry, while I was at school.

Soon writing vied with the social life I shared with other au pair girls. I might not have found the time to study for an exam or to make it to all my classes, but I always found time to read the stories we workshopped and attend the regular meetings we held in group members' apartments all over the city. For the first time in my life I met practising writers; men and women just a few years older than I who had arranged their lives around writing. An American woman spent the entire summer in a salmon-canning factory in Alaska so she could afford to sit in Paris for the rest of the year and write. None of us were published. In the middle of winter I sat in my *chambre de bonne*— a great immobile lump in five layers of clothing—and typed into the night on my portable Smith Corona with its European keyboard. By the end of the year I had forgotten about law. Paris had turned my head.

I wrote dozens of letters home and at least one body of them remains intact. On sifting through Daddo's files more than two years after his death I find that he has saved every letter I've ever written him. They start from when he left Jackie and me in Zurich in 1985 and finish with my time in New York in 1993. In one fat file lie four cities—Zurich, Paris, London and New York—and all the hopes and confidences I shared with him.

On reading the Paris letters fifteen years after I wrote them I see clearly the extent to which I adored him; what is clear, also, is that I feared he would never understand me. I told him repeatedly of how much I missed him. I told him how hard I was working on my studies and how much I enjoyed the children of the happy, grand family by whom I was employed. I dwelled on the kindness Monsieur and Madame de la Rochefoucauld showed me. I wrote that I had fallen asleep in class and been yelled at by the mad professor. I recounted the names and traits of all my friends and with them a sanitised version of our escapades. I did not tell him that I had fallen in love—with words—and that I had decided to be a writer. In fact, not once did I mention the writing group or the stories I was working on. I told him, instead, that I wished to work in publishing, which was true.

In Paris I began, as the French say, to live well in my own skin. *Je vivais bien dans ma peau.* I read extensively, passionately, I wrote, I studied (a little) and I sat up late, talking and drinking with my friends. In Paris, also, I began the process of presenting to my adored and adoring father the young woman I thought he wanted me to be.

The City of my Grandfather

That Dublin was my grandfather Ernst's city I have no doubt. I can feel him watching over us—me, Jackie and Freya—as we attend High Tea at the Shelbourne Hotel. For Emma, this had been Dublin's finest hotel; for Ernst it held close associations with the birth of the Irish Free State.

I have run down Dawson Street from Trinity College, past the bookshops in which I have spent so much time, to join them. All morning I have studied maps of the city from Emma and Ernst's time and my head is full of the patterns—a myriad of coloured veins—that the city's trams and buses once followed. In my mind I have a clear image of the different routes that Emma would have taken by foot from Fitzwilliam Square to the markets.

When I arrive Jackie and Freya are already in situ in the opulent lounge. Even my initial glimpse of the ornate room prompts that thrill of familiarity I experienced at *du Theatre*, once *L'Hôtel de Musique,* in Bern. Here at The Shelbourne in the year 2000 there are echoes of The Belvedere's sumptuosity. The high-ceilinged room is scattered with well-stuffed sofas and armchairs and the walls are adorned with bevelled mirrors and oil paintings with ornate gold frames.

When I sink back into the steady embrace of the armchair I can imagine my grandfather Ernst in the room with his newspaper and a pot of coffee. I can feel Ernst's eye on me now. Neither Jackie nor I consider the abstemious version of High Tea; we order ours with champagne. All around us are American tourists but Jackie, Freya and I are in grandfather's Dublin. Freya gets her plump little hands on a miniature bottle of champagne and quickly has it to her lips, draining the last drops. Jackie and I exchange stern glances but quickly dissolve with laughter. When we each 'arrived' at The Belvedere we were given a sip of French champagne—and we were not robust toddlers like Miss Freya. We still argue over the story; each one insisting that it was she who drank the champagne and the other who spat it.

In Ernst's city there was a great literary revival in the twenty years prior to his arrival and the Gaelic League successfully recovered a near-extinct language. Ernst had always felt that his own culture was perilously close to being subsumed by that of neighbouring Germany. In Switzerland, dialect remained in common use but few could write it and even fewer had the ability to commit the language to shorthand. Ernst had mastered both these skills. When he was introduced to Eamon de Valera—after the latter's release from prison in 1926—they conversed at some length about the transference of Celtic and Swiss-German into shorthand. De Valera had been working on a book on Irish shorthand during his stay in prison but had abandoned it when he learned that a work already existed on the topic.

Ernst shared another of the Irishman's great passions, that of swimming, and would make for the waters off the Martello Tower (which James Joyce once shared with Oliver St John Gogarty) at Sandycove with uncharacteristic enthusiasm. He—like the men who'd been swimming at the famous Forty Foot for years—would undress in a hut below the Tower and dive naked off the rocks into the choppy sea. It's a mile's swim between Sandycove and Bullock Harbour but Ernst could make the distance easily. George never accompanied Ernst to the Forty Foot, but he heard the men in the stables saying that his father swam like an Irishman, not a Swiss.

I too am a swimmer, but when I visit the Forty Foot with Jackie and Freya the chill wind of the Irish Sea reminds me of my folly in packing bathing suits for my trip. Despite the 'Men Only' sign, the three of us walk onto the rocky outcrop together. The only prospective bather waits until we've left to strip but then, curiously, follows us up towards the road naked.

One Christmas Day, after the Nahers had moved to Dublin, Ernst participated in the Swimming Race at nearby Clontarf against his wife's wishes. Emma wanted her husband at home with her and her son—and there were guests to serve. George, too, was dismayed, but for another reason; a cold prevented him from attending the race and from witnessing his father in all his glory. The day Ernst raced in Dublin Harbour there was an avalanche in Switzerland; the concurrence of these two events seemed like something of a portent. For Ernst the incident prompted renewed confidence in his adopted city. In one country snow was crashing down mountainsides with the same force that killed his brother Walter, while in the other country men plunged into icy waters in a celebration of their virility.

Graham Swift identified horse-loving as a national religion in Ireland, and if Ernst eschewed Catholicism he happily worshipped the tenets of this other religion. During his time in Dublin he never missed the Dublin Society Spring Show or the August Horse Show and was a regular at the Phoenix Park and Leopardstown tracks. When, in 1926, the Irish introduced betting shops, Emma had good reason to fear.

Ernst was in accord with yet another of the Irish male's favourite pastimes; that of never going home. The notion held by certain Irishmen that work polluted appealed to Ernst, too. As the months rolled by, Emma saw Ernst less and less, and she became widely regarded as the face of The Swiss Private Hotel. Ernst, by contrast, was associated with the stables at the 'rere' of the property and there were rumours that he mixed with members of the new republican party, Sinn Fein. At the front of house Emma worked ever harder to establish herself and her family and secure their business, while out back—as far as she was concerned— Ernst's every action, every alliance, only undermined all she had worked so hard to build.

Emma compulsively clipped newspaper articles about the New World; about Canada, the United States of America and Australia.

She studied advertisements for the Australian Commonwealth Line's migratory voyages to Australia and took note when P&O started sending its vessels to Australia via the Cape. At the time of her greatest worry about her husband and her most intense fear for her boy, she would peer through the glass of the P&O office at Lower Ormond Quay. She longed for a place where the politics were simple and where her husband might not be so inclined to surround himself with intrigue or to drown his discontent in alcohol.

Emma had been amazed to learn, on her arrival in Dublin, that women over twenty-one had had the vote since 1916. In Australia, white women had been voting since 1901, the time of Federation. It was not until 1967, however, that the indigenous population got the vote after a referendum on the issue pronounced them citizens of the land they'd inhabited for thousands of years. It would take Emma's Swiss sisters yet another four years—until 1971—to win the vote at home.

I begin to entertain the prospect of family history as a seamless blend of fact and fiction. I question each given, each story told and retold. I have grown fascinated by the way anecdotes are handed down from generation to generation. How was one story shaped? Who formed it and whom were they protecting in doing so?

Daddo only ever talked about his father, Ernst, obliquely, offering scant clues to the man's character and even fewer details from the story of his life. He told me only that Ernst was an academic and a skilled horseman. He said he should have been a journalist, could speak six or seven languages and write shorthand in each one of them. From what Daddo did not say but implied, I know that Ernst was moody, discontent and frustrated. Nobody ever actually said that Ernst was a drunk. Perhaps in living with Ernst, Daddo could not see him for what he was.

The story about Ernst in Dublin came from Switzerland. It was whispered by the elderly aunts but nobody was game to tell it out loud. The story about Ernst is that in Dublin he took up with revolutionaries, brought them into his own home and put his small son and his wife at risk. The Swiss never called him a hero.

Bono, Bona, Bonam

I LEFT PARIS IN January 1986 and returned to Australia and to Daddo's house; I would be going to university, I would be putting my head down. The plan had always been to stay away for a year, only, and—despite the rich life I was leading in Paris—I remained committed to attending university in Australia and completing a degree there. Even as I was celebrating my homecoming with Daddo and Jackie, however, I was dreaming of the next move.

I had only been home for a week when I came up with a genial plan. I would get a dog—Jackie and I had always asked for a dog when we lived with Pauline—and it would keep me at home. It would keep me in Australia which is where I believed I should be.

I answered an advertisement in a newspaper for 'cutest X Dalmatian puppies' and drove out to a shabby, semi-rural block beside a theme park called Australia's Wonderland. I knew nothing about Dalmatians, nor what happened when a blue cattle dog had jumped the fence and made his own contribution. I knew even less about caring for a dog myself. Already, however, I was certain that I should have a male. I walked across the parched field of grass that passed for a lawn and a Dalmatian bitch emerged from round the side of the house. Her teats were heavy with milk and her puppies—all twelve of them—swarmed around her. They flocked around me, too, and I grew dizzy trying to study each little face in turn.

When a woman appeared on the front verandah the bitch ambled away. Her puppies tore after her, tumbling over each other in their efforts to be near her. One puppy, however, remained there at my side, licking my hand with barely a look for its retreating mother and siblings. It was one of the males. The pup had left nothing to chance. He had chosen me.

I handed over fifty dollars and picked up the tiny, squirming thing. His body nestled on my open palm. He was white with only faint blue-black spots on his body, but he wore a great velvety black patch over his left eye and ear. He was mine.

The puppy cried all the way from Australia's Wonderland to Lodge Road, there in the cane cat basket on the passenger's seat beside me. When I parked the car in the garage and stuck a finger between the wicker bars to quiet the pup, he bit me hard with one of his sharp puppy teeth. Daddo appeared, shaking his head and saying, 'You haven't, you haven't'. I, one bleeding finger in my mouth, told him I had.

I got the puppy out of the car, lifted the basket up high and watched the resistance on Daddo's face melt as he took in the tiny creature with its dark chocolate eyes and its disproportionately large, silken ears.

'Well,' Daddo said, 'well I guess that's all right.' Daddo was the softest man I knew.

Jackie and I practised names on the pup for days. We quickly learned that he could not bear to be left alone and set up an almighty howl when abandoned. The puppy was a singer and deserved a singer's name. Bono, we would call him, for U2's Bono Vox. Daddo, despite the hours of Triple J that had been inflicted upon him, remained ignorant of the pop phenomenon. He decided that the dog's name was simply our own variation of the Latin adjective 'good' and went around reciting 'bono, bona, bonam' at the wriggling creature. Most likely he had forgotten the correct form of the adjective, 'bonus, bona, bonum'.

My head was still awash with the French I had spoken with the de la Rochefoucauld children and I found myself chattering in French to the puppy. Daddo spoke to it in *Schwyzer Deutsch*. We

were seduced and horrified in turn by Bono's antics. He proved
to be a gourmand, however, which was a sure sign of a Naher dog.
Had George and Pauline looked for these clues, I wondered,
when they brought me home as a baby?

Over the first months of caring for the naughty, beautiful Bono,
I understood that we were his as much as he was ours. Along with
the big bag of trouble came devotion, affection and a binding
focus for the three of us. Bono had made us a family again.

The Bloodletting

THEY COME, THE MEN IN uniforms, in the darkest, coldest hour of the morning. They bash on the heavy oak door with rifle butts and Emma's first thought is for the cracks in the glossy green paint. Out the back comes an echo; there are soldiers in the rear lane.

Emma and Ernst do not exchange a single word. It is as though they've been rehearsing this moment and both know their cue. They pull on their clothing and Emma goes to whisper to her son in the dark. He is not to stir from his bed under any circumstances, not without her there beside him. Emma takes the stairs slowly, to the ground floor, and pauses to gather herself. She refuses to be rushed. She looks out the window onto the garden, thinks she can see the form of her husband in the darkness and watches as the shape disappears into the stables.

As Emma walks slowly along the hallway to the great oak door—the hammering has not let up—she can hear her guests stirring in the rooms above. Nobody calls downstairs to her, nobody comes to stand by her.

Five soldiers, their heavy guns held before them, push past Emma as though she lacks substance. The group divides. Two men take the stairs to the guest rooms above and two move down to the kitchen, to the pantry where her son lies. The fifth demands to know where Emma's husband is and pushes into the sitting room to begin overturning chairs and poking his rifle into the curtains. Emma tells him only that she's going to her son. She does not watch to see where the soldier aims his gun as she dashes towards the basement.

The room Emma shares with her husband has already been ransacked. Emma stops short at the entrance to the pantry, she is still as a fallen bird. A soldier stands over her boy, holding his gun as though anticipating ambush. He has pulled back George's covers and is eyeing the bed and the boy suspiciously. The man looks up to Emma. Is the boy dead? Emma shakes her head, tells the soldier that her son is afraid. She begs that her son be left alone.

A rifle sounds upstairs and the echo of its explosion rings in the stairwell. George's eyes fly open. Emma dares not even take a breath and the soldier pushes past her. George flies from his bed, into his mother's arms, and the two stand together, waiting.

Upstairs there are footsteps and the sound of muffled conversation, of orders being shouted so fast the words are lost. Emma and her boy stand in the cold; she doubting she has ever been so still, or so afraid, in her life. Her guests are up there, she should go to them. The only thing stronger than her instinct as a host keeps her fixed in her position—her instinct as a mother. When the fear in her breast starts to quieten she feels it being replaced with something that burns her white hot . . . anger.

She expects them to come downstairs again. To interrogate her, to try to frighten the boy, to tell her they've arrested her husband. But there's nothing. Silence settles over the house above her. After a time Emma imagines the building sighing, relaxing into the silence; it's as though the house is an extension of her body. Only when she feels her son shivering in her arms does Emma's will return to her. She moves into the kitchen and lights a candle, with trembling hands fixes it in a stand. Emma and George stand with their faces pressed to the cold glass, peering out into the darkness. There's no light showing in the stables and the garden—as the curve of trees and shrubs gradually define themselves in the moonlight—appears still and empty.

She climbs the stairs gingerly, her son beside her and a candle in her hand. When she reaches the ground-floor landing she does not look too closely at the dark stain on the wall, on the patterned carpet. Notes only that whatever caused the stain, the dark wetness, has gone. The front door is hanging ajar and outside the great trees of the park are a dark, moving mass against the night sky.

With her candle held high, Emma searches the parlour and the dining room but does not bother to put things right. Upstairs she knocks on the door of the first of her guest rooms. The door is yanked open. One of her guests, the man, is fully dressed, looks ready to leave, to fight, or to comfort. Behind him, his wife clutches their own small child. Emma lies. Tells the kind, trusting English couple that everything is fine. A routine check. A soldier fired at a cat in the garden. Not to worry. All's well. The man seems relieved but the woman is unsure. She gives Emma a knowing look, tells her they'll take her boy for the night and offers to put George in the bed with her own boy so Emma can face whatever it is that she must. Emma, stunned by this rare kindness, hands her boy over and is mute with gratitude.

Alone, and stronger for it, Emma moves through the tall house reassuring her guests, reassuring herself that none have been overly disturbed. She repeats the story about the cat in the garden until it sounds hollow, until she sounds to herself like another woman speaking.

The garden, when Emma slips outside and stands in the shadows, is as quiet as the cat that, she falsely claimed, had caused the ruckus. As she walks the path to the stables an image of her son playing there on the grass flashes before her and is gone. If she knows anything it's that any happiness or comfort she has felt there in the Square will come no more.

She never enters the stables. She long ago relinquished the building to her husband . . . all the while knowing no good would come of it. In the large loft above the stalls there are half-a-dozen camp-beds and a number of packing cases that have clearly been used as chairs and a table. The remains of a meal of bread and cold meat sit on the larger of the cases as though somebody has only just been interrupted at his supper.

When Emma is satisfied that there is nobody left, that it is only herself, her boy and her guests who are in the big house, she goes with water and rags to the ground-floor landing. She doesn't need to see the colour of the dark wet stain to know that it's blood. The smell has been in her nostrils since she first passed the stain with her son. She is only grateful that there is no way the boy could recognise the odour.

Emma places a tall-backed chair on the landing, right up against the wall, where she can still see the faint tracing of the stain. Days pass, guests come and go, but there's no sign of her husband, nor of his associates. She waits up at night in the dark, staring out the window and across the garden to the stables. She detects no shadow figures, hugging the walls and seeking refuge. She does not know whose blood she has had on her hands. She might have washed away her husband's blood without even knowing it. When she sleeps, finally, it is only to be awoken by images of Ernst lying face down in a ditch by some nowhere road on the edge of town.

On the fifth day she lets her boy play in the garden in the Square. She is sorry for him, cannot bear the way he asks, each evening, whether Ernst will be there in the morning. When George has been gone for less than an hour, she turns suddenly to one of the girls at work in the kitchen beside her and yells for her to go running for her son. She would rush out herself if she were not so afraid, if she had not become so exhausted as to be irrational with fear.

She listens for her boy's return and when his footsteps sound in the hallway above, Emma feels as though a lead weight has been lifted from her chest. George flies down the stone steps to the kitchen, runs at his mother's skirts and clamps his arms around her waist. He is full of the light of outside, full of news of the world.

The gardener, he tells his mother breathlessly, has news of Ernst. According to the gardener, Ernst is enjoying a little holiday and is in excellent health. Emma, the man insisted, would know exactly what he meant.

On the sixth day Emma dresses in her finest clothes, settles her dark felt hat on her hair and smoothes her navy gloves over her swollen fingers. She takes her son to the gardener herself. She thanks the man profusely—something in his look stops the questions from tumbling out—and goes off on her mission.

Emma has a plan that involves a certain Mr de Valera. He has finally signed the oath, along with his Fianna Fáil colleagues, and has taken his place in the Dáil. Emma walks towards Merrion Square and heads for Leinster House with her head held high. She is not too proud to call in a favour from one of her husband's associates when her son's well-being is at stake.

Daddy's Girls

WE BOUGHT A BUSINESS, Jackie and I, just like that. I was in my first year of university and she was doing a demanding arts/law degree.

Jackie and I had both been living at Lodge Road while studying and working part-time jobs. No matter how much we studied, Daddo always commented on how hard we were working in our paid jobs. I was doing a Bachelor of Arts in Communications and to Daddo—as well as to countless others—this was just Mickey Mouse.

Jackie and I both worked at a bakery up on the main road in Cremorne. When we were at university, our young dog Bono regularly escaped and arrived at the premises in search of us. It was a half-hour's walk from the house and involved negotiating busy roads. Perhaps the dog had followed the smell of croissant, one of his favourite foods.

My other jobs were as a mobile disc jockey—working parties, weddings and Leagues Clubs—and as a sales assistant in a clothing boutique in a Victorian arcade in the city. My disc-jockeying career was short-lived; after I had left one wedding with the brother of the groom all my other gigs somehow lacked climax.

When the proprietor of the boutique in which I was working told me she was planning to sell up, I inexplicably found myself enquiring about the asking price. Daddo had always extolled the virtues of being self-employed, of running one's own business and really making something of it. Jackie and I—at nineteen and twenty-one—saw taking over the boutique as an extraordinary opportunity and something we should not pass by. We would be self-employed; it was the family way. Unlike our nanna, Emma, we proved adept at buying a business, but not at building it.

We petitioned Daddo to release the money our grandmother had left us in trust, imagining her delight, as well as Daddo's, at our proposed endeavour. After days of rumination and soul searching, Daddo agreed that this was an appropriate use of the money in question. Years later his closest friend confided to us that our decision to go into business had thrown Daddo into a state of nervous panic.

Ultimately he had been as proud as he was bewildered that his daughters—who were so very young—were running their own business. Even when we would come home at the end of the day to announce only one measly top sold or the failure of some outfit we'd ordered in quantity, he remained optimistic, encouraging. Evenings we would regularly sit dissecting the day, musing over the intricacies of the Australian fashion industry of which all three of us knew so very, very little.

When we sold the venture we told ourselves we had broken even. Nonetheless, Daddo insisted, going into business was really something—unlike going to university, which any long-haired hippy could do.

The Gambler

———◆◆◆———

ACTUALLY, I HAVE NO IDEA what prompted my grandparents to finally leave Dublin. Nor do I know, I confess, how the notorious bloodstain came to appear in the stairwell of the big house in Fitzwilliam Square. I know, however, that George believed a soldier once stood over his bed and that Emma chose Australia because it was so far from Dublin, where the danger lay. I know they left the Old World for the new with only a letter from Eamon de Valera to recommend them, although I do not know what she told the man when she visited him that day.

Despite The Swiss Private Hotel's dubious connections— Emma pretended there was no unrest in the city—she managed to interest another couple in the business. With her exquisite cooking, with Ernst's cellar of fine wine and with a host of appreciative guests in residence, Emma wooed the pair. Nothing she could do for them was too much—save telling them of her desperation to leave—and over a period of weeks she negotiated a good price.

Ernst had as little interest in Australia as Emma once had in Ireland. He had, however, been silenced by something new in his wife, something that seemed to have transformed her. It was fury. She could forgive and had forgiven her husband many things—despite her anger she did not stoop to list them—but she could not forgive him for putting their son's life at risk. When he returned from his time 'in hiding'—looking for all the world as though he'd been on a holiday at the seaside—she heard what he said about integrity and political conviction and about being a revolutionary and she said 'Rubbish'. While they had a small child to care for, she insisted, all of that was worthless, idealistic garbage. Ernst should, Emma told him in high colour, behave like a father for once in his life.

Emma negotiated the sale of much of the hotel's furniture as part of the deal, but in her calculations she had factored in the cost of shipping a good many items. She found she had come to care about them. There were her chests of drawers, there were her cutlery press and her massive sideboard, and there were the paintings and mirrors.

The day the deal was done, the day Emma and Ernst signed the documents transferring their business to the new people, Emma's spirits were soaring. She insisted on opening a bottle of champagne after the contracts had been exchanged and she'd carefully stowed away the pleasingly fat pile of bank notes. Ernst was surly, laconic, but this was hardly unusual. Emma, however, grew embarrassed by the silence he inflicted on the hotel's new proprietors. When they were alone, and when George was out in the Square, she asked her husband point-blank whether he intended to travel with them. Before he could answer there was a knock on the door that caused Emma to leap to her feet in alarm. When Ernst did not rise Emma looked at him suspiciously then headed upstairs to face whatever it was that awaited her there.

At the door stood a grinning man in a dark, shiny suit. He was shorter than her and she had an excellent view of the way he'd combed a few dark strands of hair over the large bald spot on his head; Emma knew that whatever he had to say would not please her. He gave his name, said he was a bookmaker, but the term barely registered with Emma. She led the man downstairs. Ernst sat at the kitchen table with his head in his hands and did not look up to greet the man who was evidently so pleased to see him.

'Well?' Emma addressed both men. 'What does this mean?'

The small man looked from husband to wife and then his gaze fixed on the champagne bottle and the four glasses. For a moment his grin broadened, then his face hardened and he began to talk. Ernst, he explained to Emma, was in considerable debt to him from betting on the horses. Ernst, he continued, had been running an account with him for over a year now and clearly there was no more credit available. If they were leaving Dublin then the time to pay was now.

Emma ignored the small man—although she was the sort of woman to treat all people with respect—and focused on her husband. She asked Ernst to tell her that none of this was true. She insisted that Ernst clear this mess up immediately. The bookmaker pulled papers from his chest pocket and thrust them towards Emma but she looked away. She had to hear it from Ernst.

When Ernst finally spoke there was none of the pride in his voice that normally characterised it. Before he'd finished his explanation, which explained very little, Emma had interrupted him. 'How much?' she demanded. 'How much do you owe?'

The bookmaker, not Ernst, named the figure and without a word to either of them Emma went into her room and closed the door. She counted the bank notes she'd just received and divided the pile almost exactly in two.

When the bookmaker left—having counted his money a painstaking three times—the couple sat facing each other. They remained silent on opposite sides of the scrubbed pine table at which Emma had worked so hard. It was nearly time for the kitchen girls to return but neither husband nor wife stirred.

'I thought I'd make good . . .' Ernst began, but Emma's gaze silenced him.

They heard the door opening upstairs in the hallway and then the voices of one of the girls and of their small boy came floating down to them. The two rose. Ernst shrugged and moved across the room to the cupboard in which they kept the jar that held the coins for the grocer. He shook out a handful of copper and went into the hallway for his coat and hat.

When Ernst passed his son on the stairs he did not even look at the boy.

In Montreal

———◆———

I TOO HAD THE travelling gene, perhaps by osmosis. I too had the urge to move on and away although I stayed at home, in Daddo's house, for nearly two years. I lasted that long before concocting a trip to New York with two university friends. I sold my small silver Honda to finance the journey; the car never worked very well anyway. In part I justified the folly, and my absence from the business Jackie and I were running together, by calling it a buying trip. Christmas was coming and unusual items—jewellery, bags, scarves—would make good gifts for the December shoppers.

In New York my friends and I stayed in a midtown apartment and ventured downtown to clubs every night. Often we came home with the dawn, flying uptown alongside the East River in a battered yellow cab. We slept late and in the afternoons we visited galleries, museums and shops. In the evening we ventured out to another club and did it all over again. Within a week of arriving each one of us had found a lover.

I decided to take a break from the clubbing and fly to Halifax to visit a Canadian friend, but was drawn to Canada for other reasons which I did not articulate. I dreamed of the land of my other father, the French Canadian, who would connect me to other parts of the world and whose work, in literature, would connect me to my real self.

On the flight north I dozed uneasily in my seat by the window.

I kept waking with an anxious start and each time I gazed out the aircraft's window I experienced vertigo.

My first glimpse of Canada mesmerised me. The clouds thinned as we made for the Nova Scotia coastline and I could, for the first time, see the snow-covered land of my other father below. As we neared Halifax I was intrigued to see that land almost dissolve; the pale blue of the snow was interspersed with the deeper blue of water and ice where Canada disintegrated to become a mass of islands. Below me was Ursula LeGuin's Earthsea. Halifax itself—when it came into view—was suitably thick with snow.

I was immediately comfortable in Canada, imagining I could feel an easy connection with the Nova Scotians. Canadians and Australians seemed to share a common sense of humour. What's more, both are large countries with relatively small populations and neither deluded by visions of its own importance. I was not spared the full Canadian experience and by the time I was to leave Nova Scotia was in blizzard.

On my way back to New York I was to change flights at Montreal. As I waited at Halifax airport for the blizzard to clear, I made a last-minute decision to break my journey in the heart of Quebec. I was so close, after all.

In Montreal, I decided, I would think of myself as Sophia Antoinette. As another man's daughter. This was the name my other mother had chosen for me, or so Pauline had told me. In Montreal, perhaps, I would meet a man who looked just like me.

In Montreal, I had arrived in a foreign city alone with nowhere to stay. I had found the University of Quebec on a free map and asked a taxi driver to take me to a hotel nearby. We pulled up opposite the university and the driver, an anglophile, proclaimed it the worst part of town and the heart of French Montreal. Elated, I told him that was exactly where I wanted to be.

In Montreal, I checked into the hotel alone and imagined I was a woman about to commit adultery. I phoned my friends in New York to say I had been unexpectedly delayed in the city because of a blizzard and a plane strike. This was a half-truth, not a lie.

In Montreal, for the first time, I dined out in the evening alone. I was twenty. In Montreal, I wished to see and be seen.

In Montreal, despite the North-American-sounding French, I was reminded of Paris again and again. My hotel was on the *rue St Denis* and I kept glimpsing café names I thought I had read before, as though in some other life. I walked the snow-covered streets of the city for so long I grew tired and confused; did I know these streets because they were smaller copies of streets I remembered from Paris? Or were they familiar because my other father knew them?

I walked the corridors of the University of Quebec staring at men's faces and at the names of professors on office doors. I studied the French names intently as though they might trigger something in me. I wondered whether, as a baby *in utero*, I had heard my other father's name. Perhaps I need only have heard it repeated now to know it again. In Montreal, I told myself, I fitted.

I had come to imagine that as well as being a university professor, my other father was a writer. There was nobody to tell me otherwise. When I caught myself making up things about him I wondered whether there were other things I had made up, too.

Had Pauline really said he was a professor of French literature? We had gone for dinner to the local Chinese restaurant and the dancing dragon had just held its bright jaws above my head. Pauline had pointed across the room at a man, said that he was the one who had presided at my birth. I rose from my seat, determined to introduce myself, to see what the good doctor might have to say. Pauline begged me not to, persuaded me to sit down by offering me a few morsels herself about my origins.

In Montreal, I lingered in bookshops reading the biographical notes on each male French Canadian writer. I imagined that my delving would lead me to the name of a professor who had taught in Sydney in the sixties. I found one or two contenders—possible only because they were professors, not because there was mention of Australia—and bought their books for no other reason. Perhaps I would recognise him in his prose?

In Montreal, I stopped short of actually making enquiries at the university, although I had visited it a number of times. I could picture myself, however, a fanciful Australian girl, asking for a man with no name who had taught in Sydney in the sixties.

In Montreal, for the first time, I resolved that one day I would find my other father. I imagined he had contributed so much to the woman I was to become.

The Only Men Standing

DADDO AND HIS parents had a last meal of fish and chips at Charing Cross because anything—even an absence of greasy food—might have awaited them in Australia. On the train for the Tilbury Docks George pressed his nose against the glass to view the great city; again he noted the coal-smoke grey of the buildings but this, from his time in Dublin, had become familiar. London's Victorian buildings, however, were not familiar enough and he longed for the Liffey and for the city he had begun to think of as home. The English accents, all around him on the train, seemed harsh beside his memory of the softer speech of the Irish.

At the docks they boarded the SS *Ballarat*, bound for Sydney via the Cape. Only Ernst looked back to the steel-grey dock scape. A postman—a young boy in an ill-fitting blue uniform—awaited last-minute correspondence between passengers and loved ones and dashed down a gangway with seconds to spare before the ship pulled away from shore. The Nahers had made their own farewells years earlier, when they left Switzerland, and in Dublin there had been only a series of polite thank yous and good lucks. A band played 'It's a long, long way to Tiperary' out on deck with such verve that it seemed determined to transform the muddy Thames.

Emma had been assured that the ship on which they would cross the world was a good, safe vessel. The ship the *Ballarat* had been named for had, in fact, been carrying Australian troops by

1915. As an ambulance transport the original *Ballarat* had been torpedoed by a U-Boat at Wolf Rock at the entrance to the English Channel and the following day, she had sunk in forty-four fathoms of water.

Not only was this *SS Ballarat* one of the fine new ships in P&O's Branch Line, but she had the benefit of an extraordinary cargo which acted as ballast. The British steel in her hold was destined to form a wondrous bridge in the new country; the construction feat itself was spoken of in hushed tones; it was an engineering phenomenon. The eight-year-old George could not imagine the wide blue harbour in this remote new land, but in his mind's eye he could easily see a bridge of such vast proportions that it might span the heavens themselves. In his feverish ship-board dreams he would imagine a great arc, hovering over deep, dark, dangerous water; it was as carefully worked as the fine linen in his grandmother's trousseau back home in Switzerland.

Ernst, and another Swiss, Charlie Bochert, assumed their positions at the ship's bar before she had departed Tilbury. He had left the task of farewelling Europe to his wife and son. Perhaps Ernst thought that, like the Irish expedition, the Australian one would be short-lived too, that a return to Europe was both imminent and inevitable. Emma and George stood on deck watching the docks recede in the gloom as they progressed down-river. Already some of the other passengers were securing their own, personal deck-chairs for the journey ahead. Later that evening the first meal on board comprised cold mutton, beetroot, bread, butter and jelly. The passengers were served tea, which, even after their time in Ireland, the Nahers did not drink.

Four days from London and Ernst and Charlie Bochert were the only men still standing when storms rendered others—captain and crew included—incapacitated in the Bay of Biscay. They had not yet left Europe. Emma looked up at the sky and out at the grey ocean and scowled at the clouds that formed around the ship and seemed so heavy with migrants' sorrow and hope. If weather could be affected by the weight of anxiety, by the sheer energy surrounding trauma, then it made sense to Emma that the Bay of Biscay should be a wild, unruly place.

Below deck in their airless cabin Emma and George took turns nursing each other. Emma ushered her son to the dining room at the height of the storm. The food was not up to much—not by Emma's standards—but the wave that crashed through the dining room windows did wonders for George. A good drenching and he was cured of seasickness for the journey's duration and filled with a fascination for the sea. Once the ship had weathered its ordeal the captain informed his passengers that without their extraordinary ballast of steel, his *Ballarat* might well have joined her namesake.

Ernst suffered in his own way, up in the saloon bar. At the beginning of his second migration in a decade he was a worried man. Below deck Emma was reckoning that as things had begun, so they would continue. She had learned to survive almost entirely by her own wits; if pushed, she might have admitted that it was easier that way. They were, of course, travelling with far less capital than she had anticipated; indeed, they would be starting again on only slightly more than they'd had when they had arrived in Ireland.

Once the ship had taken its full complement of passengers in London—others would join them in Capetown—there were close to four hundred aboard. The Nahers accounted for three of only twenty 'aliens'—the name given to the non-British—from Switzerland, Scandinavia and Eastern Europe. The ratio of British to aliens in Australia would show an even greater imbalance. Before they had even left the Thames, Emma noted that small groups of passengers sharing the same nationality had formed and clustered.

On the *Ballarat*'s passenger list Ernst was described as a hotel keeper and Emma as a housewife. Even in Switzerland, where women were half a century from getting the vote, nobody would have dared describe Emma Braun Naher as housewife. 'Master George', one of thirty-one male children, was already old enough to understand that the English he had learned in Ireland set him apart.

During the first days of the journey George befriended the sons of a coal miner, a baker, a farm labourer, a bricklayer, a care-taker and a slate splitter. The accountant's son was instructed not to mix with this rabble but the boy took enormous delight in doing so. Many of the boys travelled with their mothers, siblings and other female relatives, their fathers having gone to the colony beforehand to pave their way. At times George wished his own father had done the same thing. At times—and he was wholly ashamed of himself for having such thoughts—he wished his father absent.

Journeys by ship—Emma would make three of them in her lifetime—were the most luxurious times she knew. Each would provide moments of calm in a charged life. Aboard the *SS Ballarat* there was little toil, even for an industrious woman like Emma. George at eight required minimal supervision and Ernst—after the incident in Dublin—promised he would take responsibility for his son's education. Aboard the *SS Ballarat* Emma was not to be found parading on deck with the grand English ladies beneath their parasols, nor in the ship's lounge drinking tea with the other women and worrying publicly over her fate in the new land. No, aboard ship Emma was to be found in the ship's library satisfying her ravenous curiosity for the written word.

Ernst was supposed to be the learned one. When he discovered his wife in the ship's library, only two days out of port, he chuckled fondly at the sight of her with a book in her hands. He remarked that a few years among the Irish had evidently given her literary aspirations and went on to express his surprise that the library held French and German novels.

He took the rich green hardback from her hand, ignoring her expression of hurt. She was not reading a novel, not at all. She was reading *Saint Joan* by George Bernard Shaw. She was reading in English. Ernst snorted, returned the book to his wife's hands as though he was pleased to be rid of it. He offered to help her with the translation but she coolly declined.

Ernst straightened his waistcoat and collars, waited—in vain—for his wife to make some conciliatory comment, for an ameliorating gesture. On his way from the room he hesitated at a glass-fronted cabinet as though he too might take a book and join Emma in her reading. His parting comment was about George;

their son spent too much time roaming the ship and not enough time with his books. Ernst insisted that he would not have it.

Ernst would not have it but nor would he remain at his son's side, guiding him through the intricacies of English grammar. For that matter, he would not do it with German grammar, either. He had not needed that sort of assistance—spoonfeeding was what he called it—so why should George?

In the family's airless cabin, George sat at a table beneath the diminutive porthole, books open before him. For every minute he spent with his head bent over his books he spent five minutes gazing out across the ocean. Was that land over there? Could it be Africa, or Las Palmas? He must not miss the first glimpse of Africa. The books would be there that evening, when it was dark and there was no hope of seeing a thing from the porthole. Surely the first glimpse of an unknown continent was of greater importance than the conjugation of the verb 'to sit'? He closed the books— as if to suggest he had completed the task at hand—and went to listen at the cabin door. When all was silent in the corridor he opened the door a crack, listened for his father's footfall, and slipped out and away.

On deck the sun was shining brighter than it ever did in Dublin, brighter than the sun he remembered of earlier days in Switzerland. They were steaming towards the equator at a speed of over three hundred miles per day. Where they were going, George had been told, the sun shone all the time. On the breeze he could smell the sands of the Sahara and the smoke from a grass fire burning on some unimaginable, vast plain. Behind them, seagulls dropped down into the ship's wake, fishing for scraps from the kitchen. Ahead of them, the sea raced away; it was the future and it was calling to him.

A Mother

❦

IT WAS YEARS—SIX YEARS, in fact—before I actually took up the father quest I imagined I had started in Montreal. During that time I had finished university and started my career in publishing. Four of those five years had been spent in London, in a city in which I lived in words. I worked with books, slept in a room crammed with books and manuscripts, and in slivers of spare time I tinkered with a novel I had started writing during my final year of university. In London I met a man.

I had been interviewed by the landlord—a psychiatrist—and the two existing tenants for one of two spare rooms in a share house in Brixton. Not only was I accepted by the 'panel', but I actually wanted to live in this house. It was 1989. I only met the third of my house-mates on the day I moved in. My first impression of Paul was of a smiling, gentle man who glowed golden. He had just returned from nine months wandering Central America and his skin was the colour of the palest honey. His curly hair had been bleached blonde by the equatorial sun. An honours graduate in philosophy, he was, incongruously, about to commence his training as a chartered accountant. For many months—while both of us were involved with other people—we maintained a long, rambling dialogue about the world, about books and about films. Friendship led, as it does sometimes, to other things . . . but this, after all, is a story of fathering.

Back in Australia, in 1991, the adoption laws changed, permitting unprecedented access to previously confidential information.

I was now able to apply for my original birth certificate and my natural parents were entitled to apply for my subsequent, amended birth certificate. Jackie had obtained hers and had placed her name on the reunion contact register; her other mother had done so too. I read her letters about their reunion in fascination.

My own birth certificate, when it arrived, confirmed at least one of Pauline's claims. My other mother had called me Sophia Antoinette. My other mother—who had been twenty-two when I was born—was called Jane Chisholm. No occupation was given for her. The name of my other father did not appear. When I placed my name on the reunion contact register my other mother's name was absent. Despite my childish, wounded disinterest in the woman, this came as a blow. I imagined that once again she had not wanted me.

In late 1992 I returned to Australia after three-and-a-half years in London, leaving my relationship with the Englishman, Paul, unfinished yet uncommitted. Once again I was determined to stay, to remain, to put down roots in Sydney, the city I unreservedly loved. I needed to be near the family I had missed acutely from across the globe. Daddo, Jackie had assured me, was getting older although I hardly saw this for myself when I dashed back each year for Christmas in the sun. The dog, Bono, was no longer an adequate daughter-substitute, although when he misbehaved it was me they cursed as much as him.

On my return to Sydney I had a momentous lunch with Pauline. She wanted to know whether I had found my other mother, as Jackie had found hers. Pauline had not been part of that mother–daughter reunion, and to this day has not met Jackie's other mother. She handed me a newspaper clipping. It was, she told me, the funeral notice for my natural grandmother. The names of those who mourned her belonged to my other mother and her daughter, Ella. I watched Pauline with suspicion. I did not want another mother, one was more than enough.

But perhaps a second father? Fathers intrigued me, they gave me some comfort. I read and reread the funeral notice and thought, only, 'Give me my father'.

In spring of 1992 I was living alone in a studio apartment overlooking Sydney Harbour. It was the first time I had lived alone in my home city. I was in possession of my alleged natural grandmother's funeral notice yet I could not quite believe that my biological past—my *other* family—might be only a single phone call away. I convinced myself, therefore, that it was highly unlikely that the Jane Chisholm in the death notice was my Jane Chisholm and I thereby neutralised the situation. I was an exceedingly poor sleuth yet I schemed to glean more information. First I searched the electoral roll for women with the name I had been given; the only one listed lived in Francis Street, East Sydney. I asked a friend to knock on the door for me as we were passing one day and when nobody answered I was forced to become even more ingenious.

I phoned the priest of the church at which my alleged natural grandmother's funeral had been held, pretending to be an old friend of Jane. I told him that I had heard Jane's mother had died and wanted to be in touch again, after all these years, to pass on my condolences. He was very forthcoming; I'd find her just down the road, he told me, at the nursery she owned.

With this terrifying knowledge in my possession, I did absolutely nothing and got on with trying to make a life for myself in Sydney. Paul had been to visit—he had arrived unannounced—and stayed for a brief holiday. By the time he left we had not yet made plans for the future.

I found work as a bookseller, ran regularly down at Woolloomooloo Bay, went to the beach with friends and stayed out late into the night at bars and parties. I applied for a job working with a literary agent and attended a long interview for the position which at first brought me only manuscripts to read. I worked as a waitress for the first and last time in my life, employed by somebody to whom Daddo had once given an excellent start in the industry. Daddo did not remember the character, which was fortunate as I sullied the family name by stirring insurrection in my fellow waiting staff over our lousy working conditions. Soon my waitressing career was over and I was taking phone calls from New York about a job there with a publishing house for which I had worked in London.

Come January 1993 and my birthday, I had started to feel reckless in my possession of this information about my alleged natural mother. I decided to put my mind at rest, one way or another. It was a Sunday, crushingly hot and limply humid. I had been birthday-lunched by Daddo, Jackie and my cousin Emma, Leny's granddaughter. In the afternoon—when we were all floppy and exhausted and Daddo had disappeared to his room to rest—I suggested that the other two might like to accompany me on a clandestine mission. The three of us would drive to this nursery to have a look at the woman who was supposed to be my mother. I had not read a single scrap of literature on the protocols surrounding contacting one's natural parent, but as Jane had placed no contact veto beside her name there was no legal bar against me doing so.

I was jolly on the drive, even gregarious. I was wearing dark sunglasses and my hair was dyed red—it had been for years—and I told myself again and again that *she*, if it was indeed *her*, would not recognise me. I had no delusions about the scurrilousness of our proposed agenda; we would be there as spies. It gave me some macabre pleasure that while *she* may have been thinking of the child she gave up for adoption some twenty-six years earlier, that child would be there at her own nursery, masquerading as a Sunday plant-buyer. Jackie was far more circumspect than me and while she did not attempt to quash my excitement, it was clear that she did not share my reckless enthusiasm for the mission.

It was a good distance from Daddo's house to the nursery, but right at the last moment I wished it were infinitely further. The nursery was located on a busy road and by the time Jackie parked the car, that 17 January, my quips and brittle laughter had subsided. We three stepped out into the heat in the nursery's grounds and there were no other customers in sight. We were greeted by a heavily panting dog with long, pale, thick hair; he looked as though he should have been pulling a sled, not flopping around in thirty-five-degree heat. As we three and dog moved towards the plants a tall, slim woman approached from the office. I bolted off into the greenery..

She was squinting into the sun but I would have recognised the mouth anywhere; it resembled my own. The woman was tall, with long slim legs that I immediately envied. Her skin was tanned and freckled and her short, brown hair curled loosely as mine did when I cut it short. Like me, she had square shoulders and capable hands. I needed only the briefest glance to know that this was Jane. That she was my natural mother was no longer in doubt. It was not her height, nor the shape of her face—which was longer than mine— that gave me so much certainty; it was the way she held her mouth that was so familiar to me. I had seen the expression—lips pursed in a grimace of concentration—on my own face a thousand times.

Emma followed me and we conferred among the ficus. Em and I both said at once, 'It's her', with a manic note in our voices.

'I think she's weird,' my tone was defensive, as though the poor woman had attacked me personally. I had taken an instant dislike to her but could not have said why. Her one redeeming feature—or so I told myself—was her dog.

Out the front my mature, composed sister—demonstrating more compassion in her little finger that day than I had in my entire body— engaged Jane in polite conversation and proceeded with the purchase of a grevillea. Eventually it became necessary for Emma and me to emerge from our cover and head back to the car. All the while I had my hair over my face and my sunglasses on. I was giving Jane these sideways glances, somehow certain that she would know it was me. We were standing in the blinding afternoon sun; she must have been willing us to get on our way so she and her old dog could retreat to the shade.

The minute we drove out onto the busy road I felt like the worst kind of coward. I was the meanest, most spineless excuse for a daughter, for a woman. None of us said a word until I spotted a public telephone booth on the side of the road and I asked Jackie to pull over. I was going to call Jane. I was going to tell her who I was.

I fumbled with the coins and the holes in the dial and it took me an age to get the numbers right. I kept misdialling and had to hang up again and again and re-insert the coins, start over.

When I finally got through I told her that I had been there just a moment ago, one of the three young women. I went on to announce that it was my birthday.

There was a long silence. There was nothing at all. Eventually Jane said 'Yes?'. I was indignant, huffing and puffing in the heat. I should not have had to say any more. She should have known. Surely she thought about me on that one day of the year, if on no other?

'I'm adopted,' I continued bluntly. I mentioned, once again, that it was my birthday.

After more silence I uttered the words, 'I think you're my mother'.

There was nothing from the other end of the phone and I imagined that Jane's husband had just walked in and her marriage was falling apart somewhere on the edge of that silence.

Eventually she asked whether I had gone to The Belvedere. This was her first question to her newfound daughter. This was absolutely not what I had expected to hear.

I told her yes, I had. I could not hide the irritation in my voice when I went on to state what was obvious. That she had known how to find me . . . and yet, when she was legally entitled to, had not.

She did not say, 'I've been waiting for this moment all my life', nor did she tell me that she had searched for me.

I announced brusquely that I wished only to give her my phone number. I did not say that she had to make the next move but that was the gist of it. I gave her the information, not sure whether I had even told her my name, not sure whether she knew it anyway. I hung up as fast as I could and stood in the noisy phone booth for a few moments. I was standing in the middle of a vacant, litter-strewn lot beside a busy road.

I got back into the car and the first thing I told Jackie and Emma was that she knew where I had gone. That she had known—all that time—where I had been, who I was. For all those years she had known who I was yet I had known nothing of her. They were astounded, as it happened, but not by the fact that Jane had known the fate of her child. They were stunned by my ability to stand by the side of the road and leap back, twenty-seven years, with such glib nonchalance.

We followed the road until we reached a beach and the three of us headed into the surf. All the while I was replaying my conversation with Jane and telling myself, once again, exactly why a girl did not need a mother. I repeated this mantra to myself in the days and days and days—in fact only two or three days—that passed as I waited for Jane to phone me.

Wandering Albatross

DADDO AND HIS PARENTS' voyage to the New World was rendered sublime by the extraordinary. Certain images from that time between hemispheres would imprint themselves on Emma, Ernst and George as profoundly as a sensation from early childhood.

Just south of the equator the sea was flat as a length of glossy, cobalt silk. The spectacle brought Ernst from the bar and he found himself out there at the rails beside his son. It hardly seemed possible that the ocean could be so still; all around them was space, water and quiet. George knew a moment of rare but intense understanding with his father.

The heat had passengers—Ernst and George included—sleeping out on deck at night. Others wandered aimlessly, unable to rest, unable to focus. Some had tomato-red faces that threatened to crack when they smiled or spoke, so much sun had they taken and so unaccustomed were they to it.

The captain threw a party for the children, who were fed sweets and cordial before being paraded around the ship behind the band. Emma reminded her son of the *Solennitaet* parade in Burgdorf, in the town of his birth. There were races—featuring the egg and spoon and sacks—and in each one, the small, wiry George won a prize.

As dusk softened the afternoon sky the band would come out to play on deck and men and women danced into the night beneath the stars. One evening George broke from one of his games to stop and watch, mouth hanging wide, before his face transformed into a deep smile. His parents were one of the dancing couples.

Beyond Capetown George became fascinated with a lone albatross. He saw it following the ship early mornings and at dusk and throughout the day he tried to imagine the bird's activities, out there at sea alone. He came to imagine that the bird knew him, that the two—boy and bird—gained equal pleasure from their time spent watching each other. The young boy from the engine room told George that the bird was a Wandering Albatross and that its wingspan could reach up to ten feet. George was convinced that this bird, his bird, was even bigger. He would try to measure the span of its wings as it flew overhead by spreading his own arms wide. The albatross, according to the boy, needed dry land only to mate.

Somewhere in the Indian Ocean—longitude, latitude unknown—the men in the bar resolved to allay their boredom with a bit of spo-t. They'd shoot some birds. A rendezvous was set for dawn the fc owing morning and the use of rifles negotiated with a high-ranking member of the crew. Ernst, who had done only minimal time in the Swiss Army, admitted—when pressed—that he could shoot. He was persuaded to join the shooting party.

After only three hours' sleep Ernst's trigger finger was remarkably steady. Or so he thought as he washed his face and looked at his clear dark eyes in the mirror above the basin. The moment Ernst left the cabin George was up and dressing, slipped outside silently only minutes after his father. The sky was clear, a soft blue speckled with gauzy white wisps of cloud and the ocean dull and dark. George quickly found the shooting party and stationed himself on a deck overlooking theirs. He did not wish to attract their attention for fear of banishment.

There were the seagulls that dived and swooped at the ship's wake, ducking for scraps. The shooters took aim, began to fire. After half an hour Ernst was the only man in the party to bring down each one of his targets and George felt a mixture of pride and horror. The dead seagulls fell into the ocean in the ship's wake, spun and turned a few times in the water before disappearing. One of the shooters grew jealous of Ernst's success.

George, in his hiding place, could not watch the birds as they fell, preferred to keep his eyes on the horizon. This is when he saw the arc of white that was the majestic, gliding albatross—his albatross—off the ship's port side. He could not help himself, was compelled to show the bird to his father. Taking the steps down to the next deck, two at a time, he arrived breathless at Ernst's side. With one hand he took his father's sleeve and with the other he pointed high overhead.

The albatross—George's albatross—rose effortlessly on its great outstretched wings to hover above them. Father and son stared up, the same expression of wonder on their faces. Beside them was the movement of a gun and the disgruntled shooter taking aim. George and Ernst cried 'No' in unison but too late. George's bird, for a moment, appeared absolutely still before beginning its tumbling plunge from the sky. With a heart-stopping thud its descent was over. The great bird had landed on the deck above them. George made to run to the albatross but his father restrained him. The shooter was already striding up the steps towards his trophy, pulling at the creature's poor limp wings to pronounce a span of nine feet. The man laughed, announced that the Wandering Albatross would wander no more.

Ernst let down his guard for a moment and George broke away, tearing up the steps to stand between the man and the dead bird. He placed his hands on his slight hips and demanded to know what the man intended to do with the bird. There was talk of weighing, measuring and photographing. When George turned to his father to support his protests it was only to learn that Ernst had disappeared.

When the men finally left the bird and went to wash before taking their breakfast, George moved from the railing to kneel beside the crumpled thing. He gathered the mass of bloody feathers in his arms and was crushed all over again by the surprise of the creature's meagre weight. George stumbled down the stairs with the bird pressed to his chest, all the while struggling to contain the drooping legs, the flopping wings. Eventually he reached a railing at the ship's stern; below him there was only swirling water. He whispered a few words into the feathers—every word he knew for sorry—and lifted the body over the railing, let go. As the albatross fell its great wings spread again and for a moment there was the semblance of flight. When the bird hit the water it was quickly dragged under and was gone. For a long time George kept watch.

Not a Mother to me

I SAT UP LATE INTO the night in my studio apartment in Potts Point. The light-filled harbour was just beyond my wall of windows; it was the same stretch of harbour that every migrant ship would once have crossed. During the days and nights I sat waiting for my natural mother to phone I started receiving calls from men who were looking for a working girl. My new phone number, apparently, had once been allocated to a brothel. Their calls, when I was expecting hers, made the period all the more surreal.

When Jane finally phoned there was classical music playing in the background at her house. So great was my suspicion of her that I wondered whether she'd planned it. The conversation was brief and on my part clumsy. I had never known anybody who looked like me and I told her that was why I wanted to meet her. Nobody I knew, I claimed, had shoulders as broad as mine. Of course this was an exaggeration—I did not look like a steroidal Eastern European swimmer type—but at my lowest this was how I felt. A giant.

We clearly shared some ambivalence about meeting because we arranged to see each other only for a coffee. To suggest to share a meal, or even to meet over a drink, would have represented a far greater commitment than either of us was capable of.

I ruminated over what to wear. I thought I should appear self-possessed, smart and at ease. I chose black trousers and a black knit top that crossed at the front and sat just off my shoulders. I dyed my hair an even brighter red just for the 'fuck you!' hell of it. I had already decided that I would not like her. I wished, only, to have the name of my father.

We did not touch when we met at Andiamo in Kings Cross; not a handshake, a kiss or an embrace. Jane was wearing white trousers and a white T-shirt sporting a bold, colourful image. There were flowers on her ears. Our outfits—direct opposites—seemed to define us. Her build was much slimmer than mine and this made me somehow angrier at her.

The first thing Jane said to me was, 'You *do* have broad shoulders'. I was crushed but determined that she must not know it.

She was living in the suburbs, a single mother alone with her daughter. She had a daughter, another daughter. Ella, my half-sister, was ten years my junior. Jane had not lived with Ella's father for many years. Somehow I was dismayed to learn that she was a single mother, just as Pauline had been. Jane, however, was not the sort of mother who sat at home waiting; she had a university degree and ran her own business.

True to our intentions, we ordered coffee. We sat and sat and sat. We did not laugh, we did not cry. We presented each other— or so I thought—with a similar facade that said 'All this means nothing to me'.

I told her I hardly saw my adoptive mother any more but spoke with animation about Daddo and Jackie, presenting an image of an adoring trio. I was at such pains to keep my distance that I stated, more than once, that I would probably be moving to New York. Every move, gesture and comment amounted to one thing: don't expect anything from me.

The hot afternoon softened to dusk and we ordered focaccia. Jane told me a little about my conception. At the time she had been living in a boarding house in Bondi, a university student in a house full of travelling, partying foreigners. New Zealanders, Canadians, and she clearly the exception. He had been a big man, she told me, big-boned and solid, not fat. He had been her first lover and, although she did not say so, I guessed that she had fallen in love with him. Come time for him to move on, up to the

Northern Territory with another Canadian to find work, her period was already late. Strangely, I have trouble remembering whether she said he had known this or not.

'Would you like to know his name?' she asked. I nodded yes. 'Gus Monette—he was a French Canadian.'

She did not know where he lived; indeed she could tell me, only, that before he had come to Australia he had been a student at the University of Western Ontario in a town called London. Yes, he was a French Canadian, but she said nothing of him being a Professor of French Literature. I did not ask, clinging to my own story. As my token gesture of sensitivity towards her I was trying to hide my interest in him. I was not successful.

Jane told me that she too loved books. She had once contemplated buying a bookshop, not a nursery. Perhaps she still might. I, ungenerous, suspicious, thought she was just being ingratiating and chose not to believe her.

We had nothing to offer each other, of this I was certain. But she wanted something from me, something I did not think I could give. She said her daughter needed a sister. I happened to know that every girl needed a sister but I already had one, and three young female cousins as well. Why should I take on this other—this half-sister—whose mother would not have me?

The meeting was a disaster in all regards but one. I had my birth father's name.

I would not accept her offer of a lift home. I preferred to trust my luck in the Cross by night.

Cliff Dancing

———◆·◆·◆———

ALTHOUGH HE DID not have much exposure to other families, Daddo, as the young boy George, knew that his family was small. At times, as much as he pretended otherwise, he saw it as a family of two not three; a family comprised of mother and son. Aboard ship—while roaming the decks with a whole horde of other boys—was the first time George felt the semblance of family.

Aboard ship George had unprecedented access to his parents but still he looked to others. Among those on the *Ballarat* George befriended were two of the crew; the engineer and the engine boy. As the great vessel steamed south, George came to admire the large man—who had forearms as big as hams—in the same way he had admired the gentle Dublin gardener.

As the weeks passed and the distance between the ship and the unimaginable shoreline of Western Australia grew ever smaller, George spent more and more of his time in the engine room. He was fascinated by how things worked, delighted by the way numerous small objects could connect to become a whole other entity. As the *Ballarat* steamed across the Indian Ocean, George's study comprised more and more of gazing at cogs. He took pleasure in taking a monkey wrench in his hand and contributing to the repair of the engine that kept the great ship running.

They formed an unlikely trio, George, the engine boy and the engineer. The two small boys—for while the other boy was older than George he was no bigger—both listened in awe as the engineer huddled over a tiny gauge to explain the intimate workings of the ship's engines to them. George would squat at the engineer's side, passing him tools; wrenches as thick as a boy's wrists and fine, pointed implements which you could hardly conceive of the big man being able to manipulate. It was there in the engine room of the SS *Ballarat* that George began to dream a different life for himself. In the engine room he imagined that he too might wield a wrench, might make things work, might be able to harness power in order to create momentum. George liked the solid feel of the word 'engineer', the no-nonsense practicality of it. He also liked the fact that for all his father's learning, the word was as alien to Ernst as the country to which they were moving.

Soon George developed mixed feelings about the journey. His excitement about their arrival in the new land was tempered by an ache he suspected was sadness over leaving the ship. When they docked briefly at Fremantle, all George saw of his new country was a field of dust and an old tin shed.

The night before they berthed in Sydney the wind dropped, leaving the ship in quiet seas on a hot, full-mooned December night. With such a glowing moon in the sky and their final destination so close, neither George nor his friend could contemplate sleep. With a blanket each to soften the hard wooden deck, George and the boy lay back under a sky impossibly filled with stars. Each admitted he fancied the other boy's life over his own.

Near dawn the boys watched the full moon—bright as a thousand candles—as it sank into the land that was to be George's home. Come dawn the *Ballarat* was steaming towards the teetering stacks of sandstone that formed the mouth of Sydney Harbour. It was 19 December 1927. When the first pre-dawn light crept into the sky George rose from his makeshift bed on the deck to race to the cabin. His parents would want to know that the day and their destination approached. And George wanted to ensure that he was scrubbed and smart for their arrival.

The coast was now a series of jagged, brown sandstone cliffs and gleaming golden beaches. Beyond the beaches George could discern the silhouette of buildings. The ship was abreast of a bigger, sweeping arc of beach and his friend told George that this was the famous Bondi. Then there were yet more miraculously tall walls of sandstone warding off the ocean. There were waves crashing at the foot of the cliffs and, amazingly, the tiny forms of people; a handful of fishermen tempting the waves at the cliffs' base. The boy pointed out something moving on the cliff face itself; arms, legs, body . . . a man, skipping blithely down the cliff on a rope towards the sea. Never in George's life had he seen anything so daring as this cliff dancing. It boded well, he announced to the sea, to the sky, for his new land.

When Emma arrived on deck beside George and saw that his face was shining with awe she felt a fierce surge of hope. She put a hand on her son's shoulder and squeezed it, for his sake she was determined that they would make a go of it there. She, Emma Maria Naher née Braun would put down roots on those shores and flourish. Ernst had not yet risen.

The *Ballarat* steamed through the heads—two towering sentinels on either side of the harbour's mouth—and those on deck were met with a vision splendid. A vast harbour sprawled before them, ran off here, there in three different directions, and the reflection of light on the blue-black of the water promised a bright, solid future. Shrubs and rocks tumbled down to the water's edge. The landscape, out near the heads, was broken only sporadically by buildings, cleared land and roads. Small boats floated in bays, alive with fishermen returning from the lightening sea with their catches. As they steamed further up the harbour they passed great, dark-hulled vessels, larger than the *Ballarat*, their decks crowded with cargo.

Soon others came to join George and Emma on deck until the rails were crowded, until the entire ship's passengers were on deck, all four hundred odd of them. Ernst, however, was absent. Ernst—or so it seemed—was the only man on ship not standing there at the railings beside his wife, alongside his child.

Their arrival in Sydney was heralded by blazing sunlight and with it came a heat more shocking, according to Emma, more exhilarating, than anything they had known before. Ernst described it as barbaric, the heat, the light, the dazzling reflection from the water that made him squint, broad-brimmed hat and all. He'd been brooding about the albatross for days; although he had not shot the great bird himself he was certain that the bad luck associated with the act would settle on him, not the other. Journeys, to Ernst, were much more pleasant than arrivals. He was tempted to turn around and sail back to Europe, not because he longed to return but just to prolong the journey. What's more, he had convinced himself that it was in this new land that the ill fate would befall him.

George heard the other passengers talking about the Harbour Bridge before he saw it himself. He'd been expecting a great steel arc, spanning the water. In his mind's eye the structure was all but complete, lacking only the steel in the *Ballarat*'s hold that would join the gap. When he saw the real thing he cried out in dismay. The imagined great bridge was only two sandstone platforms on either side of the harbour with the beginnings of the steel structure crouching atop the stone on either side.

Ernst and Charlie Bochert sat in the bar until the very last moment, until the jolt of ship against wooden pile followed by stillness signalled the end of their journey.

Out on deck in the white-hot Sydney sunshine, Ernst and his friend were like two pale nocturnal creatures, prematurely expelled from their burrows. They scuttled between pools of shade on the ship's deck instead of crowding the rails like the other passengers. On exiting the bar they had taken up position to the starboard while everyone else had moved to port to view the activities on the dock. There was not much to see, Ernst noted, only another long, timber wharf and shed opposite.

Down on the dock—Walsh Bay, Berth 9—a huddle of shabbily attired locals awaited the migrants. They did not have the air of friends and family, but of men about to do business and for whom the travellers represented little more than money in their pockets.

When his son found Ernst, George was breathless with excitement. 'Did you see it? They've only just started work on the bridge . . . we'll be able to watch it grow.' George was already calling Australia their new home. His optimism, at eight, could not be quashed.

George led his father to the railing where Emma stood watching; men on the dock worked with ropes as thick as their forearms, tying and retying the ship to the piles. They pulled the ropes in tight and waited for the slack to accumulate before pulling her in again.

There was a quiet, civilised, gentlewomen's riot when the gangways were locked into place. George watched his mother being swept off without him, stood back to help first one and then another woman down the boards ahead of him, handing passengers from the ship onto land. By the time George placed his own foot on the gangway hundreds had disembarked before him. Ernst had remained on board to see to their baggage.

The waiting men had already attached themselves to other disembarking passengers. George and Emma set out down the long timber wharf alone. As they made their way forward a small, compact man appeared from inside the shed and ambled towards them.

The man who called himself Albert did not ask what was required but told them what he was offering. When he heard Emma's accent he informed them they'd be wanting the Cross because 'that's where all the foreigners go'.

Albert strode off and George trotted to keep up, all the while quizzing the man about Sydney. 'Is it wild like they say it is?' he wanted to know, and Albert pondered this. George never forgot his response and would repeat the words to himself later, as he ran errands between the Cross and Macquarie Street.

'Down here in the Rocks and over at the 'Loo it can be rough as guts. Blokes walk off the boat from London and are never heard of again. We got gangs here make your hair curl, kid.'

The man went on to question George. Surely the foreign woman wasn't his mother? George's accent was Irish and his mother's Swiss.

Ahead of them was a warehouse-lined road, congested with carts, horses and motor vehicles. Albert weaved through the throng and stopped at a shabby old trap; the beast that was to pull the cart looked more like a donkey than a horse. Emma allowed her son to hand her up into it. They pulled out and were quickly making off down the road.

They turned uphill and passed a few dusty shop fronts, broken up by roads clogged with horse traps and motor vehicles. George glimpsed a clock tower on a rise above the docks. When they reached a large area of parkland, broken by wide paths, Emma asked when they would reach the city. Albert told her that they had just passed through it. The man gestured towards a corner of parkland with one shoulder and nodded to George conspiratori- ally. 'There used to be a garbage dump there but in that corner they buried the suicides. They put a stake through their hearts before covering them with earth, you know?' George only nodded, wide-eyed, and gulped.

Beyond the park they turned on to a wider street and coming up the rear was a trolley bus pulled by six horses. George saw public houses, shops, auction houses and grand terraces on this broader street. 'William Street, lad,' their guide informed George. 'Runs all the way from the city to the Cross.'

Emma described it as familiar yet utterly different. The buildings reflected styles they already knew from Ireland, yet out of context they were alien. The light, the bright harsh light, was all wrong on those Victorian facades. Once they were at 'the Cross' and there were more trees and the streets were narrower, the fierce Sydney light did not assault them so. Albert was telling them he knew just the place for them and turned the cart into a courtyard surrounded by high brick flats.

George's smile wilted for only a moment as the man led them through a warren of corridors to two small adjoining rooms on the ground floor. The rooms looked into a light-well between buildings in which yellowed newspaper, broken bottles and a discarded pair of brown shoes attracted pigeon shit. The running water and toilet were down the hall, 'communal like', Albert told them. He named a price and Emma began negotiating. She could be charming yet insistent and walked away with an agreement to pay half the named figure.

Ernst, when Albert drove them back to the rooms later in the day, did not attempt to hide his disgust. George was running back and forth to the cart helping Albert and overheard his parents arguing in the second room which was to be theirs. Not only had 'she' brought Ernst to this infernal place, but 'she' expected him to live in two dark, squalid rooms. Emma maintained that in the height of summer, they needed shade, and went on to inform her husband that she would find them a better place soon. One could not expect more on arrival. Naturally the Australians would offer the foreigners the inferior accommodation but soon, Emma promised, she would find their place in the city.

By early evening, Emma and George had unpacked all they had means to store and Albert had brought them some camp-beds and a box of assorted pots and crockery.

At approximately 7 pm on the day of their arrival Emma, Ernst and George dressed in their finest clothing to venture out onto the streets of Sydney's Kings Cross. Emma wore the navy lace dress from Milan, the one she was married in, and Ernst his three-piece suit made of English wool. George wore long trousers and a blazer. They were in search of a café for their first meal in their new land.

It was still full light and they kept commenting to each other that surely this was unusual, this bright light, this heat, so late in the day. And Christmas only six days away.

George announced that he felt utterly weightless—still swaying with the rhythm of the boat—and kept running off then returning, full of news about what lay ahead. They passed an establishment describing itself as a tea room but it was already closed for the day. They passed a public house, its bar silent as the publican swabbed the floor and his wife polished glasses behind the bar. There were other tea rooms, other places advertising food, but all were closed. Finally they reached a shop with its doors still open and counters suggesting the preparation of food. There was nowhere to sit and eat.

Emma, in her most careful English, asked a plump, scrubbed woman behind the counter where they could eat a meal. The woman immediately picked them as 'just off the boat' and George was pleased to tell her of their six-week voyage on the *Ballarat*.

Ernst cleared his throat and, using the voice he had refined when he served George V, enquired about restaurants, even called the woman 'Madam'.

The woman chuckled and repeated the word 'restaurant' as though it was a fine piece of exotica. She told Emma and Ernst that they were in Sydney now and that she didn't think they'd find many restaurants here. There were pubs that did food, and tea rooms. At that time of night, the woman continued, she was their best bet.

'You'll have to give me your plates,' she told them. Emma and Ernst stood dumbfounded.

'Plates,' the woman was matter-of-fact. 'Plates like what you eat off. Folks bring me their plates in the morning and come and pick them up in the evening with their supper on them. They eat the food I prepare them but at their own tables. We prefer it that way here. Keeps it private, you see.'

Emma quickly pronounced this an excellent idea for fear of what her husband might call it. Employing her winning smile, she explained that they didn't have plates. Couldn't the woman help them out with some of her own, for their first night?

With a crooked grin the woman announced that she would be proud to give such fine foreign folk their first Aussie dinner. The meal—which has gained classic status in the family—comprised cold mutton, some slimy lettuce leaves, tinned beetroot, slices of white bread and a chunk of lard. Two green apples and a couple of boiled lollies were thrown in for a treat, no extra charge.

From outside, Ernst reminded his son to ask the woman for coffee, for a cup of coffee. When George repeated the request in English, the woman apparently recoiled.

'Coffee? Coffee? Oh no, we don't do that here. I don't know where you'd get that. Perhaps the Italians can tell you, when you meet them. I've heard that they drink it.'

Ernst was appalled at this latest development—this absence of coffee—it added insult to injury. Emma's spirits, however, had suddenly soared. George carefully carried a tray with their borrowed plates upon it.

Ernst demanded to know how his wife could possibly have been so pleased with herself. Emma pronounced the situation perfect; there was nothing there to eat, nowhere to eat it. That desert, she claimed, was their future, their opportunity.

Back in their rooms Emma and George made a table from a packing case and pulled up the camp-beds as chairs. From among her things Emma produced a box containing a bottle of French champagne and three crystal glasses from the market in Dublin.

Ernst took the glasses and bottle from her and placed them on their makeshift table, then he swept Emma into his arms and began to swing her around. George was giggling, was clapping his hands, and Ernst was telling Emma that this was why he loved her, that she was a spectacular woman.

Moon over Desert

———◆◆◆◆◆———

AROUND THE TIME I met my other mother they operated on Daddo's prostate to remove a tumour. The surgery, we understood, had been a success. Such was our relief we joked about the bandages that had so enhanced his masculinity. Daddo, as always, was laughing. He was making light and telling us all not to worry about him. Daddo, we kept telling ourselves, was all right.

When the offer finally came through—for the job in New York—I had been working at a Sydney literary agency for a couple of weeks and for the first time had a taste of what my adult life in Australia might have been. Not that I would have turned down a job in New York for a moment. When I phoned Paul in London to tell him I was on my way to New York, he sounded disappointed. He had, he told me, been contemplating a move to Sydney.

I told Daddo I'd been offered a job in New York and remained neutral as to whether I wished to go or not. I had only been 'home' a couple of months . . . had hardly given the place a chance. He said 'Of course you must go', just like that. He knew his daughter; I could not forego New York.

Jackie was not so sure about my going, for Daddo's sake, not her own. He was no young man, she reminded me, and we shouldn't be lulled into a false sense of security just because the operation had gone well. Daddo was seventy-four years old.

If I was to go then I must, at least, take some time with Daddo first. Some real time, not just flying visits from my bachelor pad across the harbour. Jackie persuaded us both that the moment was ripe to make one of those long train trips that Daddo had always dreamed of.

We would travel on the Ghan, the train that joined Alice Springs to Adelaide. Jackie badly wanted to go with us but could not take the time from work; instead, she funded my journey.

We flew to Alice Springs and checked into a motel. This is when I realised that Daddo was sleeping so much, but I put it down to the desert's fierce, dry heat. We walked the streets of the town in the cool of morning and late afternoon and Daddo made an effort to speak to the locals. He called it 'drawing them out' and he did it wherever he went, not only on this rare holiday. It was just that in Alice Springs, many of the locals to whom he attempted to chat were indigenous people; they were gathered under trees with their flagons of wine. The locals ignored all of Daddo's most earnest and funny overtures and he quietened, crestfallen.

We bought masks made of green netting against the flies—they went right over our heads and were drawn in at the neck with elastic—and delighted in how ridiculous they made us look and in the fact that they actually worked. At Uluru I opted to do the climb and Daddo walked around the rock's base in the company of a host of women wearing pale, floating sun-dresses. When I saw him coming towards me, once I had descended, he looked like a prophet leading his disciples through the desert. He had charmed them all. I revelled in the dry heat that touched forty degrees centigrade in the shade.

We had easy, rambling dinners and sat up late, talking about the world and all that was in it. Despite the fact that I was leaving again—and this in itself must have been a disappointment to him— Daddo made it clear that he was proud of me. I felt wholeheartedly supported. I felt loved and impossibly fortunate.

We boarded the Ghan—named for the Afghan camel trains that once made the route their own—and Daddo was as excited as a small boy. Before the train had even left the station we were seated in the sumptuous bar carriage drinking long, icy schooners of beer.

Once again I was reading in a train while the world went by, but this time it was a whole pile of manuscripts. Daddo and I shared a cabin and he elected to sleep up top, claiming it would be easier for me to read down below. Out my window there was a full moon over the desert, illuminating the orange of the sand and picking out the dark tracings of rocks and shrubs. With Daddo sleeping above me in his bunk and moonlight on the desert, I understood that above all else I had been blessed. This family, small and somehow precarious, was a gift.

Ten days later I was in New York City alone and there were icicles hanging just outside my window.

On William Street

TRUE TO HER WORD, within a matter of days Emma had found her family a home. It was a two-room apartment in what was then the tallest building on William Street, just below Kings Cross.

On Christmas Eve they moved and neither George nor Ernst had seen the apartment before they arrived with their possessions. Before Ernst had progressed beyond the small kitchen and bathroom off the hallway, George was whooping and cheering. He was telling his father that they had a view of Woolloomooloo Bay, of the whole harbour.

There was no time to stand and admire the water because their furniture—the smaller pieces, those that could be hoisted on men's shoulders and up the stairs or crammed into the small, creaking lift—was arriving. The rest of the furniture would go into storage until they had devised a suitable use for it. For now Emma and Ernst would sleep on a real bed with carved wooden head and foot from the best guest room in the Dublin hotel. George would sleep on a deep red, velvet sofa. They would store their clothes in beautifully crafted wooden chests and eat their meals from one of the most elegant of the Dublin tables. For now just for now, this was to be the high life, the life George couldn't have imagined from Dublin or from the decks of the *SS Ballarat* as they steamed across the world. For now they were a small family in their new home, there was quiet and harmony. They were in the still place before the storm that would herald the opening of their next business.

Ernst and Emma were to have the second room for their bedroom and George would sleep in the middle room that would serve as lounge room and dining room as well. George would have delighted in the room with the sparkling view, but Ernst required privacy; he would not tolerate the boy running back and forth through his room day and night.

George's first task was to unpack the kitchenware because once this was done Emma would start cooking their Christmas meal. Although they had only been in the city for a week, Emma was already well acquainted with the produce markets near Central Station and had ordered the finest cut of beef for their Christmas meal, as well as rock oysters and fruit so fresh it came with an image of the trees from which it was plucked. She had ordered wine from a merchant she found through St Canice's, the local Catholic Church, and had acquired a bottle of lemonade for her son.

Emma heated butter in a pan for a sauce, stirred in flour and stock; from the oven came the aroma of beef cooking in red wine. Soon George and Ernst were at the kitchen door, crowding the small room in order to watch, in order to be part of the sacred ceremony of food preparation. It had been months since Emma had cooked for them.

As the long, hot day eased into dusk a breeze came off the harbour and cooled the apartment, soothing their weariness. Before the meal Ernst sat in an armchair and read. George stood on their balcony and began to count the ships on the harbour, peering through the binoculars Ernst once used on his walks in the *Berner Oberland*.

Before their meal, as they sipped glasses of wine and lemonade, Emma produced Christmas gifts. For George there was a one-piece woollen bathing suit in the new fashion, with singlet straps on the shoulders and a belted waist. For Ernst there was a new ribbon for the typewriter he had carried with him for all the years Emma had known him but never used, and a finely bound edition of Anthony Trollope's writings on Sydney. George—while delighted by his bathing suit and by the promise of using it in the days after Christmas—was stricken. He and Ernst had no gift for her.

Their first Christmas meal in Australia was punctuated by George's trips to the balcony to view the changing scene outside. As lights were illuminated in Sydney's streets and around the harbour, George's eyes grew ever wider.

He pronounced it *Märchenland*, an antipodean fairyland, and went on to insist that he would stay up all night to count the lights. He had already counted the ships, of which there were fourteen.

When the meal had been savoured then devoured and Emma was so tired she could barely stop herself from twitching, the three rose to clear the table together. In the kitchen, Ernst washed the dishes and George dried them and all the while Ernst was talking to his son about mountains, about the Alps, and his boy was listening avidly. Mountains were metaphors, symbols of our dreams and our aspirations, he was telling George. The harbour would be a good place in which to swim, he acknowledged, but George should not assume it was comparable to the landscape of his homeland.

In the small, white-tiled bathroom Emma sank back into the tub with the water scaldingly hot. She had made the right choices: the apartment, the decision that when they started the new business they would not live on the premises. They would have their own place in which to be a family and they would have their business in which they would work. The two things, Emma was certain, could be separated.

When Emma emerged from the bathroom, all soft and violet-scented, she found her men at what would become their positions. Ernst was at his small writing table below the window facing the bay and George was sitting on the balcony. It was clear that they were father and son. Both held their bodies in the same way and tilted their heads just so. Both were capable of stillness, concentration and solitude.

George called goodnight to his father but was accorded no response. There was a sheet of crisp white paper in Ernst's typewriter but as yet he had not struck a key. Emma slipped off her dressing gown and slid between the sheets. Ernst rose from his table and for a moment Emma thought he might turn to the bed, turn to her. Instead he left the room, returning with a glass of some dark liquid. Emma got a whiff of whisky on the breeze and closed her eyes as her husband started to tap out a sentence on the old typewriter. On the ship, in a moment of hope, Ernst had spoken of writing articles about 'the New World' for the Bernese newspaper at which he was to have trained in journalism.

Later, when the bells of the nearby cathedral struck midnight, Emma stirred in the bed, instinctively reached across to feel for her husband. The other side of the bed remained empty and the type-writer was silent. She sat up and peered through the darkness to see that her husband was still sitting at his writing table, albeit with the lamp now extinguished. From across the room she could not tell whether he was awake or asleep. The powerful sense of the new she had been carrying with her all week began, irrevocably, to fade.

Stranger than Fiction

———◆◆◆◆———

I WENT TO LIVE IN Manhattan and moved into a loft on the Lower East Side, down below Houston; those cathedral bells that had marked Emma's days half a century earlier and had once marked my own were part of another, gentler world. I was subleasing a sculptor's home and was surrounded by her art works in their various incarnations. In the freezer were curious body pieces that she had cast as moulds from the original; one of them took the form of a flaccid penis. I was on Ludlow Street, with Katz's Deli on the corner and local landmarks like the Max Fish bar and the Mexican restaurant more famous for its frozen margaritas sold in Go Cups than for its food. Part of my tenancy involved caring for a geriatric cat and a dozen noisily fluttering doves who inhabited the loft's front window. While I was in residence not a single bird died but the cat, along with dozens of other New Yorkers, was stricken by the heat.

My publishing work—which fitted into three long days—was only a part of my New York life. The rest of the week I wrote, spending hour upon hour at one end of the sculptor's long dining table before allowing myself time out to explore the city.

New York was also a time for Paul and me; in six months he managed three short visits from London. On summer nights we would lie on the flat roof of the tenement building and gaze at the lights of the city, marvelling at the way the full moon appeared suspended between the twin towers. We still had no plans for a future together and practised long, tearful goodbyes. The word 'commitment' remained unspoken.

I was at work on what would be my first published novel, *The Underwharf*. It was the story of a young Australian woman who travelled first to London and then to New York to find the father who never knew she existed. It was not about me.

In the novel the young protagonist—who only by chance had the name my natural mother had wished to give me—searched boldly if erratically and tried to swallow all her fears in one great gulp of exuberant defiance. She was certain that she would find him, her father, but that when she did he would deny her. If he should accept her as his own she feared that her appearance in his life would prove disastrous for him.

I finally wrote a letter to my other father's former university—the one he had attended before his visit to Australia in 1966—requesting some specific information. I wrote to the head of alumni services, claiming to be a distant relative from Australia and asking for the current address for one Gus Monette. Failing that, I went on to say that I would also be interested in seeing a photo of the man. A very innocent and highly ingenious letter, I thought. A letter to which I expected no reply.

My New York life was solitary yet rich. I would rise early and go to the Carmine Street gym where I ran round a rubberised track or swam, very fast, in a small, crowded pool. I read *The Tibetan Book of Living and Dying* each morning before starting work—preparing myself for unforeseen loss—and indulged myself with cups of smoky Lapsang Souchong tea. As I wrote I paused to gaze down at the street theatre below or out towards the twin towers and soon turned back to my work again. I spent hours walking the streets and reading or spying on people in cafés, and dawdled in bookstores. I mooched around in esoteric caverns, poring over tarot cards and absorbing fragments of shamanic wisdom, slivers of crystal healing. In the evening I did the town with a couple of gay guys. My neighbour and I—he just happened to be an Australian go-go dancer—would stop for frozen margaritas as we wove our way home in the early hours of the morning. I had the precious sensation of living fully in the present, there in New York, but of extraordinary closeness through letters and phone calls to Paul in London, and to friends and family in Sydney.

At times the progress of my novel filled my body with a buzz of energy and hours could pass without me so much as rising for a cup of tea. It was on one such occasion that I was drawn from my manuscript by the ringing telephone. I had been so absorbed in what I was doing that I did not think—even for a moment—about who might have been calling before I answered. My greeting was curt; it would have been clear that I was completely preoccupied.

'Is this Gabrielle Naher?' asked a man with a rich, warm voice and a North American accent I could not immediately place.

I was suddenly very present, requesting that the caller identify himself. Before he said his name I knew, already, who it was.

'I'm Gus Monette,' he announced. 'I'm just a motorcycle-riding barrister. Who the hell are you? What do you want with me?'

I felt I was in a waking dream, it was both strange and familiar at once. All I could think of was the book I was working on and that I had somehow written this phone call into existence. Gus Monette's tone was playful and expectant.

'Can you talk now?' I asked. 'Are you somewhere private?'

'I'm in my office, the door is closed. I've got my back to my desk and I'm looking out the window,' he told me. 'Go on.'

I took a few deep breaths and could not imagine what I was going to say until I actually spoke.

'Well . . . I'm the illegitimate daughter of Jane Chisholm from Sydney, Australia,' I began.

'And you think I'm your father,' he finished.

'That's what she told me.'

He asked only for my date of birth. He neither grilled me for details of my physical appearance, nor told me where to go. When I told him my birthday he said that he'd be inclined to trust what Jane had said.

'Well, well, well.' Of all things he sounded excited. 'This is amazing news. I had a motorcycle accident last year and was badly injured. I'll never be able to father a child . . . which means that you're it.'

Gus' reaction—though it was everything I had hoped for and more—frightened me. The act of speaking to him was shocking in itself.

I told him that when he called I had been deep in the writing of a novel about a young woman searching for the father who never knew she existed. I hastened to add that it was not my story.

He, in turn, told me that after all those years he had been thinking about Jane. He'd had plenty of time to think during his convalescence and had concluded that he was none too proud of the way he had treated her. I should be kind to her, he advised, do the right thing by her.

I was suddenly irritated in much the same way I had been when Jane had asked me to be a sister to her daughter, Ella. Gus wanted me to remember that he had done the wrong thing by Jane and wanted me to make amends.

Gus asked me only a little about myself; pointedly, did I have any children? When I replied that I did not he sounded infinitely relieved.

He and his wife had been back in London, Ontario—the town in which he had attended university—for a few years. She held a good position in the university library and he was a criminal barrister and lawyer. He confessed that while he had intended to buy himself a new bike after the accident he had never got beyond the test drive. Calling himself a motorcycle-riding barrister was stretching things, then, was keeping a fantasy alive.

Gus said that he was well known in London and that the alumni services officer, to whom I had written, had called him immediately on receiving my letter. The man had implied that this was obviously a sensitive matter.

We talked bloodlines. Gus' father, he told me, was part French and part native Canadian. His mother was a Ukrainian Cossack. They, the Monette clan, were native peoples, or so Gus claimed. Both Gus' parents were alive and well and he had three brothers and one sister. My 'aunty' Kate—who lived in New Orleans, had a few tattoos and drank tequila—was only one year older than me. One of Gus' brothers, another barrister, had been working on a novel for some time. The Monettes, Gus informed me proudly, were readers, talkers and drinkers, and not necessarily in that order. I gathered they were fond of each other. Gus' exuberance was irresistible and his affection for his family both contagious and intimidating. How, I wondered, could I ever measure up?

He told me he wanted to write to me to explain some things and asked me to wait for his letter before forming an opinion of him. It would, he felt, put a few things in perspective. When we ended the call after over an hour, I realised I had no means of contacting him other than through the head of alumni services at his old university. It never occurred to me that anyone as mysterious as my other father might have been listed in the White Pages.

I sat, stunned, before rising to pace the loft. I calculated that it was the middle of the night in Sydney but a respectable hour in London, England. Paul's reaction to my news displayed the caution that neither Gus nor I showed. He advocated taking things slowly, not getting too excited, not getting too caught up in all this. Quite simply, I was incapable of taking his advice. Others I shared my news with were more excited, more intrigued, but then they did not feel the way Paul felt about me. They had not left me—three times—in one of the world's biggest cities in which I was largely alone.

I put my novel aside. I was almost disappointed, in the context of the fiction that had been unfolding on the page before me, to have had this intrusion. How was it possible to create such a story with integrity when this parallel narrative—my life—was running its own course?

Brave New World

——◆◆◆◆——

DURING THE DEAD DAYS between Christmas and New Year even Emma conceded that she could not do much to progress her business plans. Had she known that the country would close down immediately on their arrival they could have stayed in the hotel in Fitzwilliam Square over the Christmas period, taken advantage of the festive season and put away some more cash for their journey to the other side of the world.

Ernst hushed Emma, soothed her and reminded her that on balance they had done well in Dublin; the money they brought from Ireland, even less the gambling debt, came to a good amount in a city like Sydney. Emma, for one, had earned herself some breathing space. What did it matter if it was a couple of weeks before they could take premises and begin to trade? They had somewhere to live and some money in the bank.

Ernst found a barber shop in Kings Cross that was open over the holiday period and fronted up each day for a shave and trim. Once a week he had a manicure. Presentation, he told his son, was almost everything. George could hear his father's words in the morning when he was dressing, when he was combing his hair; it was only later in the day, when it was hot and he was running through unfamiliar streets and had grazes on his knees and tousled hair, that those words would grow faint in his ears.

The barber shop was run by an Italian who treated Ernst like a long-lost cousin simply because neither of them had English as their mother tongue. At the barber shop he was offered, and accepted, an espresso as part of the service. This was Ernst's first point of contact with the locals and gave him the opportunity to make his own enquiries about the city, away from the fierce optimism of his wife.

It was by one of the barber's long-standing regular clients, an artist no less, that Ernst's interest in the baths was awakened. The artist visited the baths—an old wooden structure down in Woolloomooloo Bay—each morning, swearing that it was the only way a Sydney summer could be endured. Ernst needed no more prompting and went home to look for his bathing trunks.

That evening over dinner Ernst announced his intention to attend the baths the following morning and George sat up straight and keen on his chair. He could use his new bathing suit.

Ernst immediately presented a whole raft of reasons as to why, at least in the first instance, he should attend the baths alone. None, however, withstood the steely gaze of Emma nor the exuberance of George.

Ernst was lingering at the table with his wine. Emma and George sat with him, as was their custom, but neither had further appetite.

Emma chose her moment carefully; she had, she announced, found them their premises. There were two splendid shop fronts with great plate glass windows facing onto the street in an elegant row of shops. They were on Darlinghurst Road in Kings Cross where all the fine businesses were located. There was a tea room there already and the owners were seeking a buyer, she said, someone to take over the lease and purchase their fixtures.

Ernst cut to the chase. How much was the rent?

Emma mentioned a figure quietly and her husband simply raised an eyebrow.

Emma was insistent, they would set up not one but two businesses. She said she could see it clearly in her mind. On one side there'd be a café and on the other they would sell flowers and pastries. The area had nothing like it, she continued. It was bound to be a great hit. Ernst pointed out that their decision not to start a hotel first off was in order to simplify and yet here Emma was talking about two businesses, not one. Emma talked on, undeterred.

Perhaps, she mused, they could find somebody else to run the pastry shop?

George was listening keenly. His face was a shining reflection of his mother's own enthusiasm and his eyes were dark with excitement. They left the table, with the next day's plans agreed upon, and George went straight to the kitchen to clean up before heading for his position on the balcony. Ernst, in high ill humour, told his son to leave him alone and spend the evening in his own room.

Emma followed her son into the lounge room and took his hand in hers. They would begin work on the model ship set they had bought in Dublin, back when they were first making their plans to sail across the world. Emma wanted only industry and joy for her son, and in that order.

George was awake well before dawn, in fact, he had barely slept. He had been afraid that if he slept he would not wake in time to go to the baths with his father. When Ernst finally rose—not just after dawn as he'd suggested it would be—George was wearing his new bathing costume under his shorts and shirt and the wool of the suit was already itching fiercely. Ernst obviously knew something George did not, because he was carrying his trunks and placed them in a string bag with two towels.

It was only a short walk from their flat to the bay, past rows of identical terrace houses which, Ernst informed his son, were built to accommodate the poor. If lack of shoes made children poor then George knew that they—'the poor'—were still in residence. Actually, he enjoyed playing with those children but hesitated to tell his father this.

George longed to hold his father's fine hand, to feel the warm strength of his father's fingers against his own. Instead he ran off ahead, just to be doing something, ran off ahead and ran back, did it again and again and again before Ernst told him to desist.

Ernst paid their entry to the baths and when he went to change into his bathing suit George had no idea whether he should go with his father or wait by the water. He hovered uneasily at the entrance to the changing rooms.

When Ernst strode out in his dark bathing suit George noted how well muscled his father's body was, despite its being long and slender.

Standing beside his father he, George, must have looked like a midget and a runt. Ernst was a man who took note of formalities and of protocols, and George rarely saw him without a waistcoat over his crisp white shirt, had never seen him outside without a hat on his head. Standing beside his father on the boards at the Domain Baths, each of them wearing his one-piece woollen suit with his arms and calves exposed, created a rare semblance of intimacy between them.

'Go on then,' Ernst goaded. He told his son he wanted to see if he could really swim.

George stood on the edge of the pool looking down at the dark harbour water some feet below him. In Dublin he swam at a beach and most of the time the sand was right there, visible beneath his feet just in case he should need it. There at the baths he could not see the bay's floor and was not certain—knowing what it looked like else-where—that he actually wanted to see what was below him. Across the other side of the pool, right up against the wooden fence that abutted the bay proper, other boys George's age mucked around in the water, floating, kicking at each other and generally causing a ruckus.

George walked from the pool's edge as though he had decided not to swim after all, then turned again to face the water. He held his breath, made small fists with his hands, ran as fast as he could towards the water and jumped. He had his eyes shut tight and when his calves smacked against the water's surface he was already screaming. For a moment he was sinking down, deep, deep, deep into the dark waters of the bay with no thought at all of returning to the surface. It was quiet and private down there, cooler, he thought, than any other place in the city.

When George's head broke the surface of the water he could not control the way his body gasped for air. He began to swim, or to execute his version of swimming. It was really just a forward thrashing motion but, miraculously, it served to propel him through the water. When he reached the pool's centre he turned back towards his father, one hand raised already in a triumphant wave. But Ernst was not there. Was not standing, proudly, watching his son's bravery as George had imagined he would be. Ernst was already stroking confidently, stylishly, along the outer edge of the pool. Ernst did not know that his son existed.

Guilt

———◆———

Across the world, I too was seeking the attention of a father. I received the first letter from Gustave J Monette two days after our telephone conversation in New York. It arrived special delivery and he had used his professional envelope that described him as barrister and solicitor and was marked 'Personal and Confidential'. I wondered who he thought might read it and decided that the eyes he was concerned about must have been at his end, not mine.

The entrance hall in the Ludlow Street block was dark, dank and dirty, and walking up the flights of stairs towards the bright, airy space I inhabited was like climbing out of Hades. That day I clutched my other father's letter in my hand as I took the steps two and three at a time, but when I entered the apartment I could not open the thing and placed it on a low, carved table beside the chair I liked to read in. I forced myself to change my clothes, get myself a drink, open the windows and check the answering machine. For a time I stared down into Ludlow Street, conscious that what I wanted to be a beginning might also be an ending.

When I had exhausted all the minor tasks available to me I sank into the armchair and gulped down a bottle of beer. I didn't know whether I was excited, afraid, or both. Gus' enthusiastic acceptance of me had surely been too good to be true. It was July and the evening was little cooler than the day. The whole world was still out on the street below and voices and music would float up into my sanctuary until well after midnight.

He addressed me as Gabrielle, with no salutation, the letter dated 9 July 1993. He had written in longhand on blue foolscap paper and apologised for his choice of stationery. He said that legal pads gave him some comfort. His letter—my other father's letter—was essentially about himself. He told me of the 'roller coaster' ride of emotions ranging from elation to intense guilt he had felt after our conversation.

He focused on the guilt he felt; I was quickly oppressed by it. Did he think I could absolve him?

My immediate sense was one of elation followed by profound guilt over what your mother must have experienced when I left Sydney. I didn't know what her condition was, I don't think, but possibly I did. I do have some vague and probably long repressed recollection of her telling me that she had missed her menstrual period but I honestly can't recall what she told me her solution was to be.

In any event, I believe that I was under some impression that distance was the solution as I do know that I was extremely immature at the time. She had told me, shortly before I left, that she wanted me to accompany her to her house for a holiday and I can still recall my immediate concern was that I would be stranded in the bush, surrounded by her male relatives armed with shotguns while we waited upon the attendance of a preacher.

Jane, I recalled, was from a large, remote property in western New South Wales.

In fact, I used that scenario on later occasions to avoid making any commitment to other women and indicated that the scenario did happen including the ceremony. I do recall that my excuse given to other potential mates was that I was already married and had escaped from some remote station under cover of darkness etc. That is the irony of this situation.

I don't know what the response was to your confronting her, but I do believe I should know a little about her state of mind as it would not have been an easy time for her. Our relationship was certainly brief and I was certainly not faithful to that relationship. She was aware of that and I can recall that it was brought home to her under particularly brutal circumstances. I was not a particularly nice person at that time.

Gus went on to recount details of his meeting with Jane in a boarding house in Bondi which he described as a party house.

Twenty-seven years later he remembered their first conversation, about the meaning of the words '*honi soit*' that appeared on the banner of the university paper, words he now read each day in courtrooms all over Canada. He recalled the exact address of the house and, if pressed, I imagine he could have told me the names of each of the other residents. I couldn't help wondering whether he had impregnated any other women that autumn in 1966.

As I told you in our telephone conversation of yesterday, your contacting me, although indirectly, was eerie as I had thought about those days in Bondi earlier this week. In particular I had a guilt attack over the manner in which your mother discovered my philandering. That is not something I am proud of and was not really proud of at the time.

Despite the fact that the sort of man Gus was describing to me was a 'type' I abhorred and would have had little or nothing to do with, I was intrigued, not repelled.

As I told you yesterday, I do not doubt the information that was given to you. I'll know, of course, when and if we meet, but to my knowledge, your mother was not disposed to bed swapping unlike the rest of the inhabitants of Ruapehu House. It is unfortunate that she had to endure the loneliness and pain of what was, for her, her first physical relationship with a man. If you meet her again, please keep that in mind.

At that point, after the one awkward meeting only six months earlier, in January, I had no intention of seeing Jane again and would therefore be unable to make amends for Gus' bad behaviour. Although these few brief lines from Gus' letter had shattered the myth of my creation, my heart did not soften towards my other mother. While he did not want me as a baby, he clearly wanted me then. With Jane I was not so sure.

Should you still wish to meet with me I will make every effort to see you in Toronto. After having read this if all you want is a photograph I'll provide you with one.

After the word *Sincerely* came an illegible scrawl which was either an attempt to or an attempt not to write the word 'Dad'. Then he wrote, *I don't quite know how to sign this given the circumstance. G.*

Not for a moment did I think of him as 'Dad', although I had no great problem thinking of him as one of my fathers. There was only one Daddo and he was the man who raised me, who continued to love and nurture me and whose commitment to me was sure and strong. There was no comparison.

Now that I no longer had to prepare for rejection, I longed to hear that Gus was excited about meeting me, about knowing me. I longed to hear him say that I was everything he would have wanted in a daughter. I wished he would say—without hesitation—yes, it's clear that you are mine. And it *was* clear.

Elsewhere

MY GRANDFATHER ERNST quickly took the view that things happened elsewhere. There in Australia, at the end of 1927, *The Sydney Morning Herald* ran stories on the communist push into Canton, on the dramatic sinking of a submarine off Cape Cod and on talks in the British Parliament that would have an impact on the entire world. Local news, however, comprised such minutiae as a shark sighting, an attack on a woman by a bull, a case of tick poisoning and an endless debate among the clergy about the relevance of The Book of Common Prayer.

A report suggested that even the stoic, hard-working Finns, of whom there were between four and five thousand in Australia, could not make a go of it there. They were returning to Finland in despair. Just before Christmas the Herald ran an image of a young girl and a rabbit, calling them 'our best and worst immigrants'. To be compared to a rabbit was, according to Ernst, intolerable.

Australia was altogether too Anglo, too puritanical for him. While there was a genuine drinking culture, the pubs closed ridiculously early and their clientele lacked the sophistication of that of the Dublin drinking houses Ernst had grown so fond of. As for politics, Ernst proclaimed Sydney barren. There were the trade unions, there was the communist party, but he claimed these lacked subtlety, and he had no interest in mainstream politics. Where, he asked his barber again and again, was the people's republican spirit? What, he asked Emma, did she expect him to do with himself in Australia?

Emma's unspoken reply was simple. Work for your family and raise your son. Emma was nothing if not focused. Ernst was anything but.

Their first Australian business opened in the premises Emma had found in Darlinghurst Road, Kings Cross. It was just as Emma had described it; two enormous shop fronts with large plate glass windows facing the pavement. With some practice, George could clean those windows in under half an hour despite the fact that they were so tall and he was not.

Just as she said she would, Emma employed a pastry chef, another Swiss. Neither Ernst nor Emma could fault him on his delicate *millefeuille* or his buttery croissant and he gained a reputation for his decorative work. In addition to the patisserie, the business sold flowers, which Emma lovingly arranged herself.

The previous business had been known as Sally's Tea Rooms, and as Emma and Ernst had to pay for the scant goodwill along with the fixtures and fittings, they saw some merit in retaining the old establishment's name. Neither of them could tolerate tea so they opted for the more European sounding Sally Café. In Swiss-German, the word '*sali*' means hello or goodbye, and is a warm, friendly greeting.

The Sally Café, which boasted dishes as exotic—in Sydney terms—as veal schnitzel, was Kings Cross' first European café. Before the end of its first month's trading, its continental cuisine was regularly attracting a queue comprised of other 'foreigners' and of Australians who had themselves travelled to Europe.

During the first days of the Sally Café Emma made her first Australian friend and their bond would see her right through her life. Indeed, the young doctor, Douglas Miller, would attend Emma on her deathbed half a century later. In the eulogy he wrote for her, Douglas described the Sally Café as having a warm and friendly atmosphere which was 'a great contrast to the manners of a reformatory that were so often obvious in the typical Sydney restaurants'.

George was enrolled at the local Catholic primary school where all the classes shared the one large damp room beneath St

Canice's Church. On his first day of school, in February 1928, he was quickly picked out in the playground and taunted. It wasn't the Swiss in him that the children found alien, it was his rich Dublin accent that set him apart, that seemed to lend him airs and graces. By the end of the first week he was sporting a black eye and bruised shins. The verdict in the playground was that not only did he talk funny but that his mother clearly fed him garlic and other foods that had not first been boiled before consumption.

Foreignness aside—George took none of the taunting or beatings personally—in Sydney he was happier, even, than he had been when he was aboard ship. Even in the environs of Kings Cross, where Sydney people lived in higher concentration than anywhere else in the city, there was room to run. By the end of his second week at school George was a regular at 'Cowboys and Indians', the afternoon game which was held in the bushland surrounding the stately Elizabeth Bay House. Even if he was always an Indian, George was happy to be included, happy to be almost part of a group.

In their new home in Sydney, Emma saw both opportunity and danger. While the Sally Café had gained popularity quickly, it had its limitations. It was not a venue that would lend itself to trading in the evening, even if she had been able to negotiate such a licence with the local authorities. It worried her more than she cared to admit that her husband was not gainfully employed come dusk. The pubs closed early, admittedly, but Ernst was a resourceful man and still regularly returned to their apartment around midnight smelling of wine. Emma did not care to know where he had been and she was much too proud to ask. The grass and leaves she found on his trousers were something of a clue and Emma took some comfort in the absence of all feminine odours on her husband's clothing.

He was talking, once again, about journalism. About how it had been his vocation that Emma had diverted him from. In Switzerland, he maintained, there were still people at his father's newspaper who might give him a go but in Australia it was hopeless. Not only did the local papers lack analytical commentary but there was no chance that the editor would even deign to see a foreign man. What good to him was his shorthand, in all those European languages, in a land in which migrants worked as hard to shed their own national identity as they did to earn a wage?

Before the end of Emma and Ernst's first year in Australia, Ernst had pronounced the place a wasteland. To him, it was only worth dreaming if you were elsewhere. Australia, he insisted, offered the thinking man nothing and the barbarian all.

A Courtship

———◆◆◆◆◆———

MY NEW YORK LIFE—in fact what I naively thought of as my 'adult' life—reflected my grandfather Ernst's sentiments. Things happened elsewhere, not down there in the antipodes, not in Sydney Australia. For me, elsewhere was New York, London, Paris and even Zurich.

I wrote back to my other father, to Gus. I began the letter the very night I received his letter to me. Mine was as loquacious as his, but more effusive. I did not touch on his guilt although from my tone he could easily discern that for my own part I had absolved him. The guilt he bore had nothing to do with abandoning me; it was all about abandoning Jane, my other mother.

In my letter to Gus I accused him of embellishing details of his maverick, exotic family during the course of our conversation to impress me. My imagination responded readily to his tales of the fast-living Monette brothers; big men with motorcycles. They came across as hard men who quoted poetry with as much ease and panache as they partied.

I did not admit that I was, in fact, dangerously impressed, nor that the portrait of the Monettes he had painted was enticing. Nor did I tell him that the stories he had told me about his family resonated with aspects of my own life; certain traits in myself which I recognised, now, as Monette had set me apart. I was noisy, I was wordy, I too sometimes felt larger than life. I told him—almost shyly and with no Monette bluster—about my own life.

After I had written I haunted the grimy stairwell, looking for post that might have fallen from my pigeon hole and blown into a dark corner. I was like a teenage girl in love and in a way I was in love; I was in love with the whole notion of this other father.

The tone of his second letter was indeed quite other. Now that he had confessed his guilt he could kick back and enjoy himself. His second letter was dated only twelve days after the first and yet everything with him had changed. He was a new man. He had returned from a whirlwind tour of Ontario—1500 miles in six days—high on life and on all the cycling he had done while on holiday.

Gus was as capable of teasing as I. I only hoped, as I reflected on our correspondence, that my own teasing had not been so bruising or combative. *I read your letter today and am quite grateful that you did not use the word processor. Had you done so, you would have, in all probability, not transposed the letters in 'edge'. Caught you, you would-be literatus.* He was referring to my misspelling of the word 'privilege'. I was as crushed by his 'would-be literatus' comment as I had been by Jane's reference to my broad shoulders. For a moment I panicked, out of my depth with this banter. I wished to tell him that perfect spelling and literary talent were utterly unrelated, but here my courage failed me.

In my letter I had described to him the story of my creation, of the university student and visiting professor. *What's this about 'older man'?* he countered. *To the best of my recollection Jane and I were about the same age during our brief encounter. Pederasty does not form part of my character, although I do still pant and slaver at the thought of firm young bodies. (Female only, you understand).*

I blushed, in deep water once again. I assured myself that he was not flirting with me. This was all utterly new. Daddo would never have made a sexual innuendo in his daughters' presence. In fact, Daddo regularly left the room during the sex scenes in films on TV.

Another area of your letter which astounds me is the assumption, on your part, that I am a beer-swilling rugby ruffian. In fact, that phase of my life is over and I am now an abstemious, non-violent, sensitive, kind, modest individual with a poetic soul. Who else do you know that can recite 'The Love Song of J Alfred Prufrock' with only the slightest encouragement?

He goes on to say, *Your reference to my family as a 'tribe' is, of course, offensive. Don't you know that political correctness is the most important thing in the world? To refer to anyone with aboriginal blood as a member of a tribe is most loathsome! In this instance it is true, but you can't say that as you have not yet established your bona fides as a card-carrying French, Indian, Cossack and whatever else flows through your veins. Nor do we drink hard liquor unless it is absolutely forced upon us! Beer, wine, and reefer is more to our liking, save and except brother Matt who has dabbled in almost every form of mind enhancement known in the civilized world. He is, also, the last motorcycle rider in the family as he has a penchant for Harley-Davidsons. Brother Mark has 2 vintage bikes, a 1970 Dunstall Norton and a 1971 Triumph Daytona, but he rides neither as he keeps them in pristine condition along with all of his other toys.*

How, at this stage, could I have failed to be anything but completely won over? My childhood, from that perspective, looked fey and sheltered while my adulthood was almost nerdishly dominated by books and the boozy grind of the publishing industry.

I am gratified at the thought that you were raised in a rather privileged atmosphere. I began working at age 12 and have yet to stop. Unlike the stereotype rich lawyer, I usually hover close to bankruptcy, beset upon by creditors and the minions of Revenue Canada, the income-tax predators. Thank God you aren't about to arrive on my door-step threadbare and begging, or I would have to get the dogs on you—if I could afford to keep any. My difficulty is that I prefer to work for the indigent and have a great deal of difficulty in billing people for services performed in that I enjoy my work so much. That is probably a reflection on my youth, as my father was hospitalized with tuberculosis for a few years and I was raised in poverty. Good for the sense of humour, though, especially as I always had sufficient intelligence to earn my way.

I did not point out to him that I had earned my own way since finishing school, forgetting, for a moment, that I did not myself raise the money with which Jackie and I bought our business. Come to think of it, Daddo always had an extraordinary sense of just when to surprise me with a cheque in the post.

*Another point which you made demands rebuttal. Aside from my
mother, the balance of the family does not read great literature. Alas, the
intellect that runs through my family considers absurdist writing to be the
highest form of art. We read such immortals as Kinky Friedman and
Elmore Leonard and eschew Margaret Atwood and Robertson Davies—
2 notorious Can-Lit icons. Too pedantic, don't you know. In fact, the
designated family tome is Catch-22 with Yossarian assuming heroic
proportions and brother Mark emulating Milo Minderbinder. In fact,
brother Richard and I have sent telegrams to various people pretending we
are Mark and signing as 'Milo'.*

I had read neither Friedman nor Leonard but was not about to
say so. Nor did I mention that I was not acquainted with those
characters—whose names when written in Gus' scrawl were inde-
cipherable—from *Catch 22*. Instead I anticipated the prospect of
sharing the work of one of the Canadian writers—Margaret
Atwood, perhaps, whose work I admired passionately—with Gus'
mother whom I might one day call grandmother.

*Mark has bested us time and time again. He is the only one who is
computer literate and owns, among other things, a laser printer. He has foisted
more frauds on us than I care to admit. To be fair to him, he comes by it naturally. As a teen-aged lout he drove my mother crazy by subscribing to various
offers of 'free home trials' using our home address and pseudonyms such as
Art Nouveau and Lance Slaughter . . .*

*Now that I have dispelled all the fictions you have created and further
disillusioned you I shall go back to work.*

Disillusioned? Who was disillusioned? I was hopelessly seduced.
No wonder Paul had advocated caution.

This time he signed off in a more jaunty fashion with the words
'*á bientôt*' and the scribble that came at the end of the page was
almost identifiable as Gus.

By contrast, the father figure I had been creating for my novel's
protagonist was almost saintly. His first incarnation had been as a
writer turned Buddhist monk but a judicious editor later
persuaded me to shed the monk's garb for something more
ordinary. As I worked on the novel I was reading Peter
Matthiessen; *The Snow Leopard, On The River Styx* and his essays

in *Triangle*, the Buddhist magazine. My intention had been to create a father who was well and truly outside the protagonist's reach. I wanted the invented Sophie from the novel to know the irony of finding a father who was not a father, of finding a man who could not be slotted into her young girl's dreams. I did not fail to note that my new father—my other father, Gus—was more that character than the Buddhist monk could ever have been.

My Grandfather's Liver

IN MY MIND'S EYE my grandfather's liver is as tough as a football's leather. It had certainly been kicked often enough.

Daddo, when I quizzed him about his father Ernst, was scrupulously diplomatic. He would rub his ears as he did when he was tired or anxious, a real little-boy gesture.

He usually spoke of his father in the context of work. There were, however, the few repeated stories about how Ernst swam every day at the Domain Baths, now the Andrew 'Boy' Charlton, and about how he did shorthand in all those languages and won prizes for it. He should, Daddo would say, have been a journalist. He had once been an excellent horseman.

'To my recollection my father didn't do very much in his spare time,' Daddo told me when I persisted with my questions about the man he had known, about the man my grandfather had become when he lived in Australia. 'He liked his glass of wine, he overindulged in his wine sometimes.'

Throughout my life, Daddo had told me that his father and I would have got on well. He told me his father would have liked me and I got the sense he was surprised by this. He was surprised and just a little pleased that he had raised a daughter of whom his father would have approved. He did not say that his father had not liked him but nor did he need to. Intuitively I knew that his father, my grandfather Ernst, had liked very few people.

Knowing that grandfather would have approved of me both

worried and fascinated me. Was I to feel complimented or insulted? As an earnest teenager I feared I had somehow inherited the traits of my grandfather: his bookishness, his booziness, and in the sense that I, like him, was at odds with the work culture of Emma and George. Even before meeting my other father, Gus, I could see that these traits might also have come to me through him.

The Perfect Daughter

NEW YORK BLURRED into a series of telephone conversations with Gus, my new father, my natural father. He was all the things in another father—the one I imagined when I lived with Pauline and could not have Daddo—for which I had hardly dared to hope. In the warm flush of excitement that was this new relationship the real people in my life lost colour and definition. My family in Sydney, my friends in London, Paul . . . Gus competed with them all for my attention.

My last days in Manhattan, when the summer was at its most mind-numbingly intense, were spent hanging on the fire escape looking down on Ludlow Street. At night I sipped frozen margaritas from The Hat and my heart was full to bursting with hopes and fears. I fell into bed exhausted, tipsy, all the better to sleep, I thought, and the lights of the twin towers through the window were a still point in the night. On the ceiling above my bed a small galaxy of stars and a moon glowed a sickly green. I saw them in my sleep, or perhaps I did not sleep. I rose, earlier and earlier each morning, to expend my nervous energy running and swimming and sat at the long dining table, hour after hour, racing to tell Sophie's story of meeting her father before I met mine.

Like my protagonist, I too took the train up the Hudson River to meet a stranger father and even through my excitement felt awe for the river's breadth, for its mass and colours and for the majesty of the grey towers of rock which rose from its banks. The compartment was icy and as I travelled north the cold wrapped itself around me, a shock after the city's oppressive heat. My heart, it seemed, was small, hard with fear. I blocked out the stories of my other father's family—Gus' siblings sounded impossibly smart, funny and close—in order to preserve my courage. Not for even a moment did I allow myself to wonder whether it was all too good to be true.

There was another heaviness in my heart. Something more constant, more resonant than the weight of fear. It was Daddo, my lovely Daddo. Was I betraying him? I had told him I was going to Toronto, but not why. I imagined I could protect him.

In Toronto I was welcomed by an old friend who had inadvertently become linked with my father quest. She and her girlfriend met me at the station and took me home to their bright apartment, to their pretty dog.

We three girls cycled around the flat hot city together and stayed up late, drinking and playing pool in local bars. I was immediately comfortable in the city and I saw, easily, how much energy, how much white noise, I had grown accustomed to living with in New York.

I slept little, rising early and cycling off to a local pool to swim and swim and swim lest the terror I was barely containing came spewing out. How did a twenty-six-year-old woman prepare to meet a mythologised father?

The girls took me to Kensington Markets where I bought a pair of Canadian Army combat boots, just like theirs. I decided, however, that I must have a frock. A girl preparing to meet her father must find herself a frock. I shopped with the same sort of manic zeal with which I swam, with which I drank. The atmosphere in my friends' apartment turned static with my nervous energy. I could not find the right dress.

The tone of our phone calls—Gus' and mine—had changed. Two days into my stay in Toronto and we still did not have a date to meet. He insisted on coming to Toronto from London, in western Ontario, but could not seem to fix on an appropriate day. Was he really so very busy? I had only one week before I was to return to New York, gather my things and leave for England. I was going back to Paul, I was going to finish my novel.

Casually I asked Gus how his wife felt about my existence. When he told me she did not know about me, I felt the first pang of doubt.

Gus finally found a day for me. It was right at the end of my week in Toronto and I wondered whether this had always been his plan. To meet once and ensure there was no chance of a repeat performance. What did he think I'd do? Invite myself to live with him?

I had only a pair of Canadian combat boots to show for all my shopping, for all my hopes of transforming myself into the perfect daughter.

Dagos

My grandfather Ernst could speak English with an English accent when he concentrated. Certainly, mornings when he presided over the café's tables, his accent was not noticeably Germanic. As morning slid into afternoon, however, and after the glass or two of wine he imbibed with his lunch, he sounded increasingly foreign. He somehow managed to look more foreign. Sometimes he'd forget himself, would call to his wife in the kitchen in his native tongue.

Late one afternoon two local businessmen were standing by the old cash register, the one George had already learned how to use. Ernst, who had been out late and slept little the night before, had been talking to his wife in the kitchen in Swiss-German and without thinking addressed the two customers, waiting to pay, in the same language.

'He's a dago,' one customer said to the other, returning his wallet to his pocket without having removed any money.

'No, he's a German,' the other one said, and then, under his breath, 'We conquered you lot. You've got a lot of nerve, turning up here, setting up your lousy business in competition with the Aussies nearby.'

Ernst told them he was Swiss, born and educated in a neutral country. His voice shook as he struggled to regain his George V accent.

One man told the other that that was what all the Germans said, and turned to leave.

Ernst reminded them that their account was unpaid and stepped out from behind the cash register. His voice steadier now, he told the men they may not leave until they paid their account.

The bigger of the two men stepped up to Ernst, stood in front of him with jaw set, eyes hard.

Who was Ernst to tell them, the Australians, what to do? The bigger man's voice had become as menacing as his stance. He muttered that they—Emma, Ernst and others—should not be there. Under his breath the man said that their food stank; their dago food smelled bad.

Emma appeared at her husband's side. She had combed her hair and removed her apron. She enquired as to whether she might be of some assistance and looked beyond the big man to his friend who was now standing by the door. Were they, perhaps, unsatisfied with the food, she asked, then admitted that she still had much to learn about the Australian palate.

She was smiling at the big man. Outside a lorry clattered down the road and slowly the background noise became audible again.

'You're Germans,' the big man accused, now sounding somewhat bewildered. Quietly, as though he did not like to remember such a thing, he told Emma he was a returned serviceman.

Emma told the man yet again that she and her husband were Swiss and continued levelly, soothingly. She apologised for the misunderstanding and asked that the two men accept their meal with her compliments. She placed her hand on the man's arm and confided that she had immense respect for servicemen.

The big man appeared smaller beside Emma's certainty but still attempted a threatening stare for Ernst. He turned on his heel and walked quietly to his friend by the door. The two moved out to the street together, letting their fists soften.

Ernst stormed into the kitchen. When Emma arrived moments later she found him draining a glass of red wine.

Terse words ensued. Was she, he wanted to know, ashamed of being Swiss, ashamed of her origins? She laughed at his suggestion, telling him that no, she was not ashamed of who she was. She could understand their attitude, although naturally she did not condone it. She and Ernst were foreigners. Their mother tongue, alas, derived from the language of the recently defeated enemy. Ernst poured himself another glass of wine and repeated his accusation that she was ashamed.

Emma had not once commented on the way her husband had started to call himself Ernest, nor on the way he now pronounced their surname 'n-a-a-r', so that it resembled the Irish 'Maher'.

The Lion's Skin

———————

EVEN ON THE MORNING of the day Gus and I were to meet I rose early and swam lap after lap after lap of a nearby public swimming pool. Later my friends joked that I had come to Toronto for swimming training. Exercising for the sake of it was the furthest thing from my mind; I was swimming to contain my terror, swimming to allay my doubts. Even then, somewhere at the back of my chlorinated, water-numbed mind was the possibility that after our elaborate courtship Gus might reject me. After all of this he might take one look at me and walk away.

I wore black trousers and black sandals with thick soles that had caught on the New York pavements time and time again. They were my least comfortable shoes, but they were not combat boots. I chose a black cotton singlet sporting a tough-looking cupid and over it I knotted a loose emerald-green silk shirt which gave the whole thing a softer edge. If I was sending a message it was a confused one.

My friends repeated directions to me but I was unable to get them straight in my head, I could not grasp the simplest detail for more than a moment. Gus and I were to meet in a downtown pub near the law courts. While we could not meet in his home town of London for fear of him being seen with me, it was fine to do so in a Toronto pub—he had once lived in the city and still worked in the courts there from time to time—where he might just as easily have been recognised. The secrecy was for his wife's benefit then. I left for the designated location with plenty of time to spare; the day was thick with humidity and once I had been walking the Toronto grid for a while my pretty silk shirt began to dampen and stick to my skin. I got lost.

After all those years I was running late. I was stopping on street corners and asking for directions and the anxiety that the swimming had quietened was rising again. When I finally glimpsed the bar's sign, up ahead, I wished the place did not exist. I wished myself home at Lodge Road with Daddo and Jackie and our naughty, spotted dog who was playing surrogate daughter once again.

As I mounted the steps leading up to the bar I dabbed at my damp face with a tissue. I could already imagine the scene. I would walk into a crowded, smoky room and walk from suited man to suited man. Are you my father? Are you? Is it, perhaps, you?

The bar, however, was only sparsely occupied but I did not even look at the other drinkers as I arrived. I knew this man without knowing him. Gus was the big man I knew he would be, he was leaning on the bar watching the door. He had recognised me just as quickly and took a few steps towards me as I walked across the room. In a moment a stranger's arms were around me and I felt small; for the first time in my life, or so it seemed, I was not a giant. At first his embrace was tentative, then, for just a moment, fierce, possessive.

He had told me in one of his letters that if I was really his daughter then I must be very beautiful. I had told him I was sorry to disappoint him but that I was smarter than I was beautiful. As we stood back and looked at each other I imagined that he was thinking I had not lied.

Gus was not the grizzled outdoors man I had created as a father for Sophie. He was, I noted immediately, somewhat overweight. His face was roundish, where mine was longish. We both had olive skin—his darker than mine—and brown eyes. Our hair would have been the same colour brown if mine had not been dyed red. His eyes were more almond shaped than my own; one moment they were mischievous, laughing eyes and the next moment eyes that saw the cold truth.

He asked me what I'd drink and I noticed his glass of white wine sitting on the bar. He had barely touched it. I shook out my very red hair, all ringlets in the humidity, and asked for a Bloody Mary. We moved to a round table and I sat at my other father's right hand. In my bag was a small photo album containing pictures of my family, my real family, and I clutched it for comfort but did not bring it out onto the table as I had imagined I would.

'You're my sister Kate from the nose up,' he told me, even placed his hand at the bridge of my nose so he could show me where Jane's face changed into Kate's.

'I tried to get hold of Richard.' He was referring to his youngest brother who was also a barrister. 'He's always in the courts around here.'

'So he knows about me?'

'No. I wanted to surprise him,' Gus was laughing. 'I wanted to be able to introduce him to you as my daughter when he arrived. I wanted to see the expression on his face.'

I did not say that I was horrified by the prospect of encountering more than one of those Monettes at once. Every ounce of my courage was invested in sitting there with this man who was somehow a father to me and fretting over whether he would like me or not. My drink arrived and I was embarrassed; it was the most enormous Bloody Mary I had ever seen. I wondered whether the barman had made it especially for the daughter of this big man who I knew in my bones was a drinker. The Bloody Mary was in a giant round glass on a thick stem and looked ridiculously festive with a paper umbrella, a stick of celery and a straw hanging out of it.

Gus told me, in the way of somebody accustomed to drinking, that he was not 'drinking' that day. He was sipping his wine and I guessed he would have liked to have been 'drinking', that even my silly looking Bloody Mary might have helped him then.

We ordered something to eat and he was at pains to appear frugal. Just a sandwich for him, while I ordered fish.

Quickly we were back on the subject of the marvellous Monettes. Even with my Bloody Mary in hand I felt like a pale imitation and a pretender. As well as drinking they quoted chunks of literature at each other, they had pizza-making competitions and they were fit and strong and indomitable. They had a fierce affection for each other and were larger than life and twice as funny, or this is how Gus portrayed them. He told me very little about himself.

In all the noise that was Gus telling me his favourite stories about his family again—and already some of them were starting to sound familiar to me—we reached a moment of stillness. The conversation took an illogical turn and suddenly he was talking about being in the wilderness up in northern Ontario and about coming face to face with a bear. Well it can't have been such wilderness because in the story was a railway line. In the story, which I desperately wanted to believe, Gus lay down his rifle and sat beside the railway track. The bear eventually sat down on the other side of the track. The two stared at each other for some time before something akin to a peace was gained. The bear then rose, took one last look at Gus and ambled away. This was the image of my natural father I would take from the lunch and the one to which I would cling for days and weeks and months afterwards.

Our meals arrived and Gus' sandwich had been cut into tiny triangles. He sipped his wine and lifted these morsels of food to his mouth with his great big hands and I sensed this dainty show of sandwich eating was for me. For my part, I struggled to finish my Bloody Mary and pick over my fish. I cursed myself for not having predicted all those bones.

In the silence while he was eating I told him more about myself but the stories of my own family seemed quaint beside his tales of the Monettes. I noticed him watching me carefully as I spoke about Daddo and I caught myself trying to sound less adoring. I told him, however, that I would not have changed my circumstances for the world. This made me feel somewhat less of a traitor.

He asked me again to be good to Jane when I saw her, to remember how he had treated her and to be gentle. I, defiant, told him I doubted that I would be seeing her.

When he had finished his sandwich and his glass of wine he did not move to order another drink or even a coffee. Was it over already, this meeting? And no plans made for a real reunion.

'Let's get out of here,' he said after he had paid the bill. 'Can I take you some place I really like?'

Of course, I told him, relieved, ridiculously grateful. We walked the Toronto streets to his parked Jeep and I caught him looking around as if for somebody he knew. He was tall beside me, as big and strong as a fairytale father. I wondered what his imagined daughter looked like and the extent to which I was not her.

We left downtown Toronto behind and for the first time there was quiet between us. I wondered whether we had left the Monette stories behind too. He would not tell me where we were going, he wanted to surprise me. I was both intrigued and just a little alarmed. Once we had left the city grid I saw that we were driving parallel to Lake Ontario. Whenever I mentioned Paul he scowled and muttered disapprovingly about my being involved with an Englishman. This, I decided, was just for show. This, I thought, was how a father disapproved of his daughter having a boyfriend at all.

We parked atop a grassy slope that ran all the way to the water. He strode off ahead of me, moving diagonally downhill and I slid behind him in my silly sandals that were no good for Manhattan and no good for the shores of Lake Ontario. By the time I caught up with him it was clear that we were heading for an ornate stone building on the lake shore, but for all its finery the place looked abandoned and I could not fathom its purpose.

'Do you know what this is?' he asked me, clearly expecting me to know, to be as delighted as he was by it.

I did not even hazard a guess. I did not want to be wrong.

'It's the water transfer plant from Michael Ondaatje's novel,' he announced, pleased as a child showing off some model tower he had built with his own hands.

'Oh,' I tried to sound as delighted as he. 'Which Michael Ondaatje novel?'

He did not appear disappointed that my recognition of the place was not immediate. Indeed, he seemed pleased to be able to recount the story to me.

'From *In the Skin of a Lion*,' he was striding off again in his enthusiasm. 'I love this building. You know it was built by European immigrants, just like in the book. It was built by immigrants just like my own ancestors.'

Gus was beaming. He was as passionate about the subject as he was about his family but he was calmer now, more focused. I realised that he was not trying to impress me. When I admitted that I had not read the novel he was only too pleased to give me a précis and pass on his own interpretations. I had forgotten, until that moment, that he had taught English to high school students. I could easily imagine the students he would have inspired . . . for a moment I was jealous of them.

It was in our time by the lake, in our time talking about Michael Ondaatje and his work, that I began to feel comfortable with Gus. I did not try to compete, to swap observation for observation, I just stood back and listened. I was smiling. We stood by the lake and he talked until we both noticed that the day had progressed well into the afternoon.

Again there was silence as we drove back into Toronto. I wanted to ask whether I would see him again but the words felt shabby and clichéd. Instinctively and to protect myself from disappointment I did not mention the future. I was almost as bad with Paul.

Our meeting, my day with my birth father, was over all too quickly. We were sitting in slow-moving traffic and he told me that this was probably the best place for me to get out. I obediently opened the door and climbed down onto the road. I promised I would write; as he drove away he seemed to be saying, 'I can't believe it, I still can't believe it', but I could not be sure.

I wandered Toronto numbly and stumbled into a shop in which I found 'the father dress'. It was emerald green and clung to my breasts, its skirt swished around me as I moved. I bought it in the hope that I would get to wear it soon.

When I was sitting with my friends in the early evening at the beginning of what turned into a drinking session that went late into the night I was full of stories of him, of his family. I did not know yet that these stories were like the lion's skin of Michael Ondaatje's novel, and that the man beneath the fierce skin had revealed himself only fleetingly, when he had been talking about a book.

Dame Mary

———◆◆◆———

DADDO HARDLY REMEMBERED the Sally Café but spoke with animation about the Café Claremont on Darlinghurst Road. This was the bistro-style restaurant that was my grandparents' natural progression once they'd made a go of the tea rooms.

'We moved into a flat above the restaurant,' Daddo told me and I did not ask what had happened to his mother's determination that home and business should remain separate. 'There was a lift. You could step outside the flat and into the lift and it would take you right into the restaurant.'

This was a young boy's recollection, still tinged with the excitement of lift doors opening into the restaurant so when you were working down there you never knew who might appear suddenly, unannounced.

'I did the desserts,' he told me, matter-of-fact. 'I'd get home from school and I'd be straight into it. We all had to work.'

He was ten when they moved to the Claremont and in the lane way that ran, higgledy-piggledy, between Darlinghurst Road and Victoria Street the other boys were playing cricket.

'I also took the money at the till.' Daddo remained adept at adding up figures in columns or on an antiquated calculator that spewed out figures on a curl of white paper. 'Dad looked after the customers.'

I could see my grandfather in my mind's eye. This was the best it got for him; his wife was in the kitchen, his son was at the till and it fell to him to talk to the guests.

'Mother liked the guests to have a glass of wine,' Daddo recalled. 'It was the civilised thing. Of course we didn't have a licence but she knew somebody in the force who'd tip her off when a raid was planned.'

'The writer Dame Mary Gilmore lived in the flat below ours.' Gilmore stares out at me now from one side of the Australian ten dollar note; on the reverse is Banjo Paterson. Her work was never to gain the iconic status of his.

Daddo was pleased he could add something that would have meaning for me; I had been none too moved when he'd told me they'd had viceregal patronage. 'She and mother were great friends, they really understood each other. Mum liked her.'

Later, when I read Dame Mary's letters and notes and correspondence, I fret over Emma's absence from them. Dame Mary mentioned almost everybody else, for god's sake, couldn't she at least have acknowledged that for all those years, the gracious woman with the restaurant on the ground floor had kept her well fed?

'I used to run errands for her.' Once again Daddo was pulling at his ears in a manner that reminded me of a young child. 'I'd take letters for Dame Mary through the bush, down through Woolloomooloo to Macquarie Street.'

Although he didn't know what to make of a writer in the family years later, living in the same building as one who had been knighted was clearly something.

I Wait to Ascend

I LEFT NORTH AMERICA behind me within days of meeting my other father but his stories, Gus' stories, travelled with me. I regaled my friends with Monette family tales feeling as incredulous each time I told them as when they had first been told to me. Gus had said that when he and his father got drunk together, they crawled around on the floor and spoke 'in tongues'. It's a native American thing, he shrugged dismissively.

I did not tell them that we had, as yet, no plans to meet again. If I did not speak of my doubt, of my niggling fear that Gus would disappear as suddenly as he had appeared, it might never prove founded. In truth, I did not know whether I'd been accepted or rejected.

In London Paul and I took a flat together in Kentish Town, between Camden Lock and Hampstead Heath. He travelled Europe and the Middle East for the bank at which he was now an auditor and I stayed at home, hunkering down over my novel. I scraped together a living by reading manuscripts for a literary agent, doing freelance book publicity and working as a weekend bookseller at Waterstones. To escape the cold that inhabited the flat—which I could not afford to heat all day—I ran on Hampstead Heath and the narrative of my novel fell into place in the rhythm of my stride.

Before I met Gus I had already written the part of my novel set in New York, the segments in which Sophie frets, in turn, about the possibility of her father rejecting her and the prospects of her ruining his life by appearing in it. This side of my own meeting, I assured myself that my fears had been quite unfounded. I, Gabrielle, as Gus preferred to call me, had been fortunate. He had not rejected me and was in the process of telling his family about me. When we met he had already spoken of my existence with his sister, Kate, with whom I apparently shared such a resemblance.

I did not write to him until mid-October and when I thought about it I fretted about the delay. Might he have been worrying that I, having met him, wanted nothing more to do with him? No, I told myself, I was clearly the one to worry about such things, not he.

My letter to him, one page of which sits beside me here on the desk, only recently returned to me, is light and breezy. I filled a page and a half with chatter about finding somewhere to live in London, about the great quagmire that was Hampstead Heath at the time. I gave him an account of my run-in with the author for whom I had been doing publicity, and about a trek Paul and I had just completed in the Pyrenees.

Eventually I got to the point. From where I sit now I curse that it took me so long; most of what I really wanted to say flowed on to the second page which has long since disappeared.

I told Gus that meeting him had been something of a relief. *Despite the fact that you mentioned the future acquisition of your very own shrink, you seem pretty sane, at ease with yourself and your life and your family and so the prospect of reaching 50 and perhaps resembling you doesn't seem like such a tragedy.* I pointed out to him that I had just given him a compliment but wonder now why I could not have been more direct.

I enquired how he felt about the *existence of a daughter out there in the world*. I can see it clearly now, I was fishing for affirmation. *Would your life be simpler*, I wished to know, *if I'd never sent that clumsy letter . . .?*

For just a moment I stopped fretting about whether my other father liked me or not and gave the rest of my life some attention. Paul and I still had no plans for a future. Once again, I was missing Sydney.

November came and went with no letter from Gus but I was not too proud to send him a Christmas card. I heckled him, just a little, about not having written. The least he could have done was say something polite about me. I reckoned he could have managed that, even if he didn't mean it.

By the end of January 1994, six months had passed since Gus and I had met and his long silence had thrown me back into the nervous, doubting head space that Sophie inhabited while she was in the New York loft in *The Underwharf*. I started to tell myself that he could not have liked me after all. I started to tell myself that he knew all he wished to know about me. Close the book, I told myself, let it go.

When his letter finally arrived in early February I did not know whether to be elated or wary. Something had changed, that was clear. The handwriting on the envelope was less precise, less certain, and he had taken to calling me Gaby. He had forgotten how to spell my surname.

In opening, Gus told me that the letter, the one he had actually sent to me, was draft number twelve. The one I sent him was only a third draft but then I was younger, I reasoned, and my life was considerably simpler than his. He told me that he had a waste-basket full of paper, that it was, figuratively, the repository of all of his thoughts. Finally his thinking had clarified.

Most of the first page of Gus' letter to me was about avoidance. He always thought, he told me, that things would resolve over time. If he did not mention my existence to his wife, for instance, he could relax and their relationship would not be disturbed. He went on to add that he knew that this was not possible and threw in some military terminology—boys' stuff!—about how this meant he did not have to feel embattled on all fronts. In the next paragraph he used more military jargon; this time telling me he had a tendency to keep his flanks exposed while confronting that which was before him. Although I understood what he was saying, it was certainly not what I had hoped for.

He needed to address his financial difficulties, he told me. He wanted to concentrate on one thing—one problem, as I read it— at a time. He had finally consulted a shrink who told him he was a juggler with one too many balls (no pun, Gus insisted), or one too many hands. His, Gus', theory was that things moved too fast for him in the electronic information age. He had, he insisted, become an anachronism.

As I was unaware of your existence for 26 years, you got shelved in the 'things to do' column. You were just behind income tax arrears, accumulated debt and a number of other products of my lesser inclinations. I didn't reject you or your sudden appearance, but put you in a position of priority that was somewhat lesser than your status.

So much for my fishing for a compliment . . . just one small one. I was merely a thing 'to do'.

That was enough about me. Or was it about him? Gus went on to mention that he had started taking Prozac, noting glibly that this made him a nineties type of man.

Don't give up on me just yet. As I approach and deal with each crisis in my life you will ascend in ranking until I can give you my undivided attention.

Unlike all the Monette family stories I had been sharing with anyone who would listen, I kept this letter and its contents very quiet. My sense of well-being about our meeting had evaporated. I slipped into crisis alert, ready for anything.

I could quite accept that I was not as important as Gus' tax return. I just wished he hadn't seen the need to tell me so.

Eggs and Spoons

——◆•►◄•◆——

DADDO PUT ON A high, squeaky voice in imitation of himself as a boy and tunelessly sang 'Light blue and dark blue, The colours of our school; Hand true and heart true, We'll make those colours rule; Try, boys—we'll try boys, To keep them pure and proud; High, boys—on high, boys, We'll lift their praises loud.' He was seventy-eight.

If I walk through the French doors of the study in which I now sit writing and stand on the verandah I can almost see the school that Daddo—as George—attended from 1931 to 1937. Marist Brothers Darlinghurst was once just around the corner on Liverpool Street, just there at the highest point on the hill. The Edwardian building still stands—resplendent with its curlicued verandah rails, its central stairwell, its high ceilings—but has been converted to chic designer apartments as is the way in Sydney. It retains its original name, Alexandra. Now Daddo is gone, I pass the building a few times a day, going about my own business in the streets he roamed as a child. Sometimes I slow down outside Alexandra and as I long for Daddo tears collect in the corners of my eyes. The old man who daily sweeps the pavement opposite and refers to my ancient dog as 'the pup' clutches my arm in amazement when I tell him my father had gone to the school. This kind, elderly caretaker was there himself, just a year or two before Daddo.

Back in 1929, the school magazine boasted that the school was one of the handsomest educational offices in the city and that it commanded a delightful 'panoramic view' of the city and harbour.

'We used to climb right to the top of the stairs and from a high window we could see down into the old private hospital behind,' Daddo recalled with enthusiasm. 'We could see right through the glass roof into the operating theatre.'

'It wasn't in use was it? This operating theatre?' my tone was suitably incredulous.

'Yes, it was! We used to watch the operations.'

Like so many of Daddo's childhood recollections, this one, when he presented it, sounded like a most normal pastime. While the stately building that once housed the hospital still exists, it too is now residential. I catch myself wondering who sleeps in the room that was once the operating theatre. As I walk to the café past the old school building I imagine those adjectives still echoing within the edifice's fine stone walls; *bonus, bona, bonum.*

The magazine informed parents who might have wished to send their boys to the school that its surroundings were of an 'attractive character', and it provided that quietness so necessary for 'earnest study'. In my day girls stand on the corner outside the old school building with their tatty skirts barely covering their pubic mounds. They rock back and forth on their dirty runners, either falling asleep on their feet or drugged to oblivion. It's a well-known fact that despite all that closed-eye teetering, tottering, the girls never fall down. Day and night the johns cruise in their cars, occasionally mustering the courage to hurl insults at the street workers. The pimps, too, insult their girls.

When Daddo went to school there was a thirty-five-minute lunch break. He'd run back to the Café Claremont and enter via Earl Place at the back. Emma would have just uttered the words '*Die Buobe kompt den am Twelf*', and his first course would be sitting on the neatly laid table in the kitchen when he arrived.

The moment he had finished the meal Daddo would be up and running, this time back to school for the afternoon lessons. It's almost a kilometre between the building in which the Café Claremont once thrived and the school that's no longer a school.

The school advised that the preparation of homework should take about two hours but Daddo rarely had even an hour. He reckoned he never completed his homework, even if he had managed to start it.

'Dad had me always involved in the business,' Daddo recounted. 'I used to help behind the till . . . I used to have to make the sweets as well. I remember those sweets, there were tarts . . . French tarts, choux, cream caramels, cream cakes, slices. You know, you'd have to deal them out and give them to the waitress. That kept me pretty busy. I was ten, twelve, thirteen.'

'Brother Lambert, who taught me Latin, was a great friend of Dad's,' Daddo told me. 'He and Dad would sit up drinking together at the Claremont until late in the night. When I knew it was my turn to answer a question in Latin in class the next day I'd put up my hand and rush out to the toilet. When I got back, Brother would say, "Here are two for the one you missed". I was always afraid he'd tell Dad that I was no good.'

In 1931 the school magazine claimed that 'despite the Depression the Australian school boy is still filled with gaiety and optimism'.

In his first year at Marist Brothers, when he was in Fourth Class, Daddo won the Egg and Spoon Race for under twelves. This figures: he had, after all, spent his whole life carrying food from place to place, frowning lest his father see him spill anything. Despite his work in the Claremont he won first place in History, third in Arithmetic and Reading and fourth in Writing. Overall, he achieved a remarkable third in the class which was—admittedly—small.

Throughout his junior years Daddo continued to perform, adding second place in the Balloon Race to his other honours.

The photographer who was responsible for the class portraits each year in the school magazine was annually greeted by so many pairs of freshly creased trousers and heads sporting marcelled hair. 'The crisis is at hand,' he announced. 'Endeavour to look your best and smile without obscuring your ears.'

Daddo, over the years, failed to smile in any of his school photographs although I doubt that this was for fear of obscuring his large ears. In the magazines his face matures before my eyes. When he first arrived at the school it was full and cherubic, his hair slick, lustrous and parted at the side. As his face slimmed down his hair began to curl.

'We used to gather in the back lane and play cricket,' he told me, but did not hear when I asked how he possibly found time. 'There used to be a big garage, it was in Earl Place. It housed all the trucks for Aunt Mary's grocery deliveries. We played cricket up against the garage door. There was Don Hall, we went to school together. Wally Kelly didn't have a family but lived up above the garage with another family. He became the manager of the garage. Don Hall didn't have a family either.'

'One Christmas Mum bought me a motor boat,' Daddo recalled with pride in his voice. 'They bought it with the Christmas takings. That was a great sacrifice for them. It was a great thing to own your own boat. We had it parked down in Elizabeth Bay, off the boat shed on a mooring. We used to have expeditions up towards the Parramatta River. I was nine or ten.'

'I suppose they bought it for me to keep me out of mischief. We'd clean it and take it to pieces and put it back together. I was the only one of my friends to have a boat. We always went out fishing. It was a great thrill. In those days there weren't that many boats, in those days there were about ten boats down in Elizabeth Bay.'

I asked him whether he went far in his little boat, wondering whether he had motored to Long Bay, on which he had lived, there in Cremorne, for the last twenty-eight years of his life.

'The harbour's pretty big when you're out on it, especially in a small boat.' This was a child speaking and I marvelled at the way Daddo could slip back seventy years when he wanted to, when he would permit himself. 'You've always got to think that you've got as much time coming back as going out, sometimes more. Of course our time was pretty packed because we went to school on a Saturday morning and worked, we always worked.'

'We have photographs of when I took Mum out; she was sitting in the back of the boat next to the Swiss flag.' Daddo was staring off to some distant place, there was sadness in his voice. 'It was just an ordinary little putt putt boat, but a good one. Father never went out in it, strangely, I don't recollect him in it.'

Once again we reached a blank—the blank at which we always arrived when Ernst was mentioned—and he did not want to talk any more.

Letter

◆◆◆

May 2/94

Dear Gaby,

As you will note from my handwriting, I have encountered some neurological difficulties.

My marriage has ended . . .

My practice is in disarray and I have reached the point where I will have to go on long-term disability insurance.

So much has happened to me in the past ten weeks that I am concerned I may never see you again.

I was both homicidal and suicidal for a time and was certified into a psych hospital for 10 days. I have had no fewer than 4 encounters with the local police and am facing serious charges relating to drinking and driving.

If I do recover and begin to receive disability payments in the near future, I may take time away and visit you in Europe.

My current instability seems to be worsening so don't book any plans until I have recovered.

Sorry about this news, but I feel I owe you the explanation.

Gus.

Only nine months had passed since Gus and I had met in Toronto. I am glad I do not have a copy of the letter I sent him in reply but

I believe I said something along the lines of 'There there, I'm sure it will all work out for the best'. I told him, also, that I had recently made the difficult decision to return to Australia. I explained the nature of the family crisis to hand. A cousin had been in a serious accident and I could no longer tolerate being so far from Daddo and Jackie. There was no way of disguising the fact that I was his daughter, and yet another's.

A Man

———✦———

BESIDE SYDNEY'S WOOLLOOMOOLOO Bay near the baths in which my grandfather Ernst swam each day, a small community—ordinary people who had been hardest hit by the Depression—were living in caves and tents. Up in Kings Cross my grandparents' business, the Café Claremont, was only just surviving. In Daddo's first year of high school up there on Darlinghurst hill there was only one other boy with a foreign name in his class. Those who were not faring well asked each other again and again how it was that the foreigners were making a go of it and good, honest Aussies were not.

'During the time of the Claremont it was the Depression,' Daddo told me. 'Mother used to feed the unemployed. There were always eight or ten blokes out the back waiting for handouts. Mother used to give them the leftovers. It was rather a sad thing to see these fellows; they were dependent on people giving them food. Mother was well in that. We were one of the only businesses that got through the Depression. It was 1934–35. It was very hard on everybody. Our menu was two shillings for a three-course meal, served French-style, with linen. Lobster was three pence extra, or sometimes sixpence. We had eight different veal escallops or veal schnitzels, we had four or five sirloin dishes. It became known as a continental restaurant . . . we had a select crowd.'

The world had already turned deadly serious for Daddo. He recalled running errands for his parents between the Cross and Macquarie Street, where they had an interest in a second restaurant;

he was always running. His name had by now disappeared irrevocably from the school's prize lists.

'I didn't excel myself at school,' Daddo recalled. 'Being in the catering business, one always had other things to do. Yes, I did well at football, I was always selected in the teams. We played against all the schools. I was picked to play in "the rest", it was the rest versus the premiers. I can't remember who won. Brother Norbert used to bring a case of apples out to the games. He only gave us an apple if we won or played well. We usually got the apple later on.'

'In those days they had minigolf courses,' he was pulling at his ears. 'There was one near our back gate in Springfield Avenue. It was beautiful, the Mikado Golf Course. They used to get the boys around to sweep the greens. Of course I became very proficient.'

I knew Daddo was proficient at minigolf. Jackie and I had played it with him from time to time and, like with ping-pong, he habitually sloshed us.

'We used to have a game after we'd swept the green,' he continued. 'There was a game called The Frogs. I used to be able to putt the ball into the frogs' mouths with my eyes closed, almost. It was a long distance, it wasn't just a short putt. I used to go in the competitions. I was runner-up there for quite a while. Then they stopped me practising too much because it was costing them money in prizes.'

I asked about Ernst. Did he go to the minigolf competitions? Did he ever watch his son play sport? Daddo frowned, rubbed his forehead and shook his head no. Then a memory came to him and he seemed pleased to be able to offer me it.

'On one occasion Dad took us off to Coogee,' he told this story with great seriousness. 'It was just like going to the bush. You'd come out of the bush and go onto the sand and the beach was there in front of you and there was not a bod there. It was almost like the hundred mile beach in Queensland. I think we went by car with some friends. We paddled in the water, it was not like you do today where you dive out, swim out thirty, forty metres. It was dangerous, known to be dangerous then. The sharks were well known.'

By 1936 Daddo had slipped badly behind at school and was forced to repeat the Second. In the kitchen of the Café Claremont he spoke to anybody who would listen about his dream of being an engineer. In his very limited spare time, however, he played sport instead of studying; in this he could excel. Whenever he sat to study his eyelids would drop again and again until, finally, he slept. By 1937, although Daddo's name appeared on the school roll, he no longer bothered to attend the photo sessions.

Ernst had been dismissive of his son's aspirations; George didn't have the grades for engineering and they couldn't support him through such a long course even if he had been capable. No, 'Choge'—as Ernst pronounced his name—would have to work in the business just as he, Ernst, had always had to. Daddo's boyhood, if he had ever had one, was over.

The Angelic Reindeer

I SLID EASILY FROM a late London summer into an early Sydney spring. I returned to Daddo's house in 1994 where I made a temporary place for myself in the cabana down by the bay. I slept with the lapping of the tide against the old convict-built harbour wall informing my dreams. If I know a sound that means comfort and security, it's that one.

In all, I had returned from long stints overseas to that place three times. Once again, my decision to be back in Sydney was heavily influenced by my own sense of Daddo's mortality. After all those years wandering—a third of my life—it was time to be near him. I was not choosing between fathers because there was no choice to make.

Once again I had left Paul in London with only scant plans for a reunion. We loved each other but were both mistrustful of commitment, both afraid of being trapped, of getting stuck. This time it would be London and Paul I would visit for Christmas, not Sydney and my family.

In Sydney I lived in two rooms sharing a wall of windows that faced out onto the bay. In one room there was a bed and my clothes and in the other there was a small wooden writing table, a creaking chair and a sofa. Soon every surface in the second room was covered by manuscript pages; those of my own novel and those of the manuscripts publishers sent me to appraise. Before I had left London, my novel had been accepted by an agent. Despite this affirmation, this fuel for my hopes, Daddo fretted for me, down there by the bay all on my own. He fretted for his well-travelled daughter with no job, with a nil bank balance and with a boyfriend on the other side of the world.

There was time for us now though, for Daddo and me. I would walk up the sandstone stairs to the house and lure him from his own desk for coffee. He would call down over the balcony to me, did I want some lunch? There seemed more to show for his toil than for my own: there were numerous phone calls; there were letters sent; there were meetings attended; and there were sacks and sacks of garden refuse from his early morning labour. For me there was just the constant shuffling of paper, of manuscripts coming and going, and the accompanying hum of the ideas, hopes and dreams that travelled with those pages.

I found work as a part-time bookseller and as a temp in any sort of office you could name. This was all very well, Daddo would say, but what about my career? Where was my career? Other girls' fathers wanted them to marry, to produce grandchildren, but Daddo wanted only industry and independence for Jackie and me. He, like his mother, believed that work was the answer to just about everything.

I returned to the house one day to find a note on the kitchen table in Daddo's elegant, looping scrawl. It said that my Australian agent, Jill, had called, that she had an offer for me. I ran upstairs to find Daddo in his armchair in the bedroom, Bono lying at his feet. The sun had not yet set but Daddo was exhausted.

We walked downstairs together to the kitchen table, the only place in the house from which to make important calls. We discussed the message and disagreed, Bono underfoot as usual. Daddo said it must have been a job—I had once worked for Jill—she must, Daddo insisted, have been about to offer me a job. No, this was about my novel, I argued. Jill had had an offer for my novel. I poured us both a glass of wine and dialled the numbers slowly. Daddo sat opposite, looking on eagerly through his oversized square glasses which he called goggles and which made his eyes look enormous.

Jill was there, working in the relative quiet of early evening. Her excitement took me by surprise. I was right, Daddo was wrong. She had received the first offer for my book.

Daddo was still looking on eagerly even though it must have been clear that he had misunderstood. I hung up the phone and told him the news. Yes, he said, yes . . . but what about a job?

Daddo had always believed there were too many books in the world. He would pass a bookshop and say, 'Who could ever read them all?'. At home, he was always trying to get me to put my books away in cupboards because he found rows of books on shelves unsightly.

When a deal had been struck and the contract signed, I wrote to my other father—from whom I had heard nothing in seven months—with my news. I was certain, I was absolutely certain, that this would mean something to him.

For Gus I chose a most spooky-looking Christmas card; an angel and a reindeer, both gazing off into the distance wearing expressions suggesting they had been drugged. I had not heard from Gus since May, since before I had left London.

Christmas, I wrote, ever glib, *Always seems like a good time to write to someone you haven't heard from for a while in the vague hope of eliciting a response.* I cut to the chase. Glossing over the superficial details of the writer's life—which I portrayed as being romantic—I told him that my novel was to be published. 'Would-be literatus' like hell! This, I was certain, would please him. This, I was sure, would make him proud. This, I hardly dared hope, might earn me my very own Monette story. When I allowed myself to be very honest about Gus, I admitted that I no longer expected a response.

Europa

THE MORE WORK THERE was the less Ernst worked. The more responsibility, the more he took to disappearing without explanation.

In 1937, Emma and George—mother and son—ran the Café Claremont like partners. Evenings Ernst still occupied the front of house but he had become more of a glowering presence than a force; George covered for him habitually, just as he had done as a small boy in Dublin. Eventually George took to running home between classes mid-morning, not just for lunch. Come ten o'clock his anxiety for his mother would force him to leave his desk and see him darting out through the school gates without a backward glance. None of the Brothers made a move to stop him; they knew the score with his father.

He would run down Darlinghurst Road and past the crossroads where the cars and trams were always in stasis. George, light and swift, darted between the vehicles. On these morning trips back to the Claremont he'd stand on the pavement behind the plane tree outside the restaurant so as not to be noticed by anyone inside and watch for his father. If minutes passed and Ernst failed to appear behind the glass, George would stride down the steps into the restaurant as though all this had been prearranged. He would remove his school jacket, change his tie and scrub the blue ink from his hands. Already the waitress would be setting up the tables and George would be working quickly, with precision, to make up ground.

On the days that Ernst was there, gliding between tables, his
hair svelte and glossy and his shoes buffed to a high shine, George
would turn around and run back to the school on the hill. He
would slip back into his class without a word.

As for Emma, she worked on despite a chronic knee problem.
She became known to her clients as Madame Naher and many of
them would seek her out at the servery window. Regardless of
how busy she was in the kitchen when a client came to chat she
would respond as though she too had been waiting for just such
an opportunity to converse. Emma listened to ABC radio in the
mornings, when she was working in the kitchen alone, and
remained well informed. She knew the names of the people who
made the world spin and was not reluctant to express an opinion
or to seek that of one of her clients.

It was through the servery window that Emma kept abreast of
Australian thought regarding Europe. Ernst could have told her
what was happening in the world but she did not ask, so greatly did
their opinions diverge. Once again, public sentiment was against
Germany; Adolf Hitler had led the invasion of Austria. Once again,
just like when they had first arrived in Australia, strangers would
take them for Germans and remain cool and distant.

George worked in the Claremont evenings, as well. Often he
was there all day, from 10 am right through to midnight, just like
his mother. His boat—the gift from his parents years earlier, in a
time of hope—was corroding down there in the bay, forlorn from
lack of use. The boys who had once played cricket in the back lane
had broken off their schooling and gone out to work themselves.

The first time that Ernst fell over in the restaurant he barked at
his son when George went to help him. He had staggered into a
chair, perhaps had meant to throw himself down onto it, but had
fallen spectacularly with a timber-splitting crash. Rather than face
his wife, Ernst had braved it with the customers and walked out
through the restaurant's front doors, straightening his waistcoat and
tie as he went. George followed him out onto the street but Ernst
only cursed him for his trouble. Inside George gathered the pieces
of broken chair and planned the story he would tell his mother.

The second time Ernst fell was much later in the evening and only a few days after the first incident. He had been arguing with a client, with a well-travelled Anglo-Australian businessman who had insisted that Switzerland was sympathetic to Germany. Ernst, furious, had started to speak heatedly but found that half his words tumbled out in German. Still ranting in an incomprehensible blend of Swiss-German and English he had stormed towards the kitchen. George watched his father slip in slow motion and before he could even make a step towards him Ernst came down hard, his head cracking audibly on the pale tiled floor.

Emma bustled from her kitchen and knelt down beside her husband as though this were quite the everyday occurrence. She slapped his face with more gentleness than she felt. Get up, she told him in Swiss-German, but Ernst only flickered an eyelid, mumbled. Emma and George exchanged glances and George went to his father and easily hoisted the bigger man onto his shoulders. A client had already opened the lift doors and when father and son disappeared the few remaining customers talked loudly, jovially among themselves as if determined to bolster Emma's spirits.

Later that night, when all was quiet and tidy in the restaurant and the lights had been dimmed, mother and son sat together in the kitchen. Over a glass of red wine Emma told her son of her decision. They would sell the Claremont, she announced. This could not be permitted, this behaviour, this embarrassment. Emma was at pains to tell her son that this sort of thing—with Ernst—this was not normal, this was not to be accepted. George only half listened to this talk about Ernst; he was, after all, his only father.

They would be selling the Café Claremont, Emma announced. She already knew of a keen buyer, even mentioned his name: Walter Magnus. She, Emma, would take George back to Europe for a while. George, as a Swiss, must know life in Switzerland, must understand his heritage and his history. She would book him a place at the exclusive *École Hôtelière* in Lausanne. With part of the proceeds from the sale of the Claremont she would pay his board and tuition for an entire year. This, Emma emphasised, was a tremendous opportunity. An opportunity that neither she nor Ernst had been given themselves.

If George wished to protest he restrained himself. In fact, he was silent for a long time. He watched his mother, trying to read her resolute expression. He drained his glass of wine before speaking.

He asked only what would become of Ernst. Would his father travel back to Switzerland with them? No, Emma's voice was firm. They would leave Ernst in Sydney and give him the chance to recover, to get well again, as she put it. After a short time in Switzerland with her family, with her elderly mother, Emma would return to Sydney. She and Ernst would start another business together. They would make a good start, a fresh start.

When George told his mother that he did not wish to leave them, that he felt his place was there in Sydney, working alongside his parents, Emma's reaction was passionate. 'This is no life for a young man,' Emma insisted. 'I want the whole world for you, not only this.' She gestured towards the ceiling, towards where her husband slept noisily, a few floors above them.

Flesh. Blood.

———◆◆✕◆◆———

I FOUND THE LETTER from Canada myself, in the letter-box at Lodge Road. I was probably hoping for a letter from Paul—with whom I had just spent Christmas in London—but there it was, the letter from Canada. It was mid-January 1995, just before my birthday. I was still living down there by the water, surrounded by manuscripts. I had not yet persuaded Bono, who showed me again and again that he was now Daddo's dog, to move in with me.

I carried the letter all the way down to my desk without opening it, Bono deigning to follow me. I settled by the open window and the dog, in turn, settled on my feet. I waited for my hands to stop shaking before I tore the paper.

I had known that it wasn't from Gus as soon as I had seen the envelope. The name Monette appeared on the top left-hand corner but the address was Kirkland Lake, Ontario, not London. And whoever wrote it had obviously used a word processor which was not Gus' style. I expected the worst.

Mark Monette's letter to me, the niece he had never met, was eloquent. His fine prose impressed me immediately. He addressed me as Ms Naher, told me he was writing to me at 3.30 am, New Year's Day.

He wrote that he was looking out his office window at the reflection of the night sky on snow. I paused here, at a loss as to what this might look like. More likely, I did not wish to read on. Mark's windows, he told me, faced the parcel of land that had once been home to his brother Gus—my Gus—and his first wife, in the early seventies.

Mark introduced himself as the second of the five Monette children. He referred to his elder brother as Gustave John. Mark gave me Gus' birth date, confirming that his brother had indeed just turned fifty when we'd met in 1993. He mentioned the others in sequence: Matthew, Richard and Katherine, *the very unexpected and wonderful fifth.*

Gus' mail, Mark told me, had been forwarded to his office, which was why he had my angelic reindeer Christmas card. I still held just the smallest glimmer of hope—I would not let my eyes skip on ahead down the page—Gus could, after all, have been away somewhere recuperating, or teaching up north on one of the reservations as he'd told me he had dreamed of doing.

Gus died on October 26, 1994 . . . The coroner investigating his death has ruled it natural causes: cardio-pulmonary arrest. The medical joke . . . of course your heart and breathing stop when you're dead. We will receive toxicology results sometime within a fortnight.

I stared out the window, unable to see the bay I had always loved. I felt numb, dazed. I wish I could say I was surprised. I wish I could say that it was only at this moment that my hopes dissolved.

Mark went on to speculate on the likely cause of death—the combination of alcohol and anti-depressant medication. *A combination most likely brought on by depression. Most likely brought on by the demons he would never talk about. Most likely to leave the rest of us wondering what happened to this our son and brother!*

I did not realise that I had been making a keening noise until Bono was on his feet and nudging my hands. What's all this?

Gustave died as he lived. And, I am not proud to speak of this. But, he died a messy and chaotic death. Just as he lived a messy and chaotic life. You know, death never answers any questions. It just begs more. My parents, our parents, are not dealing with this catastrophe. My brothers and sister are avoiding it rather than facing it. And, I, always been everybody's father, older brother, confidant and friend, am stuck with sorting out the mess of Gus' life. So, I have to write to you. With tears burning in the corners of my eyes.

I slid off the armchair to sit on the floor, comforted by the overpowering smell of dog.

In the Spring . . . six months ago, Gus and I spent some very sacred time together. It was sacred time, I call it that, because he finally let the mask slip enough for me to glance behind it. Gus handed me a fragment of a letter written by you, to him. It had no salutation and no closing. And, he would not at first, explain to me who had written it. But slowly, and shyly he spoke of meeting you.

Mark wrote that Gus had *a visibly painful longing to be able to proclaim that he had a daughter.*

I was cut to the core by these words and sat for a long time trying to make sense of them.

Gus wanted me to know that he had a daughter. A daughter. Flesh. Blood. But, his and not really his, at the same time.

Mark went on to tell me what Gus had never told me: that he had always wanted a child. He sketched for me the reasons why, in his mind, this had never happened.

Gus always loved children. He would treat them gruffly, but, there was shine in his eyes when kids would stand up to him and deal back what he gave them. My girls thought he was grand. Smart, sharp, knowledgeable, funny, kind and very, very sad. Yes, I was thinking, he was grand and he was all those things, including sad.

Had his brother had children, Mark reckoned Gus would have still been alive.

I was given a few of the harsh details of my natural father's final months without apology and silently I was thanking Mark for his frankness. *Ms Naher,* he wrote, *I only wish that I could tell you that I did not know that this would be his end . . . Obviously he thought he could outwit his devil. None of us can and, for someone like Gus, someone who stood on his feet in a court room and lived by his wits, the realization that the problems were far greater than he could manage came too late.*

Mark had nightmares, he told me, about his brother. That was why he was awake at 3 am on New Year's Day. The dreams, he wrote, suggested to him that he blamed himself.

From somewhere inside his pain Mark asked if there was anything he could offer me. Photographs, explanation, anything.

I was sitting on the floor hugging Bono, which he was tolerating, just. When I rose to dial the number I'd been given and spoke to Mark Monette on the other side of the world, in the depths of the northern Ontario winter, his voice was quiet and gently sad. Suicide; over the telephone he called his brother's death suicide.

The Bargain

———✦———

IT HAD ALL HAPPENED so quickly, the sale of the business, the departure. It had happened so quickly that there had not been any real
time for George to say a proper goodbye to his father or to his
friends. On the voyage back to the Old World with his mother, back
to Europe, George sat on the ship's deck, gazing out to sea, trying to
remember the last words he'd spoken to Ernst.

Then came the goodbye with his mother, which had somehow
been harder for her than for him. They had dined together, Emma
and George, in the restaurant at the *Gare de Lausanne*. The establishment's fine linen, polished silver and gleaming crystal made
them glad and melancholy at once. They saw their own standards
echoed there in Switzerland, in one of Lausanne's fine restaurants,
but silently each mourned the passing of yet another family
business in the Café Claremont. Emma had grown a little tipsy
and it made her brim with emotion. She was fretful about leaving
her son there in Europe, so far from Sydney which she had
realised was home. George, also, regretted their separation but his
eyes were on the future. He was imagining his father's pride when
his son excelled at the school there in Lausanne. George longed
for the proficiency in languages the school would bring him;
eagerly anticipated the day he would write to Ernst in French, or
High German. He could speak Swiss-German but had never
learned to write it, as Ernst had. Quite simply, George awaited the
day his father would notice him.

Emma had planned to stay in Europe for a couple of months; she knew she would not see her mother again and wanted to be at hand as George, only seventeen, adjusted to his new circumstances. The telegrams she had sent her husband, however, had gone unanswered, forcing Emma to cut short her visit and sail home. George, she knew, would be all right . . . even there in a country that was foreign to him. Ernst, however, she was not so sure about.

After her lone voyage across the world she found Ernst in reasonable spirits. He told her he had a surprise for her; he couldn't even wait for her to sit down before beginning. The week before she had arrived, he announced, he had taken all their money from the sale of the Café Claremont and invested it in a new business, another restaurant. He genuinely expected her to be pleased. Emma listened to the full story before commenting, her knuckles white where they gripped the handle of her travelling bag. She had just walked in the door. The new business was in the city, on George Street near the Trocadero. He had, Ernst informed his wife, gone into partnership with a woman who'd been working as a waitress at the Claremont.

Emma's second surprise came hot on the heels of the first; did she realise, Ernst asked his wife, that in the contract of sale she'd signed with the Claremont's buyer, Walter Magnus, she had done herself out of the right to run another restaurant?

Within weeks of Emma's return the worst had happened. Ernst and his new partner had disagreed violently. The woman had resorted to using physical violence to eject Ernst from the new premises and he had deemed the situation hopeless. As to getting some money back, quite simply there was none to be had.

Emma had resisted Walter Magnus' first, second and third offers of work but could do so no longer. The day after Ernst had left his new restaurant—on which all their money had been squandered—Emma returned to the stove, but this time as an employee in a second restaurant Magnus owned in George Street in the city. Working for the man was not so bad, Emma told herself, he was kind enough, but working in George Street was almost unbearable. Emma longed for Kings Cross' sophistication, she longed for her own hearth.

In February, Ernst came to speak to Emma while she was at work in Magnus' kitchen. He had hardly been near the place; seeing another man reap the profits of his wife's labour was something Ernst found difficult to endure. Emma had been dashing between the stove and a work bench, coating veal in egg, in breadcrumbs, positioning cheese, ham, mushrooms. That day Ernst came to her sober; she could hear it in his voice before she saw it on his face. He was wearing his best summer suit and was holding his beige felt hat before him. The hat, despite his sobriety, trembled in his hands.

He told her he'd come to say goodbye and she only managed a distracted sounding 'Oh?' in response. She was loosening some *Rösti* in the pan.

He told her he was going away and fidgeted in his pockets, resisted dabbing at the beads of perspiration on his high forehead, his upper lip.

For a moment, Emma's hands fell still and the kitchen was unnaturally quiet. From the restaurant beyond the small servery window came a hacking laugh and men's voices, raised in excitement. A chorus of horns sounded out in the world, out on George Street.

He said he would show her. He would make good again.

Emma asked only, 'What do you mean by this?' and juggled pans on the stove.

'Goodbye Emma,' he ignored her question. 'Goodbye.'

A charcoal aroma sent Emma into a flurry of activity and she worked to liberate the potato from the pan. She flicked the blackened chunks away before their flavour could ruin the dish. Holding her breath, she flipped the *Rösti* and the potato cake described a perfect arc above the pan and landed upside down with a human-sounding sigh. It wasn't until she knew her potatoes would not spoil that she extinguished the gas, shut down the entire stove, and turned to give her full attention to her husband. The kitchen, however, was now empty and through the servery window she saw Ernst chatting easily with Walter Magnus out the front.

Emma stood and watched her husband for some moments; perhaps he'd return to explain himself to her? Or perhaps there was some other, more intimate goodbye gesture he would bestow on her that could not be conveyed with words, not even Ernst's fine words? Emma waited, hands by her sides, forced herself to ignore the stove. Another woman might have shed her soiled apron, checked her hair and rushed through the restaurant to embrace him, to kiss him modestly on his barber-shaved cheek. Not Emma. She had turned from her stove for him, now the rest was up to Ernst.

Out on the street the two men laughed, bantered. From their gestures, from the way their bodies moved, she could tell they were conversing in German. Ernst took leave of Magnus easily, like a man with nothing on his mind, and disappeared out of her sight.

In the days after Ernst's departure she replayed the goodbye that was not a goodbye time and time again but could make little sense of it. She had to admit Ernst made little sense to her, perhaps he never had. She would not tell George he was gone, knew with more certainty than she knew her husband's mind that this news would upset him.

Now Emma rose from her large, empty bed at dawn to take the earliest tram to the Haymarket for supplies. For the first time since she was married, Emma was alone. Although she'd planned every other move, had masterminded every other strategy the family had implemented, she had not foreseen this turn of events. Despite the shock of it, of a solitary existence, Emma did not find this new condition a burden. To the contrary, it gave her more time to plot the next move, more time to think about the way forward in light of their drastically diminished circumstances.

Emma had been to the markets long before most of her neighbours in the building on Darlinghurst Road had risen from their beds. It was a neighbourhood of late nights, but back when Emma and Ernst had started out at the end of the twenties, theirs had been the only restaurant bold enough to offer meals after 7 pm. As the Depression eased, things had changed, but the word was still out that at Madame Naher's you could eat well late into the night. Now she was in the city she missed the familiar faces from the Cross and nearly wept when one of her regulars would make the journey across town to dine at her table.

The first Saturday in March Emma spent most of the morning working with the knives she had sharpened the day before. By 11 am, when it was time to begin her final preparations for the day's luncheon, her forearms were slick with blood from the butchering, which she sometimes preferred to do herself. Before her first customer arrived she checked her reflection and gasped to see her face, also spattered with blood, from the morning's exertions. The more she splashed water at herself, the more the blood spread.

One customer, a regular from the days of the Claremont, came to the servery window to chat to her. The gentleman enquired after Ernst as Emma worked to arrange the salads. She lied, telling the man Ernst was very well. She went on to say Ernst was working in Brisbane and that she had received a telegram from him the day before.

When the man moved away Emma was mortified that she had misled him. Her husband was in Brisbane, that was a truth. She had first learned this from the housemaid in their block of flats. Why Ernst had been able to tell the girl where he was going and not her, Emma failed to understand. What she had more trouble fathoming, however, was how he had been able to travel to Brisbane. Since he had lost all their money in December, he'd had not a penny to his name. What money he said he needed—Emma guessed he spent it on drink—came from her.

Just when Emma had convinced herself that her husband could not have gone to Brisbane after all—nine days after he had said goodbye—she had received a telegram. *Please wire two pounds urgent G.P.O. Brisbane. Ernst.* She had wired the money.

Only three days later a second telegram had arrived. *Wire two more pounds today with my dress suits. Letter on way.* Emma had forwarded the dress suits but hesitated to send the money. She had just heard the news that Ernst had sold his son's boat a few weeks earlier and kept the money for himself.

On Friday she had heard from Ernst once more. *Please do wire two by eleven must start.* For a moment, she had allowed herself to hope. Perhaps Ernst really had found a way of making good? Perhaps the next telegram would say, *Excellent opportunity for us. Please come soonest. Your Ernst?*

No telegram had come on Saturday morning and for this Emma was grateful. It made her nervous to keep withdrawing money from the bank when she was earning so little. What if she had not chosen to pay her son's school fees in advance? What if she had left that money at home with her husband?

Once the luncheon service was finished Emma found herself at something of a loss. The café in the city closed on a Saturday afternoon and did not open again until Monday. With no firm plan, Emma hung up her apron, patted her hair into place, covered her head with a hat and put on her gloves. She wandered the city's streets but did not look at the displays of fine clothing, of cakes and chocolates behind the plate glass windows. Her wanderings took her back to the Cross.

Emma negotiated the knot of traffic up near the intersection and walked with purpose down Bayswater Road. When she glimpsed the trees of Rushcutter's Bay Park she knew where she was going. The park was one of the few places in the area where the sound of the traffic, of trams and automobiles and lorries, did not intrude. At the water's edge, up against the sandstone wall, Emma lingered in the easy presence of something akin to silence. It was not until she was sitting on the wall that she realised how tired she was. As the full weight of her body pushed into the sandstone, she wondered whether she'd ever been so tired in her life. She spent the entire afternoon sitting, gazing at the water in the bay that was tinged brown after days of rain. She was not herself at all.

That evening, she ascended to her apartment—the family apartment—with no thought of food either for herself or for Mary Gilmore. She could not have stood and chatted to the writer, enquired after the woman's health and that of her son and husband, who were also in Queensland.

Emma had always been blessed with the ability to sleep deeply and well, and that Saturday night was no different. She was not a woman who had fanciful dreams only to be troubled by them during the day.

When the beating on her door came at 2 am Emma knew that this was no dream. As she knew her own name, she knew that the news that was coming to her would change the course of her life.

Before opening her door Emma covered herself in a deep red robe and swept her long brown hair up onto her head. She splashed cold water on her face but did not need waking. The policeman at her door was barely older than her son, than her George. As the man was slowly forming the words that would formally prepare her for bad news, she was making a silent bargain with God. 'Not my son, dear Lord, take anything but not my son.'

Emma's prayer, such that it was, was answered. The young policeman had come to tell her of the death of her husband the previous afternoon, on the banks of the Brisbane River.

Tears for a Lost Father

IF IT WEREN'T FOR a fistful of letters—four from Gus and one from his brother Mark—I might have invented Gus Monette. I might as well have, I thought, in the days and weeks after I had learned of his death.

I did not know how to mourn Gus. None of my friends or family had met him and I did not have even a single photograph of him. How could I have not taken a camera with me, that day we met in Toronto? It was only when I told Daddo about Gus' death—some weeks after I learned of it—and watched him cry like a small child that I realised I had not cried for my other father.

That Jackie and I had been adopted had never been a secret and the topic would arise in conversation with friends and strangers with surprising regularity. Now, when people asked me about my other parents, I would shrug awkwardly.

'Yes, I've met them both,' I would admit. People would always want to hear how it had gone and could never, or so it seemed, know enough to satisfy their curiosity.

After Gus had died this changed. I learned how to silence them. 'My father killed himself a year after we met.'

I found I could not speak these words with anything but glibness. I had always thought of myself as a capable person but I had no idea how to handle this tragedy. I did not know where to start.

Mark Monette had promised me some photos of his brother and I haunted the letter-box for them in vain. I had sent photos of myself—over which I had agonised—and I half expected to be accused of being an imposter. I would have liked, at the very least, to have been able to show my friends a photo of Gus, to have been able to prove that he had existed and that I really had known him. It's not that they doubted my word . . . it's that I doubted it myself.

Months after I had sent my photos to Canada I wrote to Mark again. He was my only connection with Gus and I trod cautiously; I did not want to lose him, too. I was writing to give him my new address—I was moving into a small flat in Darlinghurst that looked out at the towers of the city—and only in passing did I mention the photos. I was, of course, desperate for them.

My move from Lodge Road saddened Daddo. Why, he wondered, couldn't we all live together in the big house on the bay? Why indeed. Apart from the fact that I was in my late twenties and I wanted to live my writing life in private, I did not want to feel—as I did at Lodge Road—that I was somehow idle for sitting at a desk all day. Jackie and her husband Martin had lived in the flat in the bottom half of Daddo's house since they had been married four years earlier.

What's more, after eight months of living on opposite sides of the globe, Paul was moving to Australia. He had negotiated a transfer with the bank and would fix an arrival date the moment his visa came through. I still had trouble seeing ahead. Even days before his arrival I remember joking with Daddo. I told him I wasn't going to assemble Paul's clothing rail until he was in transit, just in case he changed his mind. Daddo's alarm made me think. Was Paul unreliable? The answer was no. Was I, then, paranoid?

Mark Monette eventually wrote back, thanking me for my photos. He said they made a small part of Gus' life more real for him. I did not think that by using the word 'small' he meant I was of little significance . . . but then perhaps he did.

He had said nothing about whether I looked like a Monette or not. He knew he owed me photographs but was, he said, having a difficult time with the loss of his brother. It was taking more effort than he had to deal with even organising something for me. He did tell me, however, that he was pleased to think of me as 'an extension' of his family.

During the months I waited to receive another letter from Canada, Paul arrived to live in Sydney and we chose a bigger flat for our life together. Moving gave me another excuse to write to Mark and nudge him about the promised photographs. This time I received no reply. It's fortunate that Paul and I moved so much during that period of our lives because in August 1996—nearly two years after Gus' death —I had a third excuse to write to Mark when we moved into a little house together. It was over a year since his last letter to me.

Why did I persevere when my doing so clearly caused both Mark and me pain? Perhaps because I did not know what to believe. I was clinging to the hope that one day, somehow, I would know my other father.

The silence from Canada was fuel for my paranoia. In my darkest moments I imagined that Gus Monette's life had been just fine until I appeared in it. The Monettes must have blamed me after all. They wanted to forget that I even existed.

Daddo, meanwhile, had been complaining of pain in his back for weeks and the weeks were now stretching into months. He was sleeping more and more. Christmas 1996 he sat at the dining table in a tight blue shirt, barely able to move because of the pain in his back. Even laughing seemed to hurt him. I have a photograph from that Christmas Day; he was wearing a yellow paper hat on his head and the smile on his face was clearly an attempt to hide the pain.

I was turning thirty in January 1997 and Daddo, Jackie and Paul were determined to mark the event. Despite Daddo's pain, which was not allayed by strong painkillers, they threw me a party at Lodge Road and fed and entertained forty of my friends. Daddo, his back stiff and his face held tight lest he grimaced, played the charming host. My publishing friends had not met him before and each of them commented on his kindness. They could not fail to note his devotion to his daughters. What a lovely man, they said, what a sweet, funny man. I was lucky. I had the most extraordinary father . . . who did I think I was, looking for another?

Jackie and I worked on Daddo doggedly. What did his doctor say about the pain in his back? Nothing much, Daddo would tell us. Daddo just wanted to sit it out, to wait for the pain to go away. We, his stroppy daughters, would have none of that. We arranged massages for him. They did not shift the pain. I found an Austrian acupuncturist for him and he agreed to give her a try. Once again, the pain did not budge.

Nobody said as much but I knew in my bones that he was very ill. Sometimes, late at night, I lay in bed sobbing. 'What?' Paul would ask. 'What is it?'

'It's Daddo,' I would say, 'I'm afraid of losing Daddo.'

Aliens

———•——•——

AFTER ERNST'S DEATH, Emma moved from the apartment she had shared with her husband and son for a decade. Despite the values of the time, she went to live with her 'two doctors', with Douglas Miller and Bruce Hall, in the block of flats optimistically named Del Rio. Years later, after Emma's own death, Douglas would write that she came to his apartment when she was recuperating from knee surgery. According to Douglas' widow, however, after Ernst 'went in the river' Emma went to Del Rio as a replacement for the bachelors' caretaker who had been drinking too much of the doctors' sherry. Each version of the story had its own shade of truth.

Douglas Miller's flat in Del Rio, on the waterfront at Elizabeth Bay, became Emma's refuge during the blackest period of her life. She had no assets, was legally barred from opening a restaurant in Sydney, her son was on the other side of the world and Ernst had done what he'd done.

The block of flats still stands; its Spanish hacienda style and its position there on the water must have made Emma feel quite elsewhere. Indeed, perhaps during this period she asked herself how she had managed with Ernst for quite so long.

Emma sent her niece, Leny Berchtold, the fare to travel from Switzerland to Australia. She wanted Leny to accompany George back home once he had completed his year at hotel school. Emma feared that the journey across the world alone—with all that time to contemplate his father's death—might have been more than her young son could endure.

Once her bright boy, George—now a young man—had been returned to her, Emma started to search in earnest for a new business venture. According to Douglas Miller's widow, it was a five-hundred-pound loan from her husband that enabled Emma to take the lease on what was then a somewhat dilapidated guest house in Bayswater Road called The Belvedere. Emma wished to run it as a private hotel where she would look after some 'nice people'. She envisaged serving only breakfast.

At the outbreak of the Second World War, all 'Alien Residents' were required to make themselves known. Daddo and Emma duly presented themselves at the Darlinghurst Police Station. At the National Archives I find the paperwork to prove it.

I see Daddo's alien registration form first. Stapled to the top right-hand corner is a mug shot of a young man in a suit jacket, a high-collared white shirt and a European-looking spotted tie. His hairline is already high up on his forehead, almost as high as his father's was. Gone is the cheeky grin that was so prevalent in photos of George as a small boy and in those of him as an older man, when he was my Daddo. In this photograph my young father looks knowing and world-weary for his twenty years and not so much as the hint of a smile plays on his lips. The photo is taken eighteen months after his father's death.

At the bottom of the form appear two sets of fingerprints; these are the fingers and thumbs from Daddo's right and left hands. Now that I no longer have his beautiful hands to hold in my own, I place my fingertips on the mark left by his young hands.

The photograph of Emma—a proud, handsome woman—is telling. In it she looks more dishevelled and out of sorts than I have ever seen her. Her dark hair is fixed to the top of her head in some manner but thick strands of it are loose. She is scowling into the camera; she does not look weary, she looks extremely annoyed. The print of her right hand clearly shows a scar; the trace of a knife or a razor.

I'm surprised to see that Emma made her application a month after George made his. My father, George, was eager to set things in train for his naturalisation. He was eager to prove that Australia was truly his home. He was ready to go to war.

My Grandfather, Gus

———✦———

I HAD LONG STOPPED looking out for letters from Canada when Mark Monette's arrived in April 1997. He had sent me a photo—it was the first thing I saw when I opened the envelope—but there were no people in it. Was this some sort of joke? In the photograph was an old boarded-up building of handsome proportions. It was buried in deep snow.

My last letter to him, Mark wrote, had sat on his desk for nearly seven months. He had not been able to answer it, he said, because of the ache in his heart. *The person who takes his own life dies only once,* he wrote. *For the survivors he dies a thousand times over. A-death-a-day for the rest of your life.*

Mark went on to tell me about the way his family was grieving. Things were not going well. His father, Gus senior, had suffered a couple of strokes in the last few months but *refuses to lie down and wait for the undertaker to fetch him.* Within a fortnight, however, Mark promised to deliver on his promise to me and send some photos of my own father, of my other father Gus.

Finally Mark got to the enclosed photograph. It was of the Teck-Hughes Gold Mine Assay Building and in the summer of 1973, he and Gus used to sit on its steps and speculate as to what they would do with it if they could ever afford to buy it. Now, Mark told me, he did own the building and hoped—one day—to convert it into a residence.

I still had no photo of Gus but I did have a photo of some steps on which he once sat.

It took Mark Monette a further four weeks to get the photos organised, to write accompanying explanations and to send them to me. I was not complaining, far from it. The envelope, when it arrived, was pleasantly heavy.

The accompanying text gave me the family history by numbers; Mark had placed each photograph on a sheet of paper, had given each a subtitle and date and had laminated them all. This was nothing if not a labour of love and I was taken aback. I had not dared hope for anything so special. It was nearly three years since Gus had died.

The first photograph was of my Canadian grandparents at around the time they first met and was dated 1942. They were in the prime of their youth. At some public venue—perhaps it was a fairground—they gleamed, dressed in their Sunday finest. She had dark hair in curls, a fine long figure and was squinting into the camera as though, perhaps, she could not quite permit herself to smile. There was nothing reserved about my strapping Canadian grandfather, about Gustave Etienne Monette. On his face was a dirty great grin. A square-jawed, extremely attractive man, Gustave Etienne's eyes were alight with joy.

Mark clarified a few things Gus had told me already. Their mother Anne, whom they all called Anchie, had been born to Ukrainian immigrant parents but her father, a high steel worker, died when she had been only eight. Her mother had raised her eight children herself, providing for them as best as she could by keeping a cow and chickens, gardening, and working on tobacco farms around the Niagara Peninsula in season. Apparently my Canadian grandmother had dreamed of an education, which she never received.

My Canadian grandfather, Gustave Etienne, had been raised around Ottawa and Gatineau in Quebec. Mark referred to his father as a Frenchman, said nothing of his indigenous blood but went on to tell me that Gus senior's father had been killed in action during the First World War. His mother had died when he was only fourteen. On his own, Gus senior had travelled to Ontario to find work. My Canadian grandparents—according to their eldest surviving son—met in Welland, Ontario on the Niagara Peninsula, courted and were married.

Shortly after my other father's birth in 1943, Gus senior developed tuberculosis and was institutionalised. These were hard years for the family and might have accounted for the marked difference between the image of baby Gus and that of the toddler Gus. In the baby photo Gus was enormous, large-headed, big-limbed, beefy and beaming . . . but a baby nonetheless. In the toddler photo his legs were skinny above his battered shoes and the expression on his face seemed to convey pain and a sense of injustice. Mark reckoned that as children they had been scrupulously well-groomed but 'bone-bloody-poor'.

A decade after Gus' birth things had clearly improved. Gus senior and junior stood together, well dressed in the snow. They had been photographed with Rusty the dog, to whom Gus junior is proudly attached by a rope. When my other father Gus was sixteen, he joined the sea cadets. The photo of Gus in his uniform—complete with sailor's hat—was one of Mark's personal favourites. Apparently the Navy had wanted Gus for officer training but my Canadian grandmother would not have a bar of it. *My mother didn't want this because she said the Navy would only teach him to drink, brawl and chase women. Little did she realize that that was his destiny, anyway.*

Mark told me, briefly, about his brother's first marriage to a woman who—except for marrying Gus—had been very, very smart. In the early seventies they had both taught school together in Kirkland Lake, where Mark now lived, but had left in 1975 because Gus had wished to attend law school. Separation and divorce had followed. Later Gus married one of his former high school students; she was fourteen years his junior.

The first photo Mark included of my other father as a man was as infuriatingly elusive as Gus was himself. It was a beautiful photograph of a tall, solidly built man beside a lake, walking away from the photographer towards the horizon. Taken by his first wife, the picture was labelled *Always Walking Away.*

Mark's description of his brother is the one I find myself borrowing regularly. *Gus was six-foot-two inches of bone and muscle.*

He had a brilliant mind, an agile body and a ready wit. He also had a self-destructive streak that ran through him from head to toe.

I was quite unprepared for the final photo; it was a serious, sombre Monette family portrait. It had been taken the year before Gus and I met and all the men were suited. Even Kate, my tattooed, tequila-drinking aunt, was wearing a jacket and appeared disconcertingly conservative. My natural father, Gus, looked almost as pleased with himself as he had the day we met in 1993. The photograph reminded me of something I had selectively forgotten; when I met him, Gus' hair had already been greying.

I loved Mark's physical descriptions of his brothers. Matthew, who had just turned forty-four, was *six-foot-six and about 260 pounds of muscle*. Mark's thoughts about Matt echoed Gus' own; Matt was brilliant but his mind was entirely wasted. He worked as a butcher and a truck driver, rode a Harley and hung out with bikers.

Richard, who had just turned forty, was also six-foot-six and powerfully built. *Women*, according to Mark, *find Richard irresistible*. Here I couldn't help raising an eyebrow; my uncle Richard looked disconcertingly like a younger, thinner version of Burt Reynolds. He was a criminal lawyer who had just written his first novel.

Other than the formality of the family portrait, there were two surprises for me. One of them was Kate. Gus had told me we were alike but for an adopted person there's nothing so strange, so wonderful, as finally laying eyes on somebody who truly looks like you. Most people take this physical evidence of 'connected-ness' to family members for granted, cannot even imagine life without it. When I showed Jackie the photo she glared at Kate, pointed a finger at her and said, simply, 'It's you!'.

Mark described Kate as a *BIG surprise* for his parents, but went on to dispel the myth—which had originated with Gus—that she was only a year older than me. She was, in fact, four years older than me. *Kate lives in New Orleans, teaches English part-time and does whatever comes along to survive.* Six feet tall, Kate had *a couple of great tattoos and enough life in her for ten people.*

The real unexpected was Gus senior, my natural grandfather. He did not look like me, nor I him. He looked like Daddo.

Gustave Etienne Monette looked, to me, like Daddo.

I managed to contain my excitement for only two weeks before firing off a long email to 'uncle' Mark. First I thanked him, profusely, then I asked him too many questions and finally, sheepishly, I told him I was sorry to bother him. I tried to say sensible things about the photographs, not to burble emotionally. What I wanted to proclaim, however, was not that I had an aunt who looked like me but how my other father's father and my Daddo, my real father, resembled each other. Gus senior literally shone from that photograph. I was eager to meet him. Did he, my Canadian grandfather, know about me?

Mark replied briefly to my email, saying only that he hated the medium. There were things he needed to tell me but he would do so in a letter.

I thought that sounded ominous. Would I be told that his parents hated the thought of me? Would I be told that they blamed me for what had happened to their beloved eldest child?

I waited an agonising week before the letter arrived. Mark was kind, gracious and funny. He told me he thought I had referred to his family as 'potty' and was struck by my insight. On second glance he had realised I had referred to the story he had spun for me as a 'potted family history'.

Mark's letter told me that nobody had had the nerve to tell his parents about me until he, Mark, had found out. As I had come into their lives, Mark wrote, Gus had been on his way out. This had not been the best of beginnings. My Canadian grandmother, Mark wrote, did not want to hear about me. She could not cope.

With Gus senior, whom I so wanted to call grandfather, things had been completely different. He had desperately missed his son— with whom he used to take *long boozy road trips*—and had had no problem knowing about me. *Had you ever arrived at the door he would have hugged you and welcomed you home. He was that kind of man.*

Something was wrong and before I had even read the words I was crying. It was the second death. Gus senior, my grandfather, Mark wrote, had died just a week before. He had been dying even as I had been studying the family portrait from which his face had shone with joy.

In the War

WE TOOK DADDO TO Canberra to celebrate his seventy-eighth birthday. Daddo, Jackie, her husband Martin, Paul and I drove south together and Daddo dozed in the sun. We checked into the elegant Canberra Hyatt and Daddo immediately grew animated. A combination of frugality, humility and an insider's knowledge of the industry had conspired to give Daddo an aversion to staying in fine hotels. But he was now clearly delighted to be spoiled in that way. Jackie and I watched him scrutinising the grand foyer and lounge of the art deco hotel. He took in every detail, his eyebrows raised quizzically. He approved. For Jackie and me this was a victory, because Daddo— veteran of the hospitality industry—found fault easily.

The bell boys wore plus-fours, loose trousers tucked into long socks. To one of the young men Daddo said, 'I like your poo catchers', referring to the trousers. He shot Jackie and me a wicked grin and giggled like a boy as he saw our surprise, then mock disapproval.

We had gone to Canberra for the War Memorial. Daddo had not been for many years and each one of us wished to experience the place with him. Daddo rarely spoke of his years fighting in the Pacific, in Borneo and New Guinea, and we were hungry for detail. Like every other traumatic experience in his life, when he touched upon it he would recount only the amusing parts; he extracted the smallest portion—that which was funny—from the rest that was relentlessly grim.

When we were children he had told Jackie and me about how they used to sleep in the trees in the jungle to avoid the insects, snakes and the ubiquitous mud. The boa constrictors, however, could still reach them in the trees. The enemy did not rate a mention in the war stories Daddo spun for Jackie and me; indeed, decades after the war he became a member of a Japanese–Australian friendship society and hosted young Japanese students at Lodge Road.

His cooking skills, he would tell us, had been in great demand and his recipe for shepherd's pie using layers of bully beef, baked beans and all manner of other tinned produce sounded like something I would have liked to taste. In the Army, he told us, he had learned to swear. Not that he ever swore in front of his daughters; indeed, Jackie and I would blink in surprise at Martin and his mates' stories of Daddo's expletives. They reckoned he liked to let loose, that even in his seventies he could still act like one of the blokes.

We would ask him about the real stuff of war, about death and injury. He had seen it all, we knew this, but he would not be drawn into conversation about it.

At the War Memorial in Canberra Daddo wore the thick purple jumper we had given him for his birthday and walked with a stick that he had been using sporadically since his back had started to hurt. The tools of war were clearly as familiar to him as the implements in his kitchen. While I had seen him holding an air rifle—once he had fired it into the sky several times, from the verandah at Lodge Road, because he reckoned some blokes in a dinghy had been up to no good—I could not imagine him at war. He had been in the Searchlights and rattled off the names of the planes for us. We walked among the displays of the First World War—past the photos and dioramas of Gallipoli—and Daddo shook his head, called them poor coots. He was talking about the soldiers. He knew where they had been, what they had experienced.

Eventually we came to a diorama of Balikpapan. The entire hillside, leading down to the bay, was in flames. The Allies had bombed the fuel tanks so the Japanese would not have access to them. Daddo stood in front of the display leaning on his stick. His eyes had filled with tears.

'It was like that when we landed,' he was staring at the scene with big, child's eyes. 'The water was thick with oil, some of the water was on fire. You had to jump out of the landing craft into that water and wade towards the burning shore. There were dead soldiers floating everywhere.'

Back at the hotel we retired to our respective rooms and later Daddo told us he had luxuriated in the enormous marble bath tub all afternoon and then had to struggle to haul himself out. We went out to a restaurant at which the young waitress became enchanted by Daddo—by his mischievous smile and by the many quips he'd practised on waiting staff over the years—and happily joined his banter. We were all a little tipsy and he was brimful of jokes, he was having a ball. The waitress came to take our orders and when she leaned forward to hear Daddo speak above the noise he planted a kiss on her cheek as though she had presented it to him for just that reason. They were both delighted.

When Daddo had mentioned his back pain to his specialist the doctor had been surprised only that Daddo had suffered in silence for months. Daddo had been seeing this specialist regularly since his prostate operation five years earlier, and the man had Daddo on hormone medication as a precaution, or so we understood. On learning of the back pain the specialist had booked Daddo in for a bone scan, telling him to return for the results. This was the news I feared. On the birthday trip to Canberra none of us mentioned the impending visit to the doctor and we celebrated him and his life in defiance.

After our meal we returned to the bar at the Canberra Hyatt and found ourselves a place on a comfortable sofa in front of an open fire in a grand hearth. Somehow my conversation with Daddo meandered towards the subject of children, the children I had yet to bear. Children, I might add, were not yet forecast in my relationship with Paul. Daddo told me with absolute certainty that I would be a wonderful mother. I, my voice reedy with sadness, said that I wanted my children to know him.

'I'll always be around,' Daddo told me, holding my hand. I could not help noting his careful choice of words.

GABY NAHER

The week after the Canberra trip Daddo and I went to see his specialist together. I could not say which one of us was supporting the other. Jackie was interstate on business and had left strict instructions about passing on information to her as soon as we had it. At the doctor's surgery Daddo presented the receptionist with a tablet of Swiss chocolate and as we waited he endeavoured to 'draw her out', as he put it. By the time we went in to see the doctor the receptionist's spirits had lifted and her mood was light and joyous. My palms were sweating.

With little ado the doctor informed us that the scans showed there were tumours all over Daddo's bones. His bones were spotted like a leopard's coat, he told us winningly, and Daddo and I forced a chuckle for his benefit. What did this mean? we asked, clinging to our ignorance. The prostate cancer had spread to Daddo's bones, it was the tumours on his bones that were causing the pain.

At the end of the consultation Daddo handed out yet more chocolate, a slab for the doctor and another for his 'good wife'.

We left the doctor's surgery with only a script for morphine and carefully avoided making eye contact until we were alone. In the hallway I held Daddo's arm protectively as we walked together. He shrugged, winked at me. I was fighting back tears.

'I could have been shot in the war,' Daddo quipped and I knew he was telling me that he had been fortunate.

Later, in conversations with Daddo's GP, we learned that he and the specialist had known that the cancer had spread to Daddo's bones all those years earlier, back when he had been operated on. The specialist had told Daddo that he had some spots on his bones. This news, however, had meant next to nothing to Daddo. Nobody had told him he had cancer, that was the main thing.

When the morphine made Daddo vomit and sent him spinning into a deep depression, Jackie phoned the specialist and demanded a prognosis. The man told her, brusquely, that he was trying to keep our father alive until Christmas. It was July. This was the first piece of critical information Jackie and I kept from Daddo.

The Gift of Chocolate

WE FORMED A HUDDLE. Daddo accepted. He never asked 'Why me?' nor 'How did this happen?'. He kept saying that he'd had a good life, that he could not complain.

'Are you afraid?' I would ask him. He would shake his head no. I told him he could talk about it with me—dying—if he wished. I insisted I was strong enough. There, at the real beginning of his illness, I had no idea how strong I would need to be.

We were concentrating on subduing Daddo's pain. Now it had been named, the pain in his back seemed so much fiercer. At times it wrapped its long, cold tendrils up around his neck and at other times it snapped down his legs. Getting in and out of chairs was difficult. Getting in and out of bed was excruciating. Climbing the steps—and there were many of them at Lodge Road—was a chore. Even getting in and out of the car was an operation that had to be performed with tremendous care and concentration.

Daddo did not do well on the morphine, even on a reduced dose, and he quickly lost his appetite and began to lose weight. He had used very few medicinal drugs in his life but now he rattled with drugs: morphine to stop the pain; Panadol to help the morphine stop the pain; hormones to stop the cancer spreading; Maxolon to stop the nausea; and Coloxil for constipation. Daddo was dropping weight and shrinking at once and his eyes seemed to be growing larger and larger. He would hold his hand up to his neck, just below his chin, and indicate that he was full up to there with drugs.

One of my colleagues came from a medical family and encouraged us to seek a second opinion, coached me on what we should expect from Daddo's doctors. Soon Daddo had commenced his first sequence of radiotherapy at St Vincent's Hospital and Jackie and I took it in turns to leave our offices during the day to collect him from home and drive him to the clinic. In the waiting room, despite his weakness and nausea, Daddo made an effort to engage the nurses and the other patients, to try to make them laugh. He did not have the strength to climb up onto the therapy table unaided. As I helped him undress for his treatment I could not help staring at the blue dots the doctor had drawn on his back. Those marks, a tattoo of sorts, denoted the places where the tumours on his bones were concentrated.

Back at Lodge Road Daddo vomited in the garden; he had never been a vomiter and was appalled. A close family friend came from Switzerland to help and now Daddo had a whole host of carers and unofficial nurses. True to his character, however, he hesitated to ask for a single thing. We struggled to come up with appetising meals and cranked out *Zuri Gschnatzlets*, *Bratwurst* and *Rösti* in the hope that these meals from Daddo's childhood and from The Belvedere boiler room would reawaken his interest in food. We took to eating in Daddo's bedroom; he sat in bed with a tray on his lap and the rest of us formed an audience around him, trays on our own laps. Bono—who had never been taught the difference between our food and his own—would walk between us, nudging the edge of our trays with his nose, determined, as always, to have his share. It was not only civilised, but quite jolly at times.

The day after we had received Daddo's prognosis, Jackie, Paul and I had gone shopping for two precious items. One was an electronic chair (the electric chair, as we would come to call it) which at the press of a button could lift Daddo almost to his feet. The other item was a small black tape recorder.

During those first days of shock, of aching, bewildering sadness, I would rise before dawn and work on my novel for an hour before driving across the Harbour Bridge to Lodge Road. I would spend about an hour with Daddo each day before I went to the office in which I was working as a literary agent. I had decided to interview him about his life, hoping that the experience would prove pleasurable. I was wrong. Daddo could not bear to be in the limelight or to speak about himself at any length and he literally squirmed in his electric chair as I waited for him to answer my questions. We had agreed that we'd let the answering machine pick up incoming calls but when the phone rang during our interview time Daddo would look at it beseechingly as though it was his salvation.

Despite my determination I soon bowed to Daddo's reluctance. Those were his precious days as much as they were mine; I had to keep reminding myself of this. Instead of spending time 'interviewing' Daddo in the mornings I occupied myself with simpler household tasks—folding linen, sorting kitchen cupboards—near his chair. As I pottered Daddo managed to share some memories with me but he was preoccupied by the present and the immediate future, not the past. He wanted everything to be just so, to be easy for me and for Jackie when he was gone.

Often the tape recorder remained untouched in my bag as the two of us just sat together in the morning sun. We watched the birds—rosellas and finches—in the jacaranda tree through one of the great east-facing windows.

In the office my colleagues were caring and gentle with me. As my absences for Daddo's treatments and for doctors' appointments grew more frequent others in the industry learned of my situation. Friends seemed to close ranks around me; I was surprised to feel soothed and protected. Yes, work continued, there were still demands and deadlines and too many brittle egos to manage, but there was comfort and support as well.

Daddo required more and more blocks of Swiss chocolate—Jackie worked as a lawyer for Nestlé and could easily oblige—and he rarely left a doctor's surgery or the clinic at St Vincent's without leaving chocolate behind. To my immediate colleagues he sent both chocolate and vodka. He was wretched if he could not 'do' for people.

Support, I found, came from unexpected places. After my first novel had been published—two years before Daddo's illness proper—he had phoned me one day and said, 'Your natural mother has just called. She asked for your address to send you some flowers and I gave it to her'. Simple as that. When I was two, as the story goes, and Jane had come to Lodge Road with flowers for me—masquerading as a florist—there had been heated discussion within the house as to what should be done if she ever came back. Daddo had said we should bring her in. He had felt that they should welcome her.

Gradually, after this second gift of flowers, Jane and I had formed a tentative friendship. As I got to know her I liked her more and more; she really was a reader and I took great pleasure in talking books, and the natural world, with her. I met my half-sister, Ella, who had just finished school and was training to become a nurse. Curiously I felt that she resembled my oldest friend—whom I loved dearly—more than myself. It was only once Daddo and Jackie had invited the two—my half-sister and my natural mother—to Lodge Road that things gradually became easier between us.

Now, during Daddo's illness, Jane proved herself a supportive listener and full of concern for me. She had grown fond of Daddo, as had Ella, and Jane now joined the team of drivers who took him in turn to St Vincent's for his radiotherapy.

Complications saw Daddo suddenly hospitalised and when I arrived at his bedside one evening he told me with evident pleasure that I would never guess who was nursing him. No, I could not guess. 'Your sister!' he announced, and he was clearly not speaking of Jackie. When Ella and I spoke later she told me that she could not bear to leave Daddo there 'all alone' at the end of each one of her shifts. My gratitude towards Jane and Ella is enormous.

A Monette!

WITH MY OTHER father's family I was facing a conundrum. They were mourning Gus, whom I was not sure I had ever known, and my Canadian grandfather, who had died within days of me having seen his face in a photograph. I was mourning Daddo, who was still alive.

Mark Monette had already given me his sister Kate's email address but it was she who wrote to me first. It was only a couple of weeks after her father's death.

Kate, my 'aunt' Kate in New Orleans, wrote and told me of the evening Gus had called to tell her I had contacted him. It had been an emotional conversation. He had asked Kate to accompany him to his meeting with me but had later decided to go alone.

He had told her, just like he'd told me, that I had her eyes and Jane's mouth.

He told me with pride of your accomplishments, Kate wrote, and I wondered which ones because he had never let on to me that he had been proud.

As to you writing, he said 'she's a Monette'. I read on with mixed emotions. Had I felt truly claimed as a Monette before, back when he was still alive, would it have made any difference?

As Mark did, Kate told me how her brother had wanted children and she too had her theories as to why it had never happened. She referred to his last months and in her economy with words her pain, and her brother's, revealed itself. While she was at peace with her father's death, Kate told me, she could not reconcile Gus'.

Of Gus senior she wrote, *He was a generous man and a great father. He spoiled me rotten. I am at peace with his death.* With my Canadian grandfather's warm, smiling face in my mind I once again thought of Daddo.

She asked me to write to Rick, to my uncle in Toronto. I hesitated, postponed and prevaricated. It was difficult to know what to say to the Monettes except what I had already said. I had wanted Gus in my life. I thought he was wonderful. I wished I had told him.

The Wish of a Dying Man

IN DECEMBER 1997, Paul and I moved to Lodge Road to care for Daddo. Jackie and Martin had decided that it was time to leave Daddo's house and be alone together; they had been living at Lodge Road for seven years. Clearly Daddo could not live alone—nor would we have wanted him to—and moving him from his home of so many years was out of the question.

We had discussed selling Lodge Road in the past; for some time Daddo had struggled to keep up with its maintenance. Indeed, Daddo had always been the one to instigate the conversation. None of us could imagine him, however, in a small, manageable house with a neat little garden. Try as we might, we could not see him, his towering statues, his great Belvedere furniture and his lion skin in a semi-detached cottage. Daddo's mind, if not his body, had grown accustomed to having space to roam, territory for dreaming.

His sleep had become increasingly disrupted and he would spend hours during the night staring out at the bay, gazing across at the opposite shore which he had watched change almost beyond recognition since his first glimpse of it. Without that view, that beloved landscape, his nights would have been interminable. At home he was a contented man.

Paul and I struggled to settle into our new life together; my energy was already torn between caring for Daddo and trying to keep up with my work and writing. I was afraid that if I stopped writing then I would never start again. All too well I could imagine the hole—after Daddo had left us—that writing might help to fill.

Something else had changed—in me—and I became fretful about my relationship with Paul. Watching Daddo slipping away had forced me to ask myself many questions. After years of wandering the world, with and without Paul, I wanted security and I wanted to be able to plan for the future. After years of denying that I ever would, suddenly I longed for my own family. I wanted children.

After three score years of work in the community his illness had forced Daddo, finally, to relinquish his voluntary duties for the three charities that had so occupied his time and energy. He remained a part of their worlds, however, receiving regular visits and phone calls from the men and women with whom he had served for so many years. Legacy refused his resignation; they insisted he remain 'on reserve' until he was well enough to return to them. At their monthly meetings they reported on his progress.

'The good news,' he told them, 'is that I'm still here. The bad news is that I'm no better.'

One Sunday morning he rose and left the house early. He was in a brief, energetic phase. He drove over to St Canice's in Elizabeth Bay, the church in which he had been married, where his daughters had been christened and at which both his mother and The Belvedere had been farewelled. With his fellow parishioners from his local church, he cooked breakfast for Kings Cross' homeless people and for the mob of bikers whom the church folk deemed it prudent not to turn away. None of them realised how ill he was and that was exactly the way he liked it.

One day I returned from work to find that Daddo had removed all the wrought iron hanging from the eaves around the front door for painting. He had been up and down a ladder all day and each of the wrought iron panels weighed a good five kilos. The following day he was immobilised with pain. Within weeks he was booked in for his second dose of radiotherapy.

Paul and I drifted from each other, or perhaps it was I who withdrew. All my emotional focus was on Daddo and I was running on nervous energy alone. Each day when I returned from the office I was fearful; would some awful, new medical crisis have arisen while I was away? From time to time Jackie and I discussed hiring a nurse, getting some outside help, but Daddo maintained he did not need it. He was still showering and dressing himself, most days, and on good days had the strength to negotiate the steps down to the kitchen alone. He and his 'old mate' Bono were all right together, they kept each other company. Daddo guarded his last semblance of independence fiercely.

He was planning. Daddo was watching, worrying and planning. In the evenings he would send his faithful dog to Paul. He would tell Paul he was special to Bono, that Bono waited for his return each evening. Daddo was looking out for both of them; he was making sure that even his old dog had somebody when he was gone.

Daddo fretted over my relationship with Paul. He simply could not understand why, after all of those years, we had not married. As well as he knew me, he could not understand it.

He had no regrets himself, he told me, or none to speak of. The only thing he wished he had done was to have bought that oft-imagined yacht and sailed, with his daughters, around Australia. Even at the most difficult times during Daddo's illness I was comforted to know that at its end, his life lacked only this one, mythical voyage.

Daddo longed for only one or two things during those long days in which he sat at home with his cancer. He did not seek miracle cures nor did he beg for relief from pain. He wanted his girls to be well provided for. Above all else, he wanted happiness for his daughters.

Letter to my Uncle

———◆◆◆◆———

Lodge Road
Cremorne NSW 2090

11th February 1998

Dear Rick,

During the course of our correspondence last year your sister Kate told me you'd like me to write to you. I'm sure you'll appreciate that it's a difficult thing to just sit down and write a letter to a stranger, albeit an uncle of sorts. It's taken me this long to recognise that I can't bear to be out of contact with the Monettes, so rather than exhausting Kate or Mark I'll try taking up the dialogue with you for a while.

I'm amazed at the circumstances that have prompted me to sit down and write to you today. Last night I attended the book launch of one of my clients—who also happens to be one of my closest friends—and after hours of dancing at a jazz club and at the author's apartment, nine of us went to a harbour beach for a swim. The moonlight made the water look silver and it felt silky against the skin. The beach is in the city but surrounded by a small pocket of national park and looks across the harbour towards the zoo (sometimes a tiger's roar can be heard floating across the water). When you swim out a certain distance and finally get a view to the west, past the headland, you get this sudden, magnificent vision of skyscrapers rising out of the water like towers of light. This is one of my favourite views in the world.

So I sit down to write to you on one and a half hours' sleep and with legs that ache to the bone from dancing (I'm a bit of a flamenco wannabee). Nothing makes me happier than spending an evening in the company of writers and winding down with a pre-dawn dip. Alas I'm one of the few who has to get up and straighten out and go to work in an office. I work as a literary agent by day and in the early hours of the morning I write fiction. This morning my writing time is going towards writing to you. I sent my new novel off to my agent last week and am officially in recovery for a while.

What happened to your novel? Mark mentioned it when he very kindly sent me a potted family history last year. It's brave of you to attempt a crime novel—I reckon this sort of genre fiction is the hardest to master when you're new to writing. Mark also sent a batch of photos and I'm now looking at a rather formal family portrait from 1992. With the exception of your lovely father you all look terribly serious; from what Gus told me about you, this is quite out of character.

There—I mentioned his name. Perhaps I can talk about him now? See, there's nobody here with whom I can discuss him. There's nobody here to whom I can express my disappointment and despair over never getting to know Gus or becoming close to him. When we met we were both so reserved, fiercely independent and eager to convey to the other the impression that we could both walk away essentially unchanged. You'd imagine the regret would dwindle over time, but it hasn't. You'd think that the 'if onlys' would quieten . . .

I'm sorry if this is painful for you. I can't have any sort of relationship with you or your siblings without Gus being a part of it. You know he tried to get you to come to lunch the day he and I met? I don't think he was going to give you any warning. He loved the idea of introducing his 26-year-old daughter to an unsuspecting brother. It was August 17th, 1993, and we met at the Hop and Grapes on the corner of College and Yonge. It was sweltering hot and I ordered a Bloody Mary and was embarrassed by the size of the glass and the tizzy umbrella hanging out of it. We had about five hours together. Not much at all, really.

I hope you will write back. If you don't, I'll assume I've offended you, upset you or worse. You'll point out my spelling errors as Gus did.

Gaby.

Counting Lights

———◆◆◆———

I WOKE IN THE dead of night on my old futon, the silent house looming above me, unfolding below me. I was thirty-one and I could not sleep. It seemed that I only relaxed when I was out drinking with my friends. Outside the only sound was that of the wind tugging at the leaves of the banana trees. If I waited long enough, one of Daddo's antique clocks would sound the wrong hour upstairs, or Bono would shake himself and change position noisily on his chair in the room above.

Careful not to disturb Paul, I rolled out of bed. I had taken to wearing flannelette pajamas to bed so I could rise and prowl the house without turning on lights to dress. I slipped into my woolly slippers and I crept towards the wall of windows which looked out onto the bay. The harbour was dark and the sky moonless. There was a light onboard one of the yachts and on the opposite shore a house leaked the dull blue blur of a television set. Otherwise, all was still. The sameness of that view, which it seemed I had always known, was reassuring.

I tiptoed back through the bedroom to the door that led to the rest of the house. I was painstakingly quiet but Paul stirred, mumbled anyway. 'Just going to check on Daddo,' I said, needlessly. In the dark stairwell I did not want to turn on the light to further disturb Paul but was mindful of the funnelweb spider we had caught there recently, lurking in its cold, damp corner. The stairs had been hacked into the sandstone slope on which the house was built after we'd moved in. Because of the constant flow of water down the hill to the harbour, the stairway was always damp, its walls forever weeping.

On the next floor I padded across the marble that had been taken from The Belvedere before the hotel had been razed. Bono was curled into a tight ball on his chair but groaned a little, mumbled to me in much the same way Paul had done. I stroked Bono's silky ears and he sighed. Once again I was comforted; all was well with the world.

Over the past year, since we had known of Daddo's illness, I had walked the length of the corridor into his bedroom with a keen sense of anticipation. Often this anticipation was imbued with dread. Tonight all was well, I repeated to myself as I glimpsed the blur that was me in the hall mirror. Outside the harbour was quiet. All was well.

I heard his strained breathing before I had entered the room proper. It was difficult to decide on a reaction: relief that there was breath or concern because it was strained. Daddo lay half in and half out of his electronic bed. His legs were on the floor and his torso was on the raised part of the bed. He had pulled up the quilt in a feeble attempt to warm himself. His eyes greeted me and it was as though he had been expecting me, it was as though I was right on time. It was 4 am.

'Daddo,' my voice was hoarse and I stated the obvious. 'You can't move.'

'I had to get up,' with his eyes he gestured towards the bottle on the chair by his bed.

'How long have you been like this?' I took one of his icy hands in mine and then the other. 'Why didn't you use the bell?'

'Not long, not long,' he lied, ignoring mention of the bell as he always ignored the bell itself. 'What are you doing up? You've become the ghost of Lodge Road.'

He had called me this before and when I took a step back I could see that I behaved like a ghost during that period. Floating around the house I was trying to anticipate Daddo's needs, his concerns, as he got on with the business of dying.

We talked about how best to get him back into the bed. He had grown so weak with the disease and the pain that at times he could not lift his legs the small distance from the floor to the mattress. I had no nursing training and my efforts to help him move were at best clumsy. I gritted my teeth against the pain I would cause him by moving him and I hauled both legs back into the bed. He huffed and panted and groaned. The pain was in his back—upper and lower—and now in both of his thighs where the tumours had taken hold in his once-strong femurs.

'This is a cow. I'm sorry to be a burden, darling,' he said, before he had properly caught his breath. 'Just leave me now, I'll be fine. Thanks darling. You're terrific.'

But I would not leave him, I could not. He was cold, bitterly cold, and far from comfortable in the bed. I rubbed his feet with my own cold hands. Found him a pair of blue, aunt-knitted woollen socks. I encouraged him to drink the apple juice or mineral water that sat by his bed day and night, straws drooping. He was thirsty, was always thirsty but increasingly afraid to drink for fear of having to get up too often. It was time for another dose of the slow-release morphine that kept him going, or didn't, depending on which way you looked at it.

Once he was settled, had taken his medicines and seemed warmer, I told myself that there was little more to do. I drew a chair to the bedside, got as close as I could. I held his left hand in mine, his fine man's hand, and I took comfort in its warmth, in the life I felt in it. We heard Bono's footsteps in the hallway before we saw him. The dog went straight to the bed and thrust his face under the covers at Daddo's side, waited to be stroked, fondled, told he was 'a good boofhead'. Then he came around to place his chin on my leg before flopping onto the carpet.

'Good old bummo,' Daddo smiled at the dog's single-minded pursuit of affection, comfort and food, not necessarily in that order. 'He's already been up here twice tonight. He made so much noise snuffling and scratching that I had to turn the television up loud to make him go away.'

From where I sat it looked as though there were tears in Daddo's eyes. There were tears in my eyes and I was afraid to speak because I knew my voice would shake. Jackie's sadness, and my own, upset him more than anything else. More than news that his condition had worsened and that he had to undergo further radiotherapy.

'You should go to bed, darling,' he squeezed my hand, smiled at me. 'You must be tired. You need some rest.'

'Oh, I'm wide awake now,' I tried a brave smile and felt my lips trembling. 'I'll stay with you for a while. We're both awake anyway. I like looking out at the bay at this time of night. It's so still, so peaceful.'

'I counted the lights tonight,' he swept his eyes across the opposite shore, Northbridge, and then towards Seaforth and Beauty Point. 'Six thousand five hundred and forty-something.'

We both shook our heads as though this number was somehow an impossibility.

'I started early but by the time I got halfway, people were going to bed and lights were being switched off left right and centre,' he winced as he shifted in the bed, remembered to smile, for me, once he had settled himself again. 'There were hardly any houses over there when we first arrived. Do you remember?'

I nodded non-committally. I was only a toddler when we moved from Kings Cross to Cremorne. I didn't remember the physical landscape too well but I remembered the emotional landscape. What I remembered was my parents shouting at each other in the same hallway I had just walked with such trepidation.

'Have you got a big day in the office tomorrow?' he wanted to know, and I could see he was getting tired, might sleep soon.

'Oh. No, not really,' I replied vaguely, because nothing seemed as big as this, as being here beside Daddo in the small hours of the morning when he could not sleep, when he was in pain. 'Jill's going away next week and it's always frantic beforehand. I've got a tough deal to manage . . . the usual.'

'And the new girl? How's she working out?' Daddo was at pains to give me the opportunity to discuss my worries.

'Oh, she's getting there,' I told him, but in my heart I knew that she was not. 'Should be ok.'

Daddo frowned. I looked down at the dog, stretched to pat him and he yawned as he rolled onto his back so I could rub his tummy. His tail thumped on the ground.

'He loves you.' Daddo's voice was the warmest thing on that cold night. 'He couldn't survive without you.'

'Good night Daddo,' I whispered and kissed him on his creased forehead. 'I love you.'

'Me too,' he smiled, closed his eyes.

I crept downstairs to lie in bed and sobbed, soundlessly, until sleep came.

Hero

RICK SAID IT WAS A shame that Gus had not tried harder to get him to our first meeting. Part of me was not so sure about this. I'd had only a few hours with my other father and the thought of sharing him with one of his siblings during that precious time was unthinkable and probably would have been then, too. Gus, Rick wrote, had frequented the pub in question back in the mid-1970s when he had been serving his lawyer's apprenticeship. During that time Rick had been at university and Gus used to drag him there when Rick was in town.

My uncle told me he was only eleven years old when I was born. He said he realised I was trying to paint a picture of a man I had hardly known and offered to share a few good memories with me each time he wrote. I marvelled, once again, at the generosity of Gus' siblings.

When Gus went away on his trip I would have been only nine or ten. We lived in a big old house on Young Street in Welland. I hardly knew him then due to the age difference and because he had, I think, already spent time away at university. When it was time to leave, he and a friend mounted up on a pair of 250cc Yamahas in our yard (a motorcycle so little I would be reluctant to cross town on it). I remember my father helping secure his gear with some red nylon rope, being careful to burn the ends so the nylon would not fray. My mother cried that day more than I had ever seen her cry—indeed, it is the only time I can recall her crying at all . . .

He was away for a year or so. He wrote my mother and father the most beautiful, descriptive letters about your country. I always looked forward to my mother reading them to me because they conveyed such powerful images. When he came home I was older, almost old enough that we could begin to be friends. I remember him unpacking his bag while we all sat around listening to his tales. He gave me a transistor radio he had bought somewhere along the line . . . I'm sure I could find it in my father's workshop if I went there and looked. At my age then, and for many years thereafter, he was larger than life. In many respects my hero.

The Indian Thing

—◆✦◆—

IN MY OTHER FATHER'S family—before he himself visited upon
them another, different, even more unspeakable darkness—there
was 'the Indian thing'. I ask and ask and ask until one of my
uncles, Rick, responds.

He tells me that he and Mark got their mother—my Canadian
grandmother—drunk once and confronted her with 'the Indian
thing'. Apparently Anchie had said, 'Of course your father's mom
was an Indian, don't you remember how red your aunts and uncles
were in Quebec?'.

Rick says that they had never noticed but could see what she
meant. He reckons his father never wanted to deal with it, had
only alluded that there were things about his mother and his
upbringing that were too shocking to tell.

Gus junior [my natural father] *was quite red when he got in the sun*,
Rick writes. *His looks were fairly Indian too. So, alas, were his drinking
habits . . . North American Indians cannot deal with whisky or hard
spirits. It's true after all these generations—I see it every day in the
criminal courts. Whenever my father or Gus drank hard liquor we would
say they were talking in tongues since their speech became garbled. They
would literally fall down and crawl around, too . . . If you are affected that
way by the hard stuff, that's probably why.*

Mixed in with my other father's Indian and French blood was
some from his Cossack mother. According to Rick, and to
stories Gus himself told, their mother's mother made ends meet by

bootlegging in the chicken shack behind her house.

When one of the girls I grew up with hears of my newfound genealogy, she says, yes, that's it, 'Gaby's always had an Indian look about her!'. While I think this comment is utterly ludicrous—my skin is pale and my hair is curly—I'm secretly delighted.

Kookaburra Dusk

———◆◆◆———

ON DADDO'S SEVENTY-NINTH birthday, he learned that he was to become a grandfather.

Jackie and Martin were expecting their first child. We had been out for lunch and returned home to eat cake. By the time the news had been delivered, toasted and duly celebrated, Daddo was exhausted. He sat in his electric chair, in which he had come to look tiny, and his lips seemed as red as his crimson cardigan. His skin was papery white.

When Jackie left I went upstairs to see if he needed anything. There were tears in his eyes that belied the festive red ribbon one of us had draped around his shoulders.

'Do you think I'll see the baby?' he asked me.

'There's a good chance,' I told him, and on that day I believed it.

The following weekend Jackie and Martin left for a friend's wedding on a Greek island. They would be gone for two weeks and when they returned Jackie would spend the remaining week of her holidays at Lodge Road. I could not tell what she was looking forward to more, the trip or her time with Daddo. When he had farewelled them, Daddo said, they had both been as excited as small children, despite Jackie's morning sickness which lingered into the afternoon.

Some small shift occurred in Daddo the week after Jackie's departure. In the mornings, if he was not feeling strong enough to go downstairs, I would bring the newspaper to his bed. He did not read it, not in his bed nor downstairs in his electric chair. Daddo had always been an avid reader of newspapers but suddenly he simply lost interest.

He was not idle, far from it. Each day he worked at his desk and the following morning handed me piles of letters to post. One day there were about fifteen letters to go.

I exhausted myself in an effort to interest him in food but was losing the battle. On Wednesday night I went to yoga after work and Paul cooked Daddo *Bratwurst*, which he always ate with gusto. When I returned the blokes—Daddo, Paul, Bono and Jackie's cat Oscar—were all lolling in Daddo's bedroom looking replete. Once again Daddo asked for news of my book; we were waiting to hear whether there would be offers from publishers for my second novel.

On Friday morning I persuaded him to come downstairs for breakfast but could not convince him to change out of his pajamas. All day in the office I was distracted; today was the publishers' deadline for offers on my novel but my mind kept drifting. Daddo, I felt, was fading . . . I left work early. On the way home I stopped to buy him a posh meat pie; I no longer had enough optimism to cook for him.

It was mid-winter and when I arrived home it was right on dusk. All was silent on the ground floor and I rushed upstairs to the bedroom. Daddo had just climbed into bed and the two of us sat together quietly to watch the beautiful purple dusk fading to night. When I presented him with the heated pie on a tray Daddo—who had always been a cook with boundless imagination—made big eyes at me and quipped that he had never eaten so many pies as since he'd been sick. We had overdone it with what used to be one of his best-loved treats.

On Saturday morning Daddo would neither get dressed and go downstairs nor eat. I cajoled him and eventually he agreed to rise and sit in the armchair by the bedroom window. I laid the newspaper on his lap but later it only fell to the floor, unread.

In many ways this was an ordinary day. During the course of his illness there had been days when Daddo had spent the entire day in bed. What was extraordinary, however, was that throughout the day Daddo's room was filled with a dazzling, white winter light.

I sat by the window in the glorious afternoon sunshine and ironed using Daddo's old Elna Press. Mostly Daddo dozed but as the ironing machine buzzed—I tried to release the heat before the timer sounded—Daddo smiled across at me. 'Don't worry about that, darling.' He asked me again for news of my book.

On Saturday night I gave him a truly appalling tinned chicken soup for dinner and he barely touched it. This meal was particularly unworthy of him but I was too tired and sad to think about cooking. Paul and I went out for pizza and throughout the meal I wept and wrung my hands. I could not alleviate Daddo's suffering and he—my hero—seemed to be dying before my very eyes. Was I the only one who noticed?

We arrived home and Daddo was once again stuck, half in and half out of his bed. When I eventually went downstairs to Paul I was sobbing again. We could not go on like this.

During the night I rose twice to ascend to the sick room, despite the fact that Daddo now had an intercom by his bed and had promised to use it if he needed me. At first light I was at his bedside again and again he was marooned, half in and half out of the bed. I couldn't work out whether he was barely conscious or groggy with pain. I was so distressed that my voice was hard and jagged when I asked him why he didn't use the intercom. As I lifted him back into bed, his legs a leaden weight, he started to heave and in the bucket his vomit was bloody. He was barely coherent. I smoothed Daddo's brow and tucked him in. He had trouble swallowing a drink and his medicine; eating was clearly out of the question.

My cousin Angela arrived unexpectedly to give Daddo Holy Communion she had brought from the local church. I felt bent double with responsibility and it was a relief to have someone else in the house.

When Daddo's GP arrived he sat quietly by the bed.

'I've really done it this time, haven't I?' Daddo joked, trying to make the man's job easier.

The doctor's parting words to Daddo, his patient of twenty-odd years, were, 'I wish there was more I could do for you, George'.

I led the doctor from the room and left Daddo alone. Downstairs we gathered for the verdict.

'This is it,' the doctor said. 'It could be days or weeks, but this is it.'

We had to get Jackie home, urgently, and the only question remaining was where and how to care for Daddo. I did not even need to think about it—Jackie and I had discussed it already—I was keeping him at home. We wanted him to die at home with his beloved bay just outside his window and with his devoted companions, the dog and Jackie's cat, there in attendance.

With the words 'This is it' ringing in my ears I went upstairs to talk to Daddo and to administer the dose of morphine the doctor had prescribed. I knew Daddo would ask and he did. He looked me in the eye.

'What did the doctor say?'

I looked him in the eye and replied, 'He told me I'm to keep you comfortable'.

I wondered whether this constituted a lie but Daddo had no trouble interpreting my words.

I ran down two flights of stairs and into the bathroom to howl. 'This is it, this is it.'

When I had exhausted my capacity to cry I washed my face and walked upstairs to make the terrible phone call. I tried to make myself as clear as possible to Jackie, but sobbed as I spoke. She could not or would not hear what I was saying. All the while she was telling me it would be all right, that she was coming straight home and that she would sort things out then.

I carried the phone into Daddo's room and he made a great effort to rouse himself. The first thing he wanted to know was how Jackie was feeling, how was her morning sickness? When he heard that she was coming home he said, 'I can't wait to see you'.

Downstairs Angela and Paul created a meal for us all—a better meal for Daddo than he had been offered by me in days—and upstairs I made a few more calls. I told Jackie's parents-in-law that she and Martin were coming home. Nina, Martin's mother and a trained nurse, offered her help. I—Daddo's daughter to the end—thanked her, told her I could cope. A tray appeared in the bedroom for Daddo and I was ushered downstairs to eat something myself. I left Paul by Daddo's bed, holding his hand and talking quietly to him about I don't know what. I like to imagine that Paul told Daddo he would look after me.

For a time the afternoon was peaceful again. I sat at the foot of Daddo's bed reading a manuscript, Paul was working outside somewhere and the cat and dog were curled up in the dazzling winter sun by their master's bed. As Daddo's breathing grew increasingly laboured I gave up all pretense of working and moved to sit at his bedside. I held my father's beautiful hand in mine and told him, again and again, that I loved him.

Throughout the course of Daddo's illness I had told him repeatedly that I loved him, I could not say it enough. I told him, again and again, what a wonderful father he had been to me. That afternoon I made a point of telling him not to worry about me. I told him he mustn't worry because I was strong and I could do what needed to be done. I was telling him that I would look after Jackie, and myself, too. I made a silent pledge with him, then and there, to do whatever I needed to do to give myself happiness. I was giving my father permission to die.

When Jackie's mother-in-law, Nina, arrived with a small posy of flowers and some home-made chicken soup I almost collapsed with relief. While I felt—somewhat naively—capable of dealing with the situation emotionally, technically I was at sea. Nina sat by Daddo's bed with a hand to his wrist, feeling his pulse. She chose her words carefully. 'We need to prepare ourselves,' she said.

Paul was somewhere nearby but I could not think of leaving Daddo's bedside to find him. I told Daddo, again and again, that I loved him. I told him that he was a star. I held his hand and kissed his fingers. The dazzling light of early winter filled the room. In the midst of my distress I wondered whether I had ever experienced such intense, exquisite winter's light.

Nina and I were watching Daddo's last breaths as Paul arrived carrying a huge basket of clean laundry. He was talking to me but I didn't know what he was saying and Nina hushed him. Paul assessed the scene quickly and said, 'But I was washing the car'.

Bono was the one who acted first, who knew, for certain, when Daddo had taken his last breath. The cat, true to his species, had by now disappeared. Bono heaved himself up off the carpet where he had been keeping vigil and nudged Daddo's limp right hand with his nose. Next he thrust his head right under the bedclothes and licked both of Daddo's feet. This done, he turned his back on us all and with his chin hanging to the ground went downstairs to his bed.

Paul and I sat on either side of Daddo's bed, holding his hands. 'I loved you, Georgie,' Paul whispered, but I had no words left.

Outside, the dusk—Daddo's last dusk—had nearly finished its pageant. From across the bay a flock of kookaburras burst into triumphant song and then another flock nearby answered it.

When I finally reached Jackie in the otherworld of the Greek islands I doubted my capacity to convey the news.

'How is he?' she asked.

'He's gone,' I told her. 'He's gone.'

I heard her scream and then her cries in the background. I had yet to tell her that his was a peaceful death, that somehow his leaving had been beautiful.

I kept my own vigil at my father's bedside, answering the phone and passing on the news while he was still lying there beside me. I would have liked him to stay there in his bed for one more night without pain and in peace. When they came to take him away, Paul, Bono and I followed Daddo from Lodge Road on foot in a slow, sad procession.

At dawn the next day we flew Daddo's flags at half-mast.

Mothering

⟡

THE DAY AFTER DADDO died, Paul and my oldest friend, Anna, do not let me out of their sight. Anna has brought over her baby, Eden, who is only two months old. The last time Edie and Anna came to the house Daddo had been sitting in his electric chair. He had held out his arms to the baby.

'I've been waiting for you,' he had told her simply. The two of them—the dying man and the newborn baby—had sat quietly together all afternoon. They seemed to inhabit the same peaceful place in the world.

All day flowers arrive. All day the phone rings. I am both numb and overwhelmed.

Just before dusk Jane arrives. She has cooked us a vat of minestrone and has brought us a loaf of bread. From her own garden she has collected flowers for me. She, Paul and I sit together outside the little kitchen; the bay is so close you feel you can almost reach out and touch it. From across the water the kookaburras take up their chorus and I cannot conceive of how a whole twenty-four hours has passed with Daddo no longer in my world.

I am grateful for Jane's presence at this moment. She hardly says a word and I know she hesitated, that she didn't know whether to come or not. The fact that she came means the world to me. I wonder whether this is mothering.

Pauline, when I called her the night before, seemed only angry. 'Why wasn't I told earlier?' she demanded. She had been told of

Daddo's illness . . . surely she did not expect an invitation to sit by his deathbed?

Faith

DURING THE DAYS after Daddo died I grow obsessed with the sky. The clouds seem to be putting on the most magnificent display for me and the bay on which we live is even more beautiful than it was before.

One day I'm walking Bono and look up at the sky. The sun has just disappeared behind the only small, wispy, almost bodiless patch of cloud. Instead of white cloud against blue sky I see red and blue colour on the cloud that reminds me of the way sun shines through a stained-glass window. I say 'Hello Daddo' without even thinking. I make a quick, silent promise to myself that I will always associate the play and colour of light with him. I think of the light refracting from the crystals of his chandelier, of the coloured lights he strung around the garden giving us girls a fantastical place of the imagination. And I think of the lights of the city, across the harbour, as we approached the Harbour Bridge from the north; we called it fairyland.

In the cold, dark nights directly following Daddo's death, sleep remains elusive. I wake in bed with a start and realise that there's no longer anyone to worry about; the house above me is quieter than it's ever been. Bono moved downstairs to be with Paul and me the night of Daddo's death.

I feel connected only to the dog and cannot even think of reaching out to try to bridge the gap that grew between Paul and me during the previous gruelling months.

On the second night without Daddo I lie in bed. I am fretful and find myself calling out to Daddo with my mind. In the early hours of the morning, well before the first dawn, I rise to sit with Bono and wait for the light. Night-time is no good for me; I cannot lose myself in activity.

I have been lying in bed, trying not to wake Paul, asking Daddo for a sign. I have been lying there thinking, 'If you're there Daddo, I have to know. Please show me you're ok.' He'd had enormous faith—and this contributed to his lack of fear—but I waver, I intellectualise, I doubt.

I have been trying to write Daddo's eulogy in my head as I lie sleepless in bed. The lines run through my mind easily, as though I have been rehearsing them for months. In a way I have. It seemed that as soon as I knew the nature of Daddo's illness I could already see the end. From the moment a bone scan was ordered I could already feel the chill of a time without him.

I need to know that he has forgiven me for the terrible meals I prepared for him in the days before he died. I need to know he was not hurt by my harsh words with him that Sunday morning over not using the intercom that was supposed to give me the peace of mind to sleep. I need to know that he understood I had been distressed, not angry, and that I could not bear to see him helpless and in pain. It torments me that I do not know how long he had been stuck on the edge of his bed. How many hours are there in a very cold, dark winter's dawn?

I go into my study and power up my computer. All the while I'm talking to Daddo in my head, asking for reassurance, asking for a sign. He had believed that he was going somewhere beautiful. I too wish to believe but I am just not sure.

I tiptoe downstairs to the small, cold kitchen to make myself a cup of tea and turn on the light. Out of the silence of the night comes a familiar sound. It is the Inclinator. I can hear the bottom Inclinator ascending from the waterfront. This is a comforting sound that I associate with Daddo, who used the lift between the house and the waterfront regularly. For just a moment it seems the most ordinary sound in the world until I remember that it's four o'clock on a dark winter's morning.

Even as I fumble to open the door, move outside and start calling out, I know that nobody is there. I look up and catch a glimpse of the carriage climbing to the very top of the track, where it stops on a level with the balcony. If there's somebody in the lift I'll hear the metallic clack of the gate but when the engine cuts out there is only silence. The hairs rise on the back of my neck and I run inside to shout to Paul and Bono.

Paul and I search the garden with torches. We are all spooked and Paul keeps asking me 'Are you sure? Are you sure?'. We move up to Daddo's part of the house, turn on the flame throwers—this is what he liked to call the lights—and I half expect to see him in the kitchen making himself a sandwich and pouring a beer.

I open the front door and almost fall over a floral arrangement on the front doorstep; it is from one of the two publishers who made offers for my novel the day before, the day after Daddo's death. The flowers have materialised there, on the doorstep, some time between 11 pm when we went to bed and four in the morning. Somehow their arrival seems stranger to me than the sound of the Inclinator in the dark of early morning.

In all the years we've lived at the house in Lodge Road I have never known an Inclinator to start by itself. To set them in train requires a good, strong yank on a thick cable and this is not the sort of thing that a possum or cat might achieve on a night-time patrol.

I trust my first instinct that associated the sound of the Inclinator with Daddo. Before he died a builder had been working down at the waterfront and it had frustrated Daddo that he had been too weak to go down and check the progress himself. It made perfect sense to me that he should be out surveying his domain one more time.

When the electrician comes that week I mention the bizarre Inclinator incident. The man has been servicing our Inclinator, and Inclinators all over Sydney, for decades. He was a good friend of Daddo's and the two would work together side by side. I ask him whether he has ever—in all his time working on these machines—known one to take off like that. He looks me in the eye but does not speak. He shakes his head no.

301

'Of course I thought it was Daddo playing a joke on me from the other side,' I try to make my voice sound light and amused.

'I wasn't going to say anything,' the electrician tells me, 'but as soon as you mentioned it I immediately thought "that was George".'

During that week—the first week that Daddo is gone from his home and from his daughters—I feel his presence keenly. The house is full of visitors, of well-wishers, of those who need to come and be in Daddo's space one more time, and I am exhausted. I escape into the garden to pull some weeds in peace. When I feel a gentle touch on the back of my neck I do not even turn around. I know there is no one there.

Beneath the Belvedere Bridge

My correspondence with the Monettes continues but something has shifted. I'm having trouble with the word 'father'. If Daddo was my father—and he was—then who was Gus Monette and how has he touched my life?

I have decided to take the leap; I'm going to write full time. I tell myself that if I don't do this now I never will, but the decision to leave my clients and publishing friends is painful and fraught. Watching my father die has made every moment precious. If I owe him anything it's to live by this lesson. I feel an overwhelming urge to get on with it, with my life.

I am true to my word, true to the promise I made to Daddo on his deathbed. I decide what I really want: writing and a family of my own. Paul and I drift further apart and there is so little intimacy now that talking commitment seems ludicrous. I need the space to mourn in my own time. We separate twice—both utterly miserable—before we come together again. We drive south down the coast for a weekend together. At dusk Paul proposes and before me a host of insects floats on the warm evening air, coloured light reflecting off their shining wings. I have no doubt whatsoever that Daddo has had a hand in it.

Without Daddo there Lodge Road's magic quickly fades and Paul and I decide it's time to make a home for ourselves. Indeed, Lodge Road, even with us living in it, has become so empty that the possums who have lived in the roof all those years gradually colonise first Daddo's bedroom and then the house's ground floor, both of which Bono and I determinedly avoid.

Paul, Bono and I move to a tall house in the inner city, around the corner from Daddo's old school in Darlinghurst. From our bedroom a wall of windows looks onto the towers of light that comprise the city; from the roof terrace we can see a single shell of the Opera House and one-eighth of the Harbour Bridge's span. Bono, formerly salty Middle Harbour dog and king of his street, transforms himself; within months he is a café hound with a broad local network of canine and human admirers.

On the night before Paul and I are to marry—it is May 1999—I am in the office until late, closing my final deal as a literary agent. Bono has turned agency assistant and mascot in his old age and has been at the canine beauty salon in the morning for his role as best dog at the wedding. When we leave the office for the last time the whole world is changing and the business has been sold. At home I gather my bridal clobber and walk down Darlinghurst Road to my friend's place at the Cross; I will be sequestered there for the night.

Mandy lives in a block of flats at the top of William Street—it was once the tallest building there—and this is where I am to spend my last night as a daughter. The neon sign advertising Penfolds Wine that glowed gold up at the Cross in my grandparents' day has long since been replaced with the candy red of Coca-Cola. My friend lives in the building into which Daddo, Emma and Ernst moved when they first arrived in Australia. It is the same building in which they fostered so much hope for their future, in which they wove the dreams that would become their lives in their new land.

We sit on Mandy's balcony, looking at the view that so absorbed Daddo when he was a boy. Woolloomooloo Bay, the Harbour Bridge and Mrs Macquarie's Chair are all there in their places but the lights that surround them, adorn them, have multiplied tenfold. I cannot imagine even the most ambitious of eight-year-old boys setting out to count them. The traffic hum is constant.

I have listened already to the counsel of wise women—talk of love, passion and commitment—and do so again, now. Here in this building, looking out at the harbour, I find myself listening, also, for the counsel of my ancestors. As I turn and turn again in the unfamiliar bed, I imagine the voices of Emma and of her young son George. They're whispering in the night so as not to disturb Ernst at his typewriter; they're planning a future of which I will be a part.

Eleven months after Daddo died I walk across Rushcutter's Bay Park to be married. Beside me are my sister, Jackie, and my friend, Mandy. In the absence of Daddo I can think of nobody more fitting to usher me towards a new life. By the water, under the melaleuca trees, Paul and Bono wait together with our friends; groom and best dog. Paul gleams; he wears a purple tie and shirt beneath his deep blue suit. Bono has a garland of purple flowers around his neck. During the simple ceremony Bono strains on his lead; he wants to stand right there with Paul and me, to dance on his hind legs between us and proclaim his joy. We all drink a glass of champagne beside the darkening water and the purple clouds of dusk begin to growl with thunder. As we race for the cars rain slashes the harbour and lightning strikes.

A fortnight later, we attend a service of blessing for our marriage arranged by Paul's father in the chapel at Jesus College in Cambridge. After the service we all gather for a drink in the Fellows' Garden beneath the boughs of the ancient plane tree. Soon the late spring sky darkens with purple clouds and similarly erupts the moment we've finished our drinks. I take this dramatic display as an excellent omen.

Lodge Road is behind us now, the house brimming with ghosts and far too big for us. Yet, each morning when we take Bono down to Rushcutter's Bay Park for his walk, we cross the Belvedere Bridge together. It's an ugly concrete structure, named for Daddo's hotel, but it clearly holds something special for Bono; each time he's on it he nudges Paul and me in the thigh and turns repeatedly to lick our hands. It spans the site on which The Belvedere once stood. On its northern side are a couple of Moreton Bay fig trees and a flame tree which once stood in the hotel's front garden and on the southern side is a brace of peppercorn trees that was out back. Perhaps around the Belvedere Bridge Bono can smell the scent of the dogs in his line. Is he, while on the bridge, tormented by the collective memory of all the Naher dogs?

In my collection of precious photographs I find a shot of Daddo, of my nanna, Emma, and of Winston. It is a small, sepia image. It's post-war, I can tell by Daddo's hairline. His forehead is much broader here than in the images of him as a soldier. A small white bulldog with caramel spots on its back is snuffling in the foreground; this is Winston. Daddo has the demeanour of a young, healthy man. He stands with his hands on his hips and his right foot in its brown, lace-up shoe rests on Winston's back. The small dog is a footstool on which Daddo can display his polished shoe. Winston, apparently used to such antics, is not distracted from the scent he is tracking. Daddo grins for the camera but Emma looks down at the dog as if to say, 'What you must suffer'.

Daddo wears dark, wide-legged, pinstripe trousers and from the outline of his thigh, where it pushes against the trousers' wool, it is clear that he has strong, well-muscled legs. His bright, white shirt is rolled to the elbows and you can see a crease down the front where it was folded after ironing. His forearm is muscular too and there's a large vein visible under the skin running from elbow to wrist. His arms, hands and forehead do not yet have the sunspots that he'll take with him to his grave.

Emma, by contrast, is plump and somehow earthbound. She too has strong arms and good, square, worker's hands. Her soft grey hair curls like her son's and her hairline is only marginally lower than his own. The son is all dazzling promise and the mother is there behind him, soft yet solid, ready to back him in all he undertakes. She has lost one of her men and is not prepared to lose another.

In the background is the leafy bower of a peppercorn tree. It is one of the peppercorn trees that Paul, Bono and I pass each morning on the way to the park.

I feel I have come full circle. I have seen my father out, having nursed him in his last days. Now I walk the streets he walked as a child and learn of the world he knew then. I try to take the example of his life, so fully lived, and apply it to my own. I need to know how Daddo—the world's most exceptional father—was fathered.

Beside the Brisbane River

───◆◆◆───

IN MY FAMILY, death does not go unsung. We believe in sending out our own in style, with verve and an eye to posterity. The three large photo albums bulging with pictures and ephemera from my nanna Emma's funeral is a testament to this fact. Numerous photographs of the service itself and the open casket with her in it were sent out to friends as mementos. This great weight of documentation on her death is a tangible proof to me that she existed. My three-year-old's memories of her are scant, indeed, the portrait of her I have created is based on the loving recollections of her son.

In arranging Daddo's funeral, Jackie and I were determined that he, too, should be feted. A friend took dozens of photographs for us at the church but it takes me many months before I can face them, along with all the cards of condolence, to place them in some sequence for posterity. Now there are two hefty albums alongside Emma's commemorating the event of Daddo's passing. One day his grandchildren will study them and ponder the sort of man he was. They will know, as Jackie and I knew with our nanna, how deeply he was loved and how profoundly he was mourned.

In the house in Darlinghurst I finally begin to trawl through the family archives in earnest. At Lodge Road the sheer volume of family ephemera that we had to handle when emptying the house left neither time nor emotional space for their contemplation.

I endeavour to sort the thousands of family photographs—some dating back to the days of Daddo's early childhood in

Switzerland—and keep giving up, returning them to dusty boxes and their chaos. I cull paper from the files that had already been culled before quitting the family home and my eyes still fill with tears at the sight of Daddo's handwriting, at his careful notes on letters and leaflets and scraps of paper.

I am searching for something but I'm not sure what. Perhaps it's the story within the story that every writer seeks. I make phone calls to family friends and write letters to Switzerland requesting information, trying to create some cohesive narrative that will comprise a family history. I am bothered by an absence, a sad, eerie absence. I continue to quiz people, at first hesitantly and then with more imperative. I find myself haunted by the undoc-umented man. There are neither funeral albums nor condolence cards for my grandfather, Ernst.

At Rookwood, mother and son—Emma and George—lie together in the same grave. On both their tombstones the word 'love' appears. I have no idea where to find my grandfather's resting place. I am comforted by the ritual surrounding death, by the careful gestures choreographed to honour the one who has gone. What I am unsettled by, however, is silence surrounding death.

In a damp file of Daddo's marked 'Family Ernest Naher', I find a crumpled slip of paper with familiar handwriting on it. It reads 'Mr Ernest Naher, Brisbane Crematorium, Mt Thompson, 8 March 1938', followed by a series of reference numbers. This page is pinned to a note on letterhead from the Brisbane Crematorium confirming that the remains of my grandfather were cremated there on 8 March 1938. From the look of Daddo's handwriting and the fact that the ink has barely faded I guess that he made this note during my own lifetime. I can only assume that it was after his mother's death.

I have a powerful sense of a continuum. I can easily imagine Daddo trying to make sense of Emma's archives after her death just as I am now trying to make sense of his. I can see him in his office at Lodge Road; it was the winter of 1971 and Emma had already been gone for a year. George and Pauline were trying to come to terms with living on their own, without the noise and distraction of the hotel community around them.

Through a series of phone calls to the Brisbane Crematorium and to Rookwood Cemetery, I discover that the reference numbers written in Daddo's hand on the crumpled page relate to the site of my grandfather's ashes at Rookwood. He's not in the Catholic Lawn Cemetery, where his wife and son lie, but beneath a tree near the crematorium.

A year after Daddo's death, during the winter of 1999, Paul and I travel to Brisbane together. I have a couple of media interviews to promote my second novel, which is just about to be published. Paul has some work for the bank. The view from our room is dominated by the slow brown waters of the Brisbane River and on the opposite shore the cliffs are dotted with climbers. In the morning I run along the riverbank on a path that takes me through mangroves and over sucking, slurping mud. I am accustomed to the blue-green waters of Sydney Harbour and this dark, muddy river fills me with melancholy. In places the riverbank is bleak and disused, small wastelands among the lush exotic gardens and bright glass towers.

Between interviews, I go to have lunch with another writer who was once one of my teachers. We sit by the river and talk writing, reading and, inevitably, memoir. I tell her that part of my own family history unfolded in Brisbane and repeat that my grandfather died in the Brisbane River. I am compelled, after all of these years, to learn the truth about his death and have arranged to pick up a copy of his death certificate. I confess that I expect to be disappointed. The circumstances of Ernst's death could never be as intriguing as the mystery that's been woven around it.

By the time I reach the Registry of Births, Deaths and Marriages it's just before closing and I've only minutes in which to pick up the certificate and get to my radio interview. I walk straight up to the counter in the quiet, air-conditioned room; after all these years my grandfather's skeleton will be exposed so bureaucratically.

I can barely look at the clerk or sign my name for collection of the certificate, so great is my need to read it. Before I even leave the counter I sneak a look at the page. The words that catch my eye are 'Cut Throat' and, below it, 'Haemorrhage'.

I take the certificate across the room and sit on a low bench by the window. My grandfather died on 5 March 1938, at North Quay on the Brisbane River. It's the same bleak stretch of riverank along which I ran in the morning. I shiver and wrap my arms around myself; inadvertently one of my hands has crept up to my bare throat.

This time I read it properly. I read carefully the words 'Cause of death', followed by the words 'Cut Throat' and 'Haemorrhage', which get two separate lines as though the two things are unrelated. I learn, also, that an inquest was held by the Coroner.

I stumble down the hill towards the river to the brightly lit office of the radio station. I'm startled to find myself in commercial radioland and am ushered into the studio brusquely. There's no time for small talk with my interviewer and he reads a blurb that comes straight from the publisher's press release. His tone is upbeat yet he wants to discuss the suicide I've written about in my novel.

The most direct way back to the hotel is along the riverbank. Faced with the sucking, spiralling brown waters I am overcome by an urge to hurl armloads of flowers. I want to mark my grandfather's death; I'd like to pay him tribute.

Sitting by the window in the hotel room, waiting for Paul, I pull out the certificate once again. It says my great-grandfather, Ernst's father, was a 'Book Printer' and I am unnerved by the way this small error about his occupation overlaps with my own life.

I'm dying for a drink but wait, staring out at the Brisbane River, now more than ever reluctant to drink alone. Before me is my grandfather's death certificate. I remember Daddo's words, that his father and I would have got on well.

The Baby Factory Revisited

WHEN I SPEAK TO JANE—years after our first meeting—about the place I call 'the baby factory', I learn that what I had thought were the facts concerning her stay there were wholly my own assumptions, nothing more. Contrary to what I had believed, her role at the baby's home was not to care for the newborn who were waiting to go to their adoptive families. She had been stationed in the kitchen.

Perhaps I—the surrendered child—wished to see my mother punished? Other women in her position had had to do it, look after the other babies, so why not she?

We are at her house on the Cudgegong River in Mudgee, drinking red wine late into the night. Bono and I have come to stay; I with a whole list of questions that I have wanted answered for years. I want to understand what she went through with me and, perhaps, to begin to understand how she felt. We talk on, into the evening, but I cannot ask and cannot ask.

I talk around the subject. One of us alludes to the awkwardness of our first meeting. I explain I had always believed that she had not wanted me, but that my mysterious, French Canadian father had.

I have never seen Jane angry before but she looks it now. She out and out rejects the notion that he, Gus, had wanted me, but she says nothing about having wanted me herself.

One day I hope that I will understand.

Now Jane, at times, shows me the concern of a mother towards a daughter. Now—even though we both remain hesitant and just a little unsure—I have learned to depend on her quiet support.

I have also come to tell her that I'm planning a trip to Canada.

'Will you see the Monettes?' she asks.

'I'm going *to* see the Monettes,' I reply. Has this hurt her? I cannot tell. Later, when I'm on the other side of the world and about to fly to Toronto, I receive a letter from Jane. She has written to wish me luck on my journey and courage for the meeting.

Lack of Everything

————◆◆◆————

THE FIRST TIME I SEE my grandfather's elegant handwriting, of which I know he was proud, is in the copy of his suicide note that I receive from the archives of the Queensland Coroner's Office. The envelope is addressed to the Superintendent of Police (*opp. Town Hall*) and the accompanying letter is dated 4 March 1938. The stationery is from the People's Palace Hotel, cnr Edward and Anne Streets, Brisbane.

Dear Sir,

My name is Ernest Naher born the 9/12/89. St Gallen. I'm married. My wife is in Sydney. Mrs Naher, 99 Darlinghurst Road, Kings Cross, Sydney.

I will shortly kill myself with my razor. <u>Reason</u>, lack of everything. If suitable you can use my body for anatomy researches. All my assets and debts go to my wife.

Two suitcases which are still at the People's Palace should be sent to my wife as well as the one you'll find with me.

I'm very sorry for the trouble.

Ernest Naher

In the Brisbane River

My GRANDFATHER ERNST sat on the riverbank beside his little port. It was 5 March 1938, and the weather still warm. Early on Saturday afternoon, the river was busy with boats; he hadn't expected that. He could have chosen a stretch of mangroves, could have sat among them in solitude, but he did not like the idea of being caught between their buttress roots, afterwards, in the sucking mud. He longed to float free as he had in the Aare in Bern. He imagined floating away on the long journey down-river that would take him to the sea.

Ernst sat very still on the brownish grass, his knees drawn up under his chin. Dressed in one of his fine three-piece suits—he'd had his wife send them to him earlier in the week—he laid his hat on the port beside him. Downstream cars crossed the bridge, the revving of engines shattering any semblance of riverside idyll.

A fisherman, on his way to the Bishop Island Pontoon with his crab net, greeted Ernst but received no reply. Ernst had determined to wait until the river was quiet but had not anticipated sitting there in the sun for hours while half of Brisbane—or so it seemed—strolled on the riverbank or cruised by. He had chosen the spot because at first glance it had appeared derelict and unused.

The sun was no longer high in the sky but Ernst could not make a guess at the time. In Brisbane the day lingered on and on and he had removed his grandfather's pocket-watch from his waistcoat and left it with his bags at the hotel two days earlier. His very bones ached from sitting motionless for so long and he was thirsty as a dog. He rose to his feet. The riverbank was finally free of strolling women, of skipping children.

Ernst removed a leather case from his breast pocket and laid it on the port beside his hat. When he took off his jacket he folded it carefully, lapel to lapel, before laying it on the port with the other things. Next he removed his waistcoat and placed it atop his jacket. He had to crouch down to untie his shoes as he would not lift them onto the port and risk dirtying his jacket and waistcoat. When both shoes and socks were removed and placed carefully side by side, Ernst squinted down at his pale feet; it had been months since he'd been swimming and they were a luminous white.

Trousers, shirt and vest were removed quickly and efficiently, once Ernst had checked the riverbank again for anyone who might be offended. With a steady hand he took his razor from its leather case, repositioned the case on top of the port and turned towards the river. In his white underpants Ernst walked to the low stone wall that separated water from land. He kept his face absolutely blank.

He sat on the stone wall with his feet dangling over the brown water of the river for some time. Ernst had forced thoughts of his wife and son from his mind hours ago and now there was just an emptiness; a true lack of everything.

The motor boat *Cynthia* was tied to Crouch's Landing but Ernst could not associate its name with that of a woman, with anything human. With his eyes he followed the progress of a man on a passing boat until the vessel had moved beyond Crouch's Landing. He was willing the man and his vessel away, willing a few moments of solitude so he could act.

The steel of the razor was warming in Ernst's hand and he studied the blade carefully. He had sharpened it before he had left the hotel. All he could think of now was what a relief it would be to be floating down the river in the cool water with this dreadful business over.

Mr Wilson, aboard the *Cynthia*, was the first to see Ernst in the river and he called out—to nobody in particular—that there was someone in the water. There was a man in the river.

Francis Williams was by now returning from the Bishop Island Pontoon having tied up his crab nets and taken tea. When he first saw Ernst in the river he noticed nothing unusual and took the red about his chest to be a red bathing costume. On closer inspection he realised that the red was blood and that Ernst's throat was cut. Ernst was floating right in front of where Williams had previously greeted the man who had been sitting by the port.

A third man, Theodore Trevethan, was now tying his boat to Crouch's Landing and had been alerted about the man in the river by Wilson's cry. He climbed onto the *Cynthia* from where he could see Ernst floating down-river towards Victoria Bridge. He noted that the man was not actually swimming but was just moving his arms and keeping his head above water.

Wilson then threw out a life buoy from the *Cynthia* and Ernst hesitated for only a moment before grabbing it with his right arm.

The men hauled Ernst towards the *Cynthia* and Wilson asked him what was wrong. Ernst—who never suffered fools—only groaned. The two men eventually dragged Ernst up onto the *Cynthia*, despite his profuse bleeding that would stain the timber deck. Before they had him out of the water he had lost consciousness.

Theodore Ferris Trevethan and Francis Ladner Williams both gave full statements to the Coroner, as did a policeman who said that Ernst's throat was cut 'practically from ear to ear' and who noted that the man had died only as the ambulance arrived.

In Emma's lengthy statement she was obliged to outline details of her husband's life insurance policies—one taken as recently as three years earlier—that totalled over 2000 pounds. Surely he had known that they would not have been paid out in the event of suicide?

Emma offered a more specific reason for her husband's suicide than the one he had given himself: 'business worries and his continual drinking habits'. He had, she said, given her no indication that he had been contemplating such an act.

Walter Magnus, who accompanied Emma to Brisbane to identify her husband's body, said he recalled my grandparents living together quite happily and did not remember having heard them argue. He did, however, claim that Ernst's new business partner—the former Café Claremont waitress—had given him trouble. One day she had, allegedly, gone 'hysterical' and thrown Ernst out, blackening both of his eyes.

The Coroner's report states that Ernst left the People's Palace on the morning of March 3, paying his board in full, leaving his two bags at reception and telling a Miss Black that he would return. Nobody could trace Ernst's movements—over the course of two whole days—between his leaving the hotel and appearing on the riverbank. Those two days remain lost to us and foreshadow the greater loss.

I read of my grandfather's death—which his suicide note explains not at all—and most of my questions about him remain unanswered. Daddo, however, falls into sharp focus. I can see him crying at the news of Gus' death as clearly as if that lunch following our visit to the Art Gallery had happened only moments ago. I can still hear his words: 'How could he choose not to be part of your life?'. Perhaps Daddo had felt shame—as I did over Gus—because his own father had not deemed him worth living for. I think of Ernst's motive, 'Lack of everything', and will Emma to have kept the suicide note from her son.

Despite the fascination I've always felt for Ernst—whose intellectual endeavours were looked on with suspicion by his toiling wife and son—he remained a cool, distant figure. Knowing the details of his last moments has removed that distance in a way that studying numerous photos and anecdotes has not.

What moves me, when I first read the Coroner's report, is my grandfather's dignity. There is dignity in the measured, polite tone of his suicide note and a gentlemanly concern for the strangers on whom his actions would impact. He apologises to the police superintendent for the inconvenience he knows he will cause but forgets the trauma of the poor sods who will drag him from the river. Perhaps he imagined he'd float out to sea and away, just disappear? There is also dignity in his last hours on the riverbank, during which he sat by his port in his fine suit, his hat laid carefully beside him. When he deemed it time to act he removed his clothes with care and left them neatly folded. A man of my grandfather's values would not have dreamed of ruining such a fine suit, nor would he have wanted to give anybody the trouble of cleaning it.

What lingers is the image of Ernst sitting on the riverbank with his chin resting on his knees like a boy. This is the talented horseman, the linguist, the *mâitre d'hôtel* whose restaurant once passed through five European countries in a day. This is the man who would have so liked me . . . this is my grandfather.

My Canadian Grandmother

In July 2000 I fly from London, England, to Toronto alone. Jackie, Freya and I have visited Switzerland—the country Daddo held as an example for us right to the end—and we have walked the streets of Dublin together. Paul is back in Sydney with Bono. Each day he cycles home from the bank at midday to have lunch with our old dog who is unaccustomed to solitude.

Long before I decided to place the story of my other father alongside that of my father and grandfather, I realised that if I was going to meet the Monettes it must be soon or never. How easy it would have been to let go of them, to return my other father to his mythic status. My delay has meant that not only have I missed meeting my Canadian grandfather—the only one of four grandfathers whose life span coincided with my own—but I have missed 'uncle' Matt too. Matthew, the third of the Monette brothers, died two months before my scheduled visit.

On the flight from Heathrow I am sat next to a Glaswegian nuclear physicist. I have moved from my window seat to accommodate a mother and child and the flight attendants, in their gratitude, shower attention and booze on me. The Glaswegian physicist thinks he has it made; he thinks we're going to drink our way across the Atlantic. I am sorely tempted.

We descend onto Canadian soil through cloud so thick that at times I cannot see the aeroplane's wing and I have a strong sense of not having any idea what I'm getting myself into. As we taxi along the runway I look out into the fog and driving rain and contemplate turning around when I reach the terminal and taking the next flight back to London. It has occurred to me, on more than one occasion, that I might learn things on this trip that I do not wish to know.

I exit customs, scrutinising the gathered faces for someone looking for—or looking like—me. I follow the other passengers right through the crowd until I spot Rick Monette. He's not pressed up against the rails in the arrivals hall like the others awaiting friends and family. No, Rick Monette—tall, tanned, broad-shouldered, with almond-shaped eyes and a high forehead just like my own—is standing well back. We recognise each other instantly, embrace awkwardly, but embrace nonetheless. In Switzerland my relatives kiss three times, cheek after cheek after cheek.

As we walk in tense silence towards the car park, I ask how either of us knows whether we've greeted the right person. How do we know that the other is the person we were waiting for?

I climb up into Rick's four-wheel-drive vehicle that I soon learn is a 'truck' and he drives us out onto the 401, an essential Toronto road that seems to lead just about anywhere you might care to go. I resist burbling at him. I've already told Rick that I feel nervous. He has barely uttered a word. I want to know all the important things right away, right now. Will his mother—my grandmother—meet me? Is Kate coming from New Orleans? He says we'll talk about all those things in the Monette way, over a drink. This sounds ominous but I'm thirsty.

It's the Canada Day holiday and as we drive through residential streets I cannot fail to notice the proliferation of red maple leaves flying from porches and implanted in front lawns. I feel like the prodigal daughter.

I check into my bed and breakfast; Rick has invited me to stay with him and his partner, Connie, but I've said no, maybe later. He's worried about the neighbourhood in which my b & b is located. He's a criminal lawyer and many of his drug dealer clients live close to where I'm staying.

I don't even change from my travel clothes, simply leave my bags, before we drive on to his house to settle in Connie's garden, drinking beer. Connie tells me, later, that the moment she arrived home from work and saw me sitting there with my Old Milwaukie, drinking straight out of the can, she knew I was 'one of them'. She knew, she said, that I was a Monette.

She herself is long and slender, a former ballerina. Her blonde hair falls to her waist and her smile is warm and kind; I feel immediately at ease with her. For all her softness, she is sharp and astute—she works as an architect.

Connie's garden is where the action is; its trees and purple and white flowers are alive with birds and insects. In the evenings the racoons come to fling small blue glass pebbles out of the fountain. Nobody knows why the creatures do this but I am charmed.

Rick wants me to stay with them. Points upstairs to the spare room beside his study and says 'That's your room there'. He's only just met me and I could be an axe murderer or as troubled as any of his clients but he wants to give me the keys to his house. I resist. For the first two days I need the distance provided me by the guest house.

Last week, Rick tells me, he went to see his mother Anchie in Welland, specifically to tell her of my visit. He had been holding my photos in his hand as he spoke but he didn't even have the opportunity to present them before Anchie started screaming at him. Rick, I soon learn, has a very soft centre, despite his daily dealings with all manner of Toronto lowlife. His mother's reaction to his attempt to reintroduce the subject of her Australian granddaughter caused him tremendous pain. What's more, he tells me, Matt had made a point of saying that he should not unbalance Anchie further by raising the subject of Gus' daughter with her once again. With the weight of hindsight, Rick looks on this as one of his brother's last wishes.

I am in Canada to meet the Monettes but my seventy-six-year-old grandmother denies my existence and refuses to be reminded of it. I've had four grandmothers but only knew one of them—Emma Naher—who died when I was only three years old.

At some point during my visit to Canada—probably while sitting in Connie's garden drinking beer from a can—I learn that

Anchie first heard of my existence at Gus' wake, directly after her first son's funeral. The Monettes were sitting around drinking when Mark announced that he would have to inform Gus' daughter. Anchie insisted there was no daughter and Kate seconded Mark. From that day to this, Anchie refuses to hear of me.

Gus senior, known to his children as Lucky Pierre, would have been a whole other story. Lucky Pierre, according to Rick, said he would have loved to meet me. I am told that he was a charmer, a womaniser and a big-hearted Frenchman. We would have gotten on just fine.

Flesh of our Flesh

RICK AND I ARE sitting in the garden one afternoon and I'm telling him about my first few conversations with Gus and the circumstances of our meeting. I explain how overwhelmed I had felt by Gus' first reaction to me.

'He told me he didn't have any other children,' I tell Rick. 'He also told me that because of the motorcycle accident he'd just had he'd never be able to father a child. I was *it*. That's what he said.'

'Motorcycle accident?' Rick asks.

'Yes, motorcycle accident,' I repeat. 'Before I contacted him he said he'd had a terrible accident and that he'd spent a long time recuperating. As a result of the accident, he told me, he'd never be able to father a child.'

My uncle slaps his thigh, laughs. It takes a lot to make serious Rick laugh but he's laughing now, and enjoying it. I'm not.

'He told you he was impotent?'

'Well, he didn't use that word but that was the gist of it.' I'm a little embarrassed discussing my other father's masculinity in this way.

Rick picks up his mobile phone and punches in some numbers.

'Mark?' he barks. 'Gus told Gaby he was impotent from some motorcycle accident.'

Rick listens and then there's more thigh slapping and laughter. These Monettes are pretty different, I'm thinking.

When Rick ends his call he looks absolutely delighted.

'What?' I fear I have just revealed his brother's deepest, darkest secret.

'He didn't have any terrible motorcycle accident,' Rick tells me. 'He just fell off his bike drunk on the way home from the pub one night. That was it.'

When Mark arrives he's wearing his wavy hair down to his shoulders and has a badly sunburned face from a recent fishing trip. I try to imagine how it must be for him, to meet his dead brother's adult daughter for the first time. He's full of emotion; excitement and wistful sadness. I have just learned that Mark is a funeral director, a detail that was omitted from Gus' stories. He takes me out in his 1966 Corvette. 'Made in the same year as you were,' he tells me and he's right. I just wish I looked as good for my age.

Mark and I have a whole day alone together—having dined with Rick and Connie the night before—and I am a little anxious that we won't find anything to say to each other. We will, after all, be sober for at least a few hours. Actually I am pleased to have learned that Mark is in death and is as interested in it as I am. With him I can talk death more frankly than I can with most. I am still coming to terms with the beauty of Daddo's passing; it seems that I cannot exhaust the topic for myself.

We drive from north Toronto to the St Lawrence Market and instead of taking us ten minutes it takes nearly an hour. Neither of us knows the way but the slow traffic and heat inside the small car are both conducive to talk. Inside the markets we walk aimlessly yet appreciatively between food stalls. We are waiting to be tempted. We buy beef sandwiches, dripping with juice and mustard; mine helps with the hangover I've had every morning since the day after I arrived in Canada. We sit on a bench, watching the passing parade and wolfing down enormous sandwiches. Later Mark tells Rick that I eat like a Monette. I imagine making myself a little checklist and ticking off the ways in which I belong.

We climb back into the Corvette to drive off to I don't know where. Mark doesn't know where either, even when we get there.

We park at a beach on the eastern edge of the city and the place has an easy, mellow feel to it. The sand is coarse and brown but the water in the lake—there were it meets the land—is cool and clear. We are in a small inlet off Lake Ontario and we look across at a forested shore. This place has a similar feel to the piece of lake shore Gus took me to the day we met.

'Do you regret having met Gus?' Mark asks me as we're strolling along the shore.

I'm immediately disarmed and think carefully before answering. Is there a hidden meaning here, a trick?

'Not for a minute. Absolutely not. Finding Gus was one of the best things I've ever done,' I tell Mark and this is the truth.

Mark looks at me in surprise, in some disbelief, his sunburned forehead cracking and the coloured fish on his shirt mocking me.

'I wasn't very comfortable with myself before I met Gus,' I tell Mark and I'm aware of how curious my words must sound. 'Up until then I felt that I never quite fitted in the world. I don't expect you to know what I mean.'

'Even with George and Jackie?' Mark wants to know and I feel immediately traitorous.

'In a way we were all misfits together,' I tell him, but I don't say that I was the biggest misfit of them all. 'They're both such good people. Jackie's kind and very beautiful and has these gorgeous dimples in her cheeks. Daddo was small and wiry and I towered head and shoulders above him. I wasn't like either of them. I was harder and sharper and bigger. I was always uncomfortable with myself physically. I know that teenagers are often that way but this seemed like something different.'

Despite Mark's perplexed expression, this confession—of sorts—makes me feel good. In fact, I feel screamingly happy.

'Before I met Gus I felt obscenely large,' I shrug because beside Mark I'm not large and beside his brother Rick I'm almost diminutive. 'And I used to dye my hair red. For years I was trying to create the illusion of being somebody else. I was uncomfortable in my own skin.'

Things are different for me now and I suppose Mark only needs to look at me to know this. Gradually, over the last few years, I've become proud of my broad, square shoulders. I've learned to appreciate my strong legs that can carry me over the hardest of terrains, day after day after day. And now that the shape of my face has changed, has become longer and forms a distinct point at the chin in the way Rick's does, I am beginning to see where I came from. Now that I don't dye my hair any longer I recognise that somewhere in there, in my eyes, my high forehead, in my colouring, is the blood of my French-Indian grandfather and my Cossack grandmother. I have Jane's mouth and her capable hands.

I turn the conversation back to Mark's pivotal question about whether I regret having met his brother.

'I can't help but wonder whether it was good for Gus to have met me.' It's taken me some time to compose these words. 'I mean he'd been living his life for fifty years before I turned up. He met me and then killed himself a year later.'

'That had absolutely nothing to do with you,' Mark says firmly. 'He was already well and truly on the way by the time you contacted him, not that any of us realised it then.'

'I don't have many regrets in my life but I have a profound regret regarding Gus. I didn't tell him how much meeting him meant to me. Or how wonderful I thought he was. He played it cool and so did I.'

Talking to Mark is easy. He's a good listener, asks gutsy questions and never makes the mistake of trying to tell you what he thinks you want to hear. I appreciate this.

'You know, it's not as though he gave much away himself.' For some reason I find that I need to stress this point. 'He never responded to me as a daughter, if you know what I mean. He never told me that he thought I was all right or that he was even just a little bit proud of me. And I badly wanted to hear that stuff.'

Mark remains silent. Like his brother Rick, he doesn't bullshit about the serious stuff. Mark had told me in our one telephone conversation, after Gus' death, that meeting me had given Gus tremendous pleasure. Conveying details of my life and achievements to his brothers and sister had too, but this is not the same as having heard Gus speak the words.

I tell Mark that Rick is certain Gus knew about me. I tell him Rick reckons it was clear that his brother couldn't leave Australia fast enough. Mark says, 'No way. Absolutely not.' As far as he's concerned, there's not even a skerrick of doubt. Mark insists that had Gus known about me he would have mentioned it to him.

'Why are you being so nice to me? Why are you doing all this?' I ask Mark and am appalled by my question once I've spoken it, embarrassed by the gratitude I feel towards the Monette brothers.

'Because you're flesh of our flesh,' Mark says simply.

Gus and George

———◆◆◆———

RICK AND CONNIE take me on the Monette tour of the Niagara
Peninsula. In three days I'll get to see every sacred Monette site
and plenty that aren't too sacred as well. We're all hung over after
another night out with Mark. Once I'd had a few drinks and
started to carry on a bit my uncles kept exchanging glances with
each other and saying, 'Just like Kate!'.

We've discussed a scheme whereby I get to see my grandmother even if I don't get to speak to her. Maybe Rick could take
her to a restaurant in Welland and I could be sitting at a table
nearby? We don't progress this plan, agreeing that the crying
woman at the nearby table—me—would resemble Anchie's
daughter far too closely.

We drive west out of Toronto through miles of flattish
farmland. Rick comments that this is the hilly part of Ontario.
The landscape is dull and fails to meet my notion of what Canada
is all about. I catch myself babbling inanely. We lunch in a bar in
Ontario's own Stratford, where the smokers and arctic air-condi-
tioning vie to irritate us. I'd be calmer if I'd ordered a beer with
my sandwich, as Rick and Connie did, but I'm already dehydrated
after a week of Monette-style bonding. All the Monettes seem to
drink is coffee or alcohol.

As we drive on, towards London, I really start to feel grim.
'We're going to see Gus,' as Rick puts it. That is, we're going to
visit his grave. I feel as though I'm going to perform an intimate

act with somebody I've never met before. I remind myself that I'm the guy's daughter and challenge myself to feel something, to feel anything at all.

I contemplate suggesting a stop for flowers on the way to the cemetery but end up asking whether we should bring a bottle of red wine instead. Rick has it all planned and pulls up outside a beer shop on the edge of town. Connie and I sit in the truck waiting and I turn around to tell her I think she's brave to be accompanying us on this journey. I say brave but I think I mean heroic.

Connie is perplexed by my comment about her bravery and bats it back to me. '*I'm* brave?'

Rick returns with a bag of ice and a dozen cans of beer. He packs them in a small cooler bag he's brought from home; he's put some thought into all of this. Unlike me. I start to feel panicky. We make a tour of Gus' university, where Rick also studied. I'm impressed by the grand stone buildings but I'm finding it difficult to concentrate.

We're going to the grave of my other father, the one I never got to know. He's the father I never had an opportunity to love. I don't know how I should react. My fear is that I'll feel absolutely nothing, which seems like a far worse outcome than being overwhelmed by emotion.

I have to keep reminding myself of how this must be for Rick. He's been back at the cemetery once, only, since the burial. There was some bad blood between the two brothers before Gus died. From the way I've heard that Gus was behaving I don't know how there could not have been. It crosses my mind that in bringing me to his brother's grave Rick might find some peace.

We drive into Mount Pleasant Cemetery, all grey and pink granite tombstones embedded in rolling green lawns. I'm afraid now. We skirt lawn after lawn and I find myself hoping that we won't be able to locate the damn thing, that we won't find Gus' stone. We find it, of course we find it. This is an organised Canadian cemetery, nothing like the French cemetery in which William Butler Yeats was buried and then promptly lost.

We stand beside the car, Rick duly distributing cans of beer before the three of us trudge across rows of graves to the stone that says MONETTE. It reads '1944 to 1995, son of Anne and Gustave'. This is no easy, peaceful place. Daughter and brother stand here cradling unresolved issues with the deceased.

I am struck by the wording on the stone; 'Gustave John, son of . . .' Not husband of, not brother of, and certainly not father of. The word 'love' is glaringly absent but Rick assures me later that this is the Anglican way. The Monettes were once Catholic, but in a bid to appear more 'Canadian' they had converted.

At the end my other father brought isolation on himself and misery on others. This despite being brilliant, having three adoring brothers, a doting sister, loving parents and a woman in his life. That's to say nothing of a newfound daughter who wanted to look up to him.

Rick, Connie and I stare dumbly at the tombstone, the beer cans making fists of our hands. I feel more than out of place, I feel lost. Connie wanders off—she never met Gus—to leave Rick and me to our business. I move forward to the stone and tentatively finger the rope twist that borders the wording. Rick gives an annoyed shrug and says that was Gus' wife's doing.

Rick looks down at the grass which is sick and patchy on the grave itself. All around the cemetery the grass on the other graves is green and healthy.

'The grass can't grow on my brother's grave,' he mutters, then laughs. 'It's being poisoned by the alcohol leaching from his body.'

I return to the foot of the grave and sit on the patchy grass. I am sitting at my other father's feet. Rick moves forward to pat the stone and moves away. The chipmunk that was playing by my side has disappeared and I am sitting alone at the grave of the father I hardly knew. I've sought advice from Daddo over the last two years, from beyond the grave, and so I try talking to Gus. I make a couple of pathetic attempts but find that every sentence that forms in my head opens with the words 'what if'. I receive no answers. I am Gus' daughter but was never his daughter. There's no changing this.

Minutes drag by and although I feel utterly miserable I still cannot cry. Did I expect to get something from Gus—here at his grave—that I didn't get from him in life? Gradually I begin to sense that I am no longer alone. If I am very still I can feel it; a presence.

It's not Gus, though, it's too familiar. In my mind's eye I can see two figures sitting at Gus' grave; my own and that of a white-haired man, his knees drawn up beneath his chin. Daddo, in some form, is there with me and as always his presence is warm and comforting. I haven't felt Daddo's near physical presence since the days immediately after his death and keenly recall the light touch of an invisible hand at the nape of my neck. My first thought is that he is there for me, that he's there to support me through this necessary ordeal. Daddo, however, also needs to pay his respects. Daddo, also, needs to express gratitude. We three—father, daughter, father—are irrevocably bound.

Here at my other father's grave I experience a moment of near dazzling illumination. This father quest could and should only lead back to George, my Daddo.

Afterword

————◆—◆◆—◆————

THIS BOOK DOES NOT attempt to present a biographical account of the life of my grandfather, Ernst Naher, nor of my fathers, George Naher and Gus Monette. Indeed, George's great life is drawn only within the parameters of his time as a father, and as a son. This is, however, an account of how I was fathered and of what I know of the way my true father, George, was fathered. If I have failed to paint truly vivid portraits of Gus and Ernst, it is, perhaps, because of the context in which I have placed them: that of their roles as fathers.

The memoir is, also, an attempt to understand what makes a father. Is it commitment? Is it an ease in one's self? Or is it, simply, the legacy of the life one has lived?

Mark Monette writes to me, once I've left Canada, to say that the stone I saw in the cemetery in London was not really a monument to his brother. Gus' true monument, he tells me, is a bursary Mark established at their old school in Welland, the school at which they both learned to read. Half the bursary is donated in Gus' name to a graduating student who is nominated and voted for by the entire student body and school staff. The other half of the bursary is donated to the school library to purchase books in Gus Monette's name.

My ancient dog, Bono, hangs on—despite the vet's expectations and my own—until I have finished my manuscript. He is fifteen years and two months old. His death, the day after I have sat down to read the completed draft of this book, prompts another journey to Rookwood Cemetery. Jackie, Paul and I visit Daddo's grave, which he shares with his mother. Surreptitiously, we sprinkle Bono's ashes on the lush, green grass.

When we have reunited Daddo and Bono, we head for the crematorium to find Ernst. His plaque, I am told, should be at the foot of an oleander tree. 'Do you think she knew that oleander was poisonous?' I ask Jackie of Emma, who would have chosen this tribute. Ernst's plaque, when Jackie finally spots it, has outlasted the poisonous tree and is now sheltered by an azalea, which looks none too healthy itself. The plaque states only my grandfather's name and the dates of his birth and death. The word 'love', once again, is absent.

At the end of this long cycle of loss, Paul and I drive down the south coast to a place that has become sacred to us. We stay on a wildflower farm between the hills and the sea. We have visited this dazzling, sylvan place many times, always with Bono. Just up the road is the place where Paul proposed. It is there, too, not even a month after Bono's death, that we conceive our first child.

Darlinghurst
26 March 2001